THE ORIGINS
of
ENGLISH
SURNAMES

THE ORIGINS
of
ENGLISH
SURNAMES

Joslin Fiennes

ROBERT HALE

First published in 2015 by
Robert Hale, an imprint of
The Crowood Press Ltd
Ramsbury, Marlborough
Wiltshire SN8 2HR

www.crowood.com

www.halebooks.com

This impression 2017

British Library Cataloguing-in-Publication Data
A catalogue record for this book is available from the British
Library.

ISBN 978 0 7198 1652 9

Printed and bound in India by Parksons Graphics

For Janet Hermans,
a much-loved friend

CONTENTS

INTRODUCTION

THE WELL-KNOWN AND everyday, the small cogs that keep machines turning, are often taken for granted. Surnames belong to this group. We all have one. We use it all the time. If we pay attention to it, it is to find out about others with our name, like our ancestors. But look at the meanings and sources of surnames and take them together, and they turn out to be a rich record of a much broader subject – society. Single names stand sentinel, but groups of names open the gates to the city.

It was in the retiring rooms of magistrates' courts, while looking at the daily lists, that I first began to really look at surnames, wondering how Prettijohn came to be and how you could inherit Freer when friars were meant to be celibate. A great deal of time later, spent poring over dictionaries, medieval records and modern books and being bent like a hoop over the underside of a church choir seat, I discovered a new world.

It is a world that is unique. Most English surnames emerged over some 150 years before AD 1400. And each surname means something. These two facts were my starting-gun.

Their timing means that most describe a people who were largely illiterate. Surnames exploded into the records in the late fourteenth century, and document a unique history of ordinary medieval society during a short period of extraordinary social change. The roots of the names tell you the language people spoke then. It is a well-stirred mix of Old English, Middle English and Norman French, with some Norse and Celt, in which it is English that dominates. To see it in context, Norman French was the language of power and rank until Henry IV made English the tongue of kings at the end of the fourteenth century when most surnames already existed. But the vigour and wit, range and colour of the English mix of surnames show why the language had the capacity to win out in the end. These names were the final triumph of English over French and grounded the culture of England forever.

And their meanings led me into a lost society. They tell the story of the fading of English feudalism. Occupational names are about what people did; names describing the countryside and places in it tell where they travelled; nicknames record what people noticed, thought and laughed at; and those from first names document memories of earlier cultures. You see traditional life co-existing with great opportunity, some people on the land and at the manor, others moving into rural industry and urban crafts and trades. Some surnames record Norse still entrenched in the old Danelaw, but others show people travelling along trade routes across England and out over the Channel.

The deeper I looked, the more patterns I saw. Country names describe a feudal peasantry co-opted by fine titles; other groups record specialization and rural industry, fashion and luxury work showing mobility, growing prosperity and consumption. The same sea routes from the Mediterranean that brought in spices and damask via Weymouth, a small port on the south coast of England, were travelled by the Black Death. At the same time, you see attitudes, an obsession with appearances and rank, scorn for the elite (particularly the church), and a great deal of humour underlying the most innocent-looking of names. Names document memories of ancient myths and the heroes and gods within them. The easy way in which people turned to metaphors to describe their neighbours brought along symbols from a terrifying world view that had united Anglo-Saxon England with Scandinavia and northern Europe.

The language of surnames shows how the Norman invaders had infiltrated English society. English surnames often record traditional, small-scale and less skilled activities. The Normans brought a sophisticated hierarchy of management to feudal manors and estates, larger-scale merchants, higher-skilled crafts and suppliers of luxuries. But co-existing translations of many names show people confidently moving between the two.

This book is about English medieval names. It excludes names from later migrations, such as the Huguenots in the sixteenth century, and most Scottish and Irish names, especially those beginning with 'Mc' or 'Mac'. The majority of Scots and Irish with these names arrived in England in the eighteeenth century with names documented only from the fifteenth and sixteenth centuries that were, in any case, generally from a very different clan culture. But included are those names the Scots and the Irish were called in the Middle Ages: for the Scots this is often Scott, one of the more popular names; for the Irish it is Irish and Ireland. I also exclude Welsh surnames, established mostly in the sixteenth century, although, again, I do cover the names the Welsh were called in medieval England. Many modern Welsh names are from Norman personal names – Roberts, Williams, Thomas – but in medieval times most Welsh immigrants were known as Wallis or Walsh.

The sample of surnames taken from the telephone directory for South-East Devon for 2007–8 closely tracks the surnames used in an earlier study by C.M.M. Matthews from the London Directory, so it can be taken to be fairly representative of the population as a whole. Telephone directories still worked then as a source of English names because most people still had landlines, although with mobile phones, internet communication and ex-directory numbers, they are becoming less and less comprehensive.

Surnames have many facets; some will shine brighter than others for each of us. After all the insights surnames provide into the social and economic history and culture of ordinary medieval society, it is the vivacity, energy and imagination of the people behind the choices of these names that I most enjoy. There are those that tell of people like us: some descriptive, some mocking and some you cannot be completely sure of. There is Swift who might be slow, the Bramble who is painfully difficult, and the Toogood who may be just that. And there is always visual humour – look at the Waghorns and Catchpoles, Benbows and Littlejohns. There are the Greeleys, whose skin is like wet snow after hail, and the Mackerells who have red scorched skin on their legs.

Listen to the names, and you get an ear for medieval cadences and an eye for their images. Ordinary medieval folk light a trail that leads to the King James Bible and Shakespeare through their directness, their imagery and their ability to communicate ideas and wit. Surnames allow us to track the real people in medieval society much further back than other records allow.

This book discusses the different groups of surnames in a way that takes us deep into medieval society, from its economic and social structure to its inherited culture. Thus, the first chapters on occupational, topographical and locational names (Chapters 1–4) explore how surnames record physical lives, what people do and where they travel. Then, through nicknames and first names, Chapters 5–8 record the attitudes and beliefs that appear in people's comments about each other's looks and behaviour, their absorption of Christianity, and their memories of pre-Conquest mythologies. By investigating what English surnames have to tell us about ordinary medieval English society, this book will reveal not only the origins but the people behind our surnames.

CHAPTER 1

VOICES FROM THE PAST

GEORGE BUSH AND Bob Hawke, Mick Jagger and Margaret Thatcher, James Watt and Benjamin Britten. We know these have all been at the top of their chosen careers in the English-speaking world at one time or another. And their surnames tell us what we might not know: that their ancestors all began at the bottom of the social hierarchy in the Middle Ages.

Bush lived near a bush, perhaps one with a defining feature or shape. It is a country name, the name of a villager. George Bush's ancestors did serious and successful work at distancing themselves from their rural origins. Hawke, meaning just that, comes from a hawker, carrying the bird on the gauntlet on his left arm as he goes hunting with his lord. Or the name could be symbolic for the bird and mean someone powerful, rapacious and evil, drawing on Norse traditions and the footfall of earlier cultures. Jagger is a pedlar. First records of the name show it comes from the West Riding of Yorkshire, and Mick Jagger can indeed trace his ancestry back to that county. And the Iron Lady has her name from the medieval thatchers who, albeit in smaller numbers now, continue to thatch houses just as they did then. James Watt, engineer and scientist, is called after an abbreviation of Walter. Wat is a poor man's name; it heads the list of peasants participating in the Peasants' Revolt of 1381 in John Gower's poem *Vox Clamantis*.

13

Originally Britten was probably a Breton, coming to England to raid or to trade, staying long enough for the name also to become a nickname for someone who boasts and swears (a deadly sin). One contemporary source has it that the Bretons are:

> ... the greatest rovers and the greatest theeves,
> That have bene in the sea many one yeere[1]

At the very least these surnames show how far their bearers have come. But along the way they bring those first namesakes back, telling us what they did and where they came from and how they were viewed by their contemporaries. And the words behind the names – Old English, Old French, Norse and Celt – show the languages that were part of spoken English in the Middle Ages as well as what each contributed to the way of life.

A Unique Record

English surnames turn out to be a unique record of a specific period in medieval England. They carry rich stories about the people who create them, knitting up the shreds torn by time in our bindings to the past. They are important because of when they appear and who they describe. They capture a society emerging from a time of famine, war and plague that leaves no other such comprehensive record. This is not about the Scots, Welsh or Irish, who take names later in very different societies.

Almost all English surnames are medieval. Landowners with estates to protect have them by about 1300, and everyone else follows. Few new ones appear after the end of the fourteenth century. So they record a relatively short, discrete, time period, when there are Smiths, Taylors and Clerks, but no Solicitors or Lacemakers, who come too late (lacemakers only catching their boats from Holland in about 1550).

The vast majority of names apply to illiterate ordinary people who leave virtually no other records of their own. The surnames they choose tell an exuberant and wide-ranging story about their lives that captures not only the physical world in which they live, but also their cultural attitudes and inheritance. Surnames contain social and economic history, documenting feudalism and change, diversification, specialization, new callings, trade and travel. They record people who are pragmatic and close to nature yet have an obsession with appearances, a keen eye for pretension and an ear for neat expressions. There are the names telling of people like us: some descriptive, some judgemental and some mocking – particularly about those who preach, tax and rule and presume to qualities they do not have. There is the visual humour in the Waghorns and Catchpoles and always the risk of the irony of opposites in the Angels and the Lyons. And in the names of heroes, gods and symbols of magic from inherited myths survive the ancient cultures that are still in peoples' collective memories.

These names show the vigour, depth and flexibility that enables English to supplant Norman French and Latin as the language of power in England by the turn of the fourteenth century. In the linguistic roots of names you see that Old English dominates. When something needs to be said, English can say it. Yet it is inclusive; Old French names bring hierarchy to service, scale and quality to crafts and trades while some Norse and Celt names survive to tell of old callings. Surnames capture in amber the spoken language of a largely illiterate people. In it, you can find the colour, agility and wit of earlier geniuses with words.

Norman French, Latin and occasional English records of the educated and the powerful give us most of what we know about the Middle Ages. The thoughts and plans of medieval monarchs, bishops and administrators are in their reports, letters, treatises and poetry; what happens to them is in charters and deeds, ecclesiastical records and inventories as they expand their estates, send knights and soldiers to fight in the king's armies and provide dowries for their daughters. Ordinary folk – the vast majority of the population – are the shifting shadows of these records; now you see them, now you don't. If they do not disturb the peace or run away from their manors, if they do not let their animals stray or brew ale without a licence, and, crucially, if they are too poor to pay tax, they do not appear at all. Even when they do, their lives are haphazard bit appearances in those records that chance happens to preserve. Geoffrey de Leya, a Devon serf, is documented buying freedom for himself and his two sisters for sixty marks of silver in 1238 and a week later paying another twenty marks for two estates, all at a time when peasants on the land are earning just a penny (1d) a day (one mark is worth 13s 4d)[2]. No further records tell how he has come by such enormous sums, or what happens to him and his sisters later.

But understanding the attitudes, beliefs and aspirations of ordinary people is as important as knowing the ambitions and ideals of the elite. History is made by what the ruling class believe the rest will let them get away with as much as by what they want to do. After the first outbreak of the Black Death, despite strong and repeated legislation, people simply leave the land and landlords without labour have to let arable farming revert to pasture. Within a generation, the Peasants' Revolt of 1381 shocks the ruling class and strengthens the hand of the ordinary man further; serfdom is to wither away in the fifteenth century. As does Norman French as the language of power. Ordinary people are developing their own ideas and the self-confidence to express them – in English. These are shown in the surnames they are taking.

Corralling the Names

Surnames describe life, a disorderly topic. But scholars have attempted to give a sense of order by providing a classification. There are essentially four groups of names:

1. Occupational names (e.g., Thatcher and Jagger)
2. Nicknames (e.g., Britten and Hawke)
3. Topographical and locational names that describe the countryside and the places in it (e.g., Bush and Britten again)
4. Those taken from first names (e.g., Robin, Osborn or Morgan).

There are, of course, many overlaps as over time names adopt more than one meaning and straddle more than one group. Ware can work at or live by a weir, but the name might also be occupational or topographical. Wood, for example, could be topographical or a nickname because *wod* means frenzied or wild in Old English.

Pye could be a keeper or seller of pies, or someone who is vain, so could be an occupational name or a nickname. Rare surnames tend to become absorbed in more common ones that sound similar. Crocker, for instance, combines the name for a potter and the unusual nickname from *crève-coeur*, a ladies' man or heart-breaker. Finally, classification is not necessarily definitive. Someone called Bristol might be a carpenter, and a Carpenter might be the son of a carpenter, but he himself may be a cooper. Some records help here, documenting 'Bristol, le tailleur', for instance. Some names have dominant meanings that help classification. For others, you just have to live with the ambiguities. And, indeed, ambiguity turns out to reflect a fundamental quality of medieval society.

An extreme example of overlapping meanings is Pike, a fairly common name, strong in the west of England, with no variants to complicate the story. From its Old English root it could refer to the fish, to someone who catches or sells it, or someone who behaves or looks like it (perhaps someone with a long nose). On the other hand, it could refer to the weapon (a pike or pickaxe), someone who makes or uses that weapon, or a soldier who carries one. But the Old English could also mean someone living by a peak or hilltop. Then again, when the name comes from its Old French root *pic*, it means someone who looks like a woodpecker (with a pointed nose this time). If from the Old Norse *pik*, it means someone who is tall and lanky. Finally, via its Old French and Middle English root it can be from Pic, a Germanic first name. So Pike could be classified anywhere: occupational from the Old English; a nickname from the Old English, Old French and Old Norse; topographical from the Old English again; and a personal name from Old French and Middle English roots. Not many names gallop off in all directions like Pike, but many go off along at least two different paths, often, but not always, from combinations of words with different roots.

How Surnames Emerge

It is obvious why surnames had to happen. The Celts, Anglo-Saxons and Norse in England originally had only one name. Such names were tremendously varied. The Domesday book is packed with wonderfully evocative Anglo-Saxon Wulfstans and Wulfrics, Godwins and Baldwins, Aelmers and Aelfrics – wolf-stone and wolf-rule, good friend and bold friend, famous noble and elf or noble ruler. With the Normans at the Conquest came a bunch of remarkably less imaginative and less varied single Norman names, which the English rapidly substituted for their own. In a thirteenth-century collection of deeds from Essex, some 64 per cent of the people recorded held one of six Norman names, with 20 per cent being either John or William and the rest Robert, Richard, Geoffrey or Thomas.[3] The invaded were paying homage to the invaders by taking their names.

With so many Johns and Williams, Roberts and Richards, people have to differentiate themselves. As early as the eleventh century, some land-owning Normans begin to add to their first names the name of their most important holding. The habit spreads among the English; more types of name appear and these gradually become hereditary. Nobody knows exactly why, but we can make some assumptions. Under the feudal system where every man owes homage and service to his lord, heirs – even of serfs – can still, for a fee, inherit a tenancy, so being able to prove identity through a surname is important. At the same time the growing numbers of craftsmen and traders might depend on personal reputations and their children would benefit from the same surname if they want to carry on the same business. Then people need, or are required, to identify themselves for other reasons – perhaps to prove they have paid taxes or court fines. Surnames might also emerge simply because they become fashionable or emphasize the notion of family.

We can see the stabilization of surnames actually happening in the records. At first, they often have prefixes; people identified by where they live can be called 'atte-' or 'under-' or 'by-' something. Eventually these prefixes disappear or become absorbed. Thus, by-the-Ford becomes Byford and under-the-Hill, Underhill. Think of Attree. The first 'atte Tree' might be known by the tree near his home; perhaps an unusual one – an elm among oaks or a tree that still stands after being struck by lightning. He might be a free tenant with a small piece of land to pass on when he dies, so his son would keep the name and give it to his children, even though they could by then be Attrees and have moved many miles from that special tree in the first hamlet.

Popularity seems to play a role in which names survive; Smiths and Taylors come from across England and there are too many for the names to die out. Aspirations are involved. Some surnames, particularly ironic or offensive nicknames (Cuckold or Snot, for instance) have simply not survived. Yet others have; think of Crook, which can mean mentally or physically deformed, and Orme, the universally disliked and feared serpent, and it is a mystery why. Unless later generations simply forget what these names originally meant and take them for granted, as we do now.

The survival of surnames is chancy, affected by how many sons inherit them and the impact of disease and migration. They can be hard to track, because spelling does not settle down until the nineteenth century and depends on the hearing of the recorder as well as the pronunciation of the speaker. This is particularly true of foreign names. Then information about surnames depends on records, and early records of peasants' names are particularly sparse. This affects especially indigenous personal surnames, which seem to have belonged largely to those who fall out of the recording net of tax and court in the Middle Ages. It is hard to establish a chronology for them; pre-Conquest records are rare; only Arden and Berkeley can be traced back to pre-Conquest Englishmen – the first an Aelfwine, and the second a Harding.[4] Even records of these names from between the Conquest and the fourteenth century, when a surge in written documents occurs, are scarce. Finally, many names are difficult to track because they change form, combine with others with different meanings, or simply disappear.

An important caveat is that names do not necessarily identify families or blood-lines. Many surnames from our Norman invaders are still with us – the Boons and Bruces from La Manche, and the Percys from Calvados, for instance. These names could just possibly be held by the original families, but the only likely direct descendants in the male line of men who fought at Hastings are the Maletts.[5] It is much more likely that today's Boons and Percys come from servants or tenants of the original families, villagers from places called after them, or with some other tenuous connection. Then, in fourteenth-century London, apprentices routinely take the surnames of their masters. Many of the same surnames – occupational names, nicknames and topographical names like Wood or Green – arise in different counties and are from multiple families. Even well over half the place names originally producing surnames occur in different counties. The evolution of surnames complicates the link between family and name yet further. People can change their names, typically to inherit property. And surnames themselves evolve, particularly foreign ones, as they adapt to local pronunciation and spelling.[6]

Co-opted into the Structure

In the fourteenth century, surnames show how English fingers are unpicking the threads binding society to feudalism. It is a disturbed time. Two centuries of growth, followed by a series of catastrophic harvests from 1315 to 1322, when average yields in England are believed to have been the lowest for over a century, accompanied by sheep scab and cattle plague, are together thought to have killed half a million people. This is followed by a run of plagues beginning in 1348. The population is estimated to have fallen from some 5–6 million in the early 1300s to some 2.2–3 million in about 1380 and is to remain low until about 1540. The king still depends on support and finance from the people, and the aristocracy, a tiny fraction of the population, depends on the peasants for labour and rents. But with fewer peasants and a failing war with France, the system is under stress.

Some occupational surnames record how the old feudal pyramid of land-based wealth is still being held up by its wide base of servants at the manor and workers on the estates. Surnames show how this system operates. Look down the list and you see that the essential structure hinges on numerous and differentiated management jobs. There are virtually no names for everyday activities like ploughing or weeding. At the top are the lord's men, gentry or above like him – the Stewards and the Chamberlains at the manor and the Bailiffs on the estate. Below come the servants and farmers with oversight functions and specialized responsibilities: at the manor the Ushers and Sargeants, Butlers and Cooks; on the farm the Reeves, the Haywards, the Wards and the many herdsmen, Shepherds and Cowards or cow-herds, the Woodwards and keepers of bridges and weirs. Management cascades down to ensure the landlord's life is well organized and his properties are productive.

Key to the dominance of the ruling classes is the appearance of awe-inspiring magnificence. This requires the public display of hospitality, hunting and retinues of servants. Many surnames record the specialists who manage the lord's symbols of rank at the manor, his horses and falcons, food and wine, and his animals, forests and parks on the estate. Foresters and Parkers are popular names, and there are many names for grooms, from Marshall to Palfrey, and for hunters, like Hawke and Falconer with their many variants.

These surnames tell us a great deal about the feudal system. First, the productivity of the land and the status symbols there and at the manor are both crucial to the landlord. Second, micro-management is key. The few co-opt the many by devolving responsibilities from organizing the whole estate to keeping a cow or two. Intriguingly, the popularity of these management names and their survival may also suggest the co-option plays on peoples' aspirations; they want to be seen to be part of the structure.

Other surnames record skills: Carpenters and Stonemen, Thatchers and Smiths, Carters and Ashburners, among others (see Chapters 2 and 3). Many will reflect part-time activities and the realities of medieval farming. Basic skills to make and repair are required to keep estates functioning, but when crops fail and herds are decimated by disease, skills could also make the difference between life and death from starvation. Surnames tell us little about farming and a lot about the value added by diversification in the countryside as farmers hedge their risks through craft-making and skilled service at the manor.

Lives on the Land

Surnames show that people live in close communities. Descriptive nicknames, for example, the Longs and the Barrels (for corpulent), could be given by strangers. But many others, for example, Sharp and Pratt (the smart and the cunning), Moody and Blythe (the brave and the merry), could only come from friends or neighbours. And the many '-sons', such as Robinson, Johnson, Wilson, tell us that people know their fathers. The linguistic roots of names show many communities can stay for centuries in a particular area. Early records of Norse names show a vast majority moving from single name before the Conquest to surname some three centuries later in the same areas. Like paths threading through long grass to a distant wood, many local modern names still lead back to local medieval namesakes. This is a finding of regional genealogical work as well – hard to believe after six centuries of incoming and outgoing, wars and plagues, but it is a fact. Norse surnames are still concentrated in the Danelaw, where the Vikings and the Danes consolidated their power in the ninth and tenth centuries. Wool tramplers still broadly follow their medieval distribution: Fullers in the south and east, Tuckers in the south-west and Walkers in the north. Genealogical research in Lancashire, the West Riding of Yorkshire and elsewhere finds that at the end of the twentieth century a large percentage of surnames, many from local places, are still recorded close to their medieval origins.[7]

And most people in the Middle Ages are still agricultural. The many nicknames of birds and animals show they are sufficiently close to nature to be able to match the habits of those around them to the looks and behaviour of wild creatures. Despite occupational names that show migration to towns, the most popular group of surnames records our hills and woods, rivers and weirs, farms and villages. Few record urban landscapes.

Some names describe farming practices. Surnames incorporating '-ley', like Bradley, Buckley and Riley, describe land clearance, and Barnet describes quite specifically clearance by burning, all documenting the effects of population growth during the early fourteenth century before the effects of famine and plague take hold. All the names describing woods, forests and individual trees suggest that these are scarce, so useful for identification, and valuable. The Hay names – Hay, Haywood and variants – record later land enclosures. Names ending in '-ton' – Horton, Milton and Worthington – describe farms. Names tell about barns, outlying dairy farms near pastures, and valleys with pigsties. A bunch of other names record features that would inhibit farming (for example, Brimblecombe, the brambly valley), rough land, heath, marsh, and so on.

The church plays a large part in peoples' lives. Many surnames are taken from the names of saints, who are very popular in medieval England. Ships are called after them, and many trades, occupations and social groups have patron saints. It is hard to separate saints from kings and statesmen in the more popular names, but well-known medieval saints like Thomas à Becket, Hugh of Lincoln and James of Compostela will have influenced the use of even these. At the same time, many less common names like Martin and Lambert can be traced back to a particular saint. While there are indigenous names for saints, like Cuthbert, Edmund and Petherick from Petroc, most take the Norman form of the classical/biblical name – Gregory from Gregorius and Bennet from Benedict. The medieval English accept the Norman dominance of the church, perhaps because, since the Synod of Whitby in AD 664, the English church had always been more continental in outlook. But names for the top levels of its hierarchy are Old English rather than Norman French, suggesting that the ecclesiastical elite was absorbed into the native ruling class before the Conquest, while saints' names across cultures are largely classical/biblical as many continental saints become part of English devotion and local saints opt for non-English names.

The Upper Classes from Below

Nicknames demonstrate a strong reaction against the ruling classes. Behind King and Lord lies scorn for the arrogance and vanity of the aristocracy. With Prior or Abbot, Monk or Bishop, people are laughing at the hypocritical worldliness of a church that presumes to give them moral guidance on abnegation and humility.

Contemporary literature is scathing about the hypocrisy, avarice, greed and philandering of the church, particularly of the priests and monks who come into everyday contact with ordinary people. Resistance to the powerful appears in the odd record of the serf who will not work or who refuses to leave his land, but ironical nicknames show people across the country engaged in mocking their secular and religious betters. Since irony is only funny if others see the joke, these names demonstrate the mockery is widespread. Medieval church carvings in side chapels, on high bosses, on the underside of seats in choir stalls, are peopled with bishops as lusty apes, greedy hogs and womanizers.

Some of these names can also be descriptive. Some Kings could have come from a King of the May Day pageant; some Bishops from the custom of electing a boy chorister to act as a bishop. But generally when a ploughman or a small trader is called Pope or Abbot, Earl or King, we can safely assume that it is in mockery.

There is an edge. The humour must partly have been a way of coming to terms with reality, with the same perspicacity and wit we see in medieval carving. But partly it shows the growing self-confidence of a people who feel able openly to criticize their rulers. And for some, the mockery in these names is bitter. During the second half of the fourteenth century, England is losing the war with France and the population is undefended from coastal raiding, attacks on shipping in the Channel and is subjected to increasing demands for taxes. Ordinary people blame an inept, extravagant and corrupt government, in which senior ecclesiastics rule alongside the hated aristocracy. During the Peasants' Revolt in 1381, which was concentrated in the east and the south of England, abbeys, bishops' palaces and senior ecclesiastics are targeted as well as the secular elite, and rebels kill Archbishop Sudbury, the chancellor, along with the treasurer, Sir Robert Hales.

Engineering Change

Feudal ties are losing tension; moorings are slipping. Many surnames show the new lives of skilled craftsmen and traders straddled between countryside and the growing number of towns. The many nicknames describing height, strength and speed record the importance of physical labour. Those telling of intelligence and astuteness, fraud, vanity and hypocrisy describe attributes needed for and encountered in a more complicated world.

Ironically empowered by the high death rates from famine and plague, people are leaving the manors for the towns and for the new cloth-making industries, developing skills to become full-time Carders and Weavers, Taylors and Merchants. The mid-fourteenth century is a watershed for rural England. At the end of the thirteenth century, England mainly exports raw materials, predominantly wool, but also animal hides, lead and tin. From 1303, an export tax on wool, combined with innovations in cloth preparation and disruptions in Flemish cloth production, mean that by the end of the fourteenth century English cloth exports rival wool. Both the wool and cloth businesses are grounded in the countryside, powered by artisans. At about the same time English wool exports, previously handled by foreigners, particularly Italians, begin to be taken over by English merchants, channelling their wool through mainly foreign staples that settle in English-owned Calais from 1392, a convenient system for facilitating taxation for the monarchy, giving cloth yet another boost.

Surnames show how old specializations are consolidated and new ones are emerging. From Hacker to Turner through Sawyer and Carpenter, woodworkers are moving from making crude mattocks to housing and sophisticated joinery. Shearers and Cisore are handing over scissors and ribbons to Taylors and Glovers, Capes and Cappers. A building boom fuelled by an extravagant church allows Stoniers to rise to become professional Masons and even Masters, architects of vast building projects. The Hundred Years' War is taking the Bowmen from the parks and making them Archers, giving more jobs to specialists producing the bows – the Arrowsmiths, Stringers and Bowyers. Specialization can be vertically integrated, each task feeding into the next. The Taylors work with cloth that starts as wool teased by the Tozers, combed by the Carders, woven by the Webbers and Weavers and so on, until it is bundled up and taken off by the Packers. Cloth-making has become an industry with a tight structure; the surnames show it.

Growing prosperity makes it worthwhile for people to invest in the skills and equipment needed to become specialized. Ordinary people are becoming richer and are engaging in conspicuous consumption. Occupational names record Spicers, Vinters and those producing sophisticated fashions and jewellery alongside necessities. There is more discrimination; people want joinery, not carpentry, dedicated milliners and embroiderers. The eating of meat is spreading, and the surnames show how the meat profession is developing. Butcher and its equivalents of Bowker, Shinner or Skinner are all names for a butcher. Shinners and Skinners come from the Old English and Old Norse and mean what they say, flayers of meat, all that the Anglo-Saxons needed. Butchers, from *boucher*, come with the Normans; they are the larger operators who get involved in fattening pastures for the live cattle, slaughtering and selling.

The names of people at a time when they must be the first or second generation holding them show that tailors and suppliers of luxuries like Spicers and Glovers do well. When you have talent, opportunities exist even in medieval times to rise in the world. Robert le Taylour of Shrewsbury has, in 1309, the status goods of the elite – a forty-shilling riding horse, fine clothes, silver and jewellery.[8] But even people with humble names have in their tax inventories meat, silver, jewellery and brassware. And those with quite lowly names can become distinguished. Thomas Fartheyn is a Steward of Exeter from 1315–21, his name recording that he owns or comes from a tiny place. Drapers and Merchants grow rich on the cloth and wool trade, challenging the aristocracy in wealth and power. But the many surnames of small-scale tradesmen – Pedlar, Jagger, Chapman – show prosperity fingering all of medieval England. The English are marching out of bondage.

The English Travellers

Early medieval records of locational names in a given place show that up to a third of the population can come from somewhere else. All sorts of people move. The names of ships' captains docking at the port of Topsham, near Exeter, in the late thirteenth century include Cook, Webbe, Spicer and Baker. Records from early fourteenth-century Shrewsbury show people in the city hundreds of miles away from their original home. Feudalism is not the strait-jacket we might imagine. Some of the travel in these names will have been transient, much of it local, but many of the surnames track the paths of our trade down English staging posts and out across a network of routes over the Channel. These names of foreign places record how closely integrated medieval England still is with continental Europe and they describe the structure of the trade that makes English Merchants and Drapers rich.

Surnames recording English towns and counties show that trade wealth is widely distributed across the country. As well as names from major commercial centres like London and Winchester, they record people named after the great English cities built on the wool and cloth trade: the older wool centres of Lincoln, Ludlow in Gloucestershire, Boston in Lincolnshire, Bristow (Bristol) and Kendal in Cumbria, and the newer cloth centres of York, Warwick, Gloucester, Lancaster and Derby. Names of smaller places from around the English coast – Dover, Hastings and Wight from the Isle of Wight – are likely to record the pattern of in-shore trading from larger ports like Southampton, Lynn (King's Lynn), Hull, and the East Anglian herring centres. Snape, for instance, named after that tiny place on the Alde in Suffolk, is here to remind us of its grander past as a fishing entrepôt.

The Foreign Travellers

However distant the sources of imports, surnames tell us that trade comes via the Low Countries and northern or western France as far south as Gascony, but not much further. The surnames of foreigners recording where the wool and cloth go to be sold are our Callises from Calais, Bridges and Brugess from Bruges, our Brabsons from Brabant, as well as our Flanders, Franks and Flemings, Hollands, and so on. Contemporary writing describes goods from Spain, Portugal, Brittany, Prussia, Genoa and Holland going to the fairs in Flanders and Brabant to be exchanged for England's wool and tin. These are the exotic goods we see in our medieval shipping lists: figs, oil and quicksilver from Spain; salt, wine and canvas from Brittany; beer and bacon from Prussia; silver plate from

Hungary; cloth of gold, silk and black pepper from Genoa; spices, apes, marmosets and 'things not induring that we bye' from Venice and Florence. Our Janaways, or Genoese, are among the rarer names from further afield, representing the Italians contemporaries described coming 'Into this land with divers marchandises/In great Caracks ...'.[9] Janaway and the names mentioned previously all suggest that foreigners come here with this trade. Some might be direct exporters but most will be associated with the wool and cloth that is bought in exchange.

Slipping down the wake of these wool and cloth traders come other foreigners. The Bretons, Bretts, Brittains and all their variants may have come as direct exporters of their own goods or as adventurers and pirates. Our Pickards are associated with Picardy, a source of woad, the popular blue dye used universally in the cloth industry before the Hundred Years' War, suggesting that Picardians could, at least for a time, have controlled or at least facilitated this trade here. Other surnames recall the new wine trade with France that evolves at the end of the twelfth century after Henry II marries Eleanor of Aquitaine. These include our Gaskens, or Gascons, Champness from Champagne, and Burgoynes, as well, perhaps, as the various names for the French, because at some point the English do not bother much about specific origin, and call people French, Francis or France, regardless of which region they hail from.

There are many surnames that record travel from the places that the Normans are still attempting to subdue – the Scotts, a popular name, and the Welsh and their many variants (which can also just mean foreigner), as well as other English names taken particularly by the Welsh, and the Irish and Irelands (fewer variants for them). Some will have come for trade too. The Scots, according to contemporaries, are seen 'draping of her wolles in Flanders' and send fells, hides and fleeces there via England. From the 'wild Irish' the same source says come all sorts of hides and skins, fish, including salmon, wool, silver and gold used by London jewellers.

From across the warp and weft of these names emerges the great story of the Middle Ages. It is not about costly wars or internecine royal struggles, but the army of cottage spinners and weavers, small traders and craftsmen who, with what must have been the tacit acquiescence of the ruling elite, are beginning to break their feudal ties and create the foundation of English prosperity for the next three centuries. Land, still the prime asset, is in the steel grip of the aristocracy and the church. But money in the fingers of those below is prising this grip open. The meanings of surnames in records tell a story of social mobility, of peasants becoming great merchants within a few generations of their first namesake.

Values and Attitudes

Surnames do much more than give such broad facts about the economic realities of ordinary medieval life; they tell us what people make of the world around them. They record that difficult concept – culture.

Values and aspirations are captured in the choice of name. Although the survival of surnames is haphazard, it is probably fair to say that the most popular surnames today like Smith, Taylor, Brown and Clark, and particularly those with a number of variants, record what medieval people notice and value. Groups of names record the importance of agricultural responsibilities, the specialization of crafts and fashion, and a people at all levels obsessed with appearances and the symbols of status.

Topographical surnames show the English to be deeply and consistently pragmatic. They tell not of the beauty or grandeur of nature but of features with earning potential from rivers and woods, farms and communication routes. Why do the people in Cumbria not name someone after the silver lake they live by, or those in East Anglia record the wide sky above the farm? Where Celts and Scandinavians find spirits in groves and waterfalls, the medieval English see sources of subsistence and income.

Nicknames are perhaps the best record of medieval attitudes towards the world around them. They record the morals and ideals of church and knight, but also the reality of human frailty; a curiosity about deformity and a recognition of cruelty and evil, and, in the many names with several nuanced meanings, human complexity. Names show how medieval people love to take an idea,

29

then shred any precision into ambiguity. Humour is ever-present. Just as Littlejohn is a giant, so Perfect, Humble and Wise could record the neurotic, arrogant and stupid.

The thinking behind these names, particularly the symbolic nicknames, can be hard to interpret; time has done an impressive job at cutting us loose from the culture producing them. But contemporary writing and art can help to guide us back. One source is William Langland's *Piers Plowman*, published in different versions between 1370 and 1386, in English, and the most popular poem of its day. Langland is a Lollard and anticlerical; Geoffrey Chaucer's *The Canterbury Tales* of 1384 is less obsessive, wider-ranging, and more tolerant. Other writings include church sermons, Thomas Wright's *Political Songs*, which puts together medieval writing and poetry, and work on Celtic and Christian symbols. Medieval art, particularly church carving, is a rich source of information on attitudes and values.

These surnames, chosen by people for people they know, come up close. From the numbers in this group that have survived, our medieval ancestors notice personality traits as much as physical attributes. Popular surnames record complexion and hair colour, giving us the Browns, the Whites, the Reads (or redheads), and the Fairs. Many others list a village pump of people like us – the good and the lively, the show-offs and the rowdy, the giddy and the obstinate, the spendthrifts and the gossips, the clever and the simpletons. Barrat and Tranter, which associate trade with fraud, record a healthy mistrust of the proliferating traders. By extension, it is likely that because surnames may also record the unusual, the many names for the good-humoured and the short, the dark-skinned and the stupid, could mean that most people are dismal, tall, fair and shrewd.

Rather, abstract nicknames, such as Humble, Meek, Dove, Lamb, Wise and Curtis (for courteous), reflect the moral teachings of the day in the Bible, stories of chivalry, political songs and morality tales. People like to be known as they aspire to be. Many of Chaucer's more virtuous pilgrims come from this group. But there are many more surnames for the savage and the violent, the cunning and the fraudulent, the avaricious and the blasphemous, the gluttons and the lechers. Abstract ideals are outweighed by a recognition of human frailty, so much more real, interesting and entertaining. These names present a people who could come out of Aesop's fables – who know what is right, fail much of the time, and laugh at themselves by naming the failure as it walks by.

There is a fascination with distortion. Surnames record people with deformed bodies, noses, faces, hands, heads, legs, feet. These could simply identify odd-looking people, or they could be more sinister – we simply have no way of knowing for sure. Churches are full of carvings of people with distorted faces or other body parts that are believed to be there to frighten or propitiate. Some names associate physical and mental or moral traits. While Belcher is fair-faced and happily disposed, Dodd can be lumpy or stocky and stupid, so a lump for a body and a lump for a brain, and Crook is crookedly built and cunning or fraudulent.

Memories

The many personal surnames with multiple Norse, German and English roots show how deeply the culture of Anglo-Saxon England was entrenched in Scandinavia and northern Europe. All these languages have common Indo-Germanic roots, and people carrying these names had moved regularly for trade (as well as booty) between Scandinavia, northern Europe, the British Isles and the islands beyond for centuries before the Norman Conquest.

But it is more than just the words. Surnames can tell of ancient migrations, creating patterns of later settlements. Those with Scandinavian, often Norse, and Irish or Gaelic roots – Coleman, Gill, Neal and Brian – tell us that Vikings went to and probably settled Ireland before coming to north-west England, Cumbria, and over the Pennines into Yorkshire. Celtic names such as Morgan, could be Cornish, Old Welsh or Breton, showing how the Celts were driven back to the edges of land masses by successive Roman, Saxon and then Scandinavian invasions, to be brought back to the heart of England by the Bretons with the Norman invasion.

Many surnames record that medieval people have active memories of ancient cultures. Symbolic names like Raven or Wolf carry echoes of the magical predators of Norse legend. More potent evidence is in the surnames from the old first names that gave way to the Johns and Williams of the Conquest. Like a forest fire that smoulders underground to flare up much later far away from its first outbreak, many of our personal surnames – Godwin, Gamble and Griffin – have Old English, Scandinavian and Celtic origins, carrying the stories of earlier invasions and assimilations.

Background of Myth

Legend and myth arising across northern Europe and Scandinavia give cultural depth to these names. In the early days of the naming period, there is a great revival of interest in transcribing oral folk culture. The most important and comprehensive is the Danish recording of Icelandic and Scandinavian legends in the twelfth and thirteenth centuries that have become the bedrock of most of our knowledge of Norse and Teutonic mythology. *Beowulf* and other Anglo-Saxon and early Welsh poetry are recorded at about the same time. The *Chanson de Roland*, the best-known Norman *chanson de geste,* is written down in about 1100. Visual evidence of England's integration into this continental culture is the 'Franks casket'. Made in Northumberland in about AD 700, it shows a scene from the life of Weland, the smith of Norse and Teutonic myth who fashioned wondrous jewellery and weapons for the gods.[10]

Many of our personal names today come directly from these legends. Harold, mainly from the Norse *Haraldr*, but also the German *Hairold* and the Old English *Hereweald* is only one example of many. Harold was the name of Norse kings; Harold Wartooth, called after two massive tusks protruding from his mouth, was a Norse hero, a favourite of the god Odin, who battered him to death after a long and eventful life. The meanings of these names show times of conflict. Across all languages march names that mean war, battle and victory. They record the need for heroes, courage and strength, protection, magic and gods. They describe a time of political and social instability when people looked to their leaders and gods for salvation. And, indeed, pre-Conquest England was a disturbed place. The Irish Norse and the Danes advanced over 200 years in a pincer movement from west to east, culminating in the battle of Brunanburh in AD 937 when Aethelstan and Edmund finally stopped their advance and England was unified at last under an Anglo-Saxon king. But continued Danish raids gave no relief from conflict and the need for successful warrior kings.

It is hard to know now how much of this culture is known to the namers. The emergence of surnames from Norse single names in the old Danelaw suggests a traditional society there, and traditional societies have long memories. Surnames and physical relics show Norse was still used, and language carries culture. The revival of indigenous names, particularly those with multiple roots, shows that the legends and epics of pre-Conquest Anglo-Saxon culture are still in peoples' memories in the fourteenth century. Like parents today choosing first names, some must simply use a surname they like and some a name with an historical or sentimental connection. Our Elliots, Levetts and Woolvetts record, six centuries after it was written, the only English epic that has survived, *Beowulf*, and the heroic tribe of Geats from northern Europe. The Geat in our names is meaningless unless you know the epic. So although we cannot tell how much people know of the legends when they take names from Cuthbert or Thor, Ottar or Harding, at the very least the choice of these indigenous names is a cultural statement and at the most many would know something of their mythological background.

The number of these indigenous surnames contrasts with the sparseness of early records of them in contemporary literature. *The Canterbury Tales* and *Piers Plowman* have many classical/biblical and Norman names, but few Norse, Celtic or even Anglo-Saxon ones.[11] This suggests that the majority of the population has a far stronger connection to Anglo-Saxon, and, by extension, northern continental culture, than has the literate elite.

An intriguing aspect of the indigenous surnames is how far the emergence, particularly of the Norse surnames, is influenced by pagan culture. The church is a massive presence in the private and public lives of medieval people and many nicknames and saints' names demonstrate deep faith, despite a realistic cynicism towards ecclesiastics. But fourteenth-century England is a frightening place. The agricultural crises from 1315 to 1322 and several bouts of a new and terrifying plague from 1348 kill over half the population. Lives change in a way that must seem cataclysmic in such a traditional society. Perhaps the names of heroes and victorious kings, and particularly gods and magic, fill the same need for protection that people had felt centuries before. Surnames like Pagan and all the Wild names, as well as the personal names from the god Thor, might be the evidence.

Picture-making and Laughter

People use imagination to understand, explain and comment on their world. Some of these surnames are symbolic; when the name, for instance, of a bird or animal is used instead of an epithet. At one level, these surnames can just be descriptive: Crow is black and Swan white, Crane long-legged, Fox deceitful, and the wonderful Winch can be someone with a twisted bouncing walk rather like the flight of a lapwing. Other lovely images are Cardon, or thistle, for the difficult, and Bramble for the obstinate. At another level, these names tap into the associated meanings of the symbol from experience and legend, and reflect close observation of the natural as well as the human world. Names like Hawke, Wolf or Kite – the savage, violent and cruel – have echoes back to Norse and Celtic traditions, reminding us that this is a society vulnerable to death and destruction, with the simultaneous recognition that people can have the uncompromising cruelty of nature. The symbol vastly expands what the surname tells us.

But the tail switches. Wit lurks around the edges of these surnames. Many may seem to show a mostly straightforward and pragmatic people who tell what they see, giving us Carpenters, Browns, Rounds and Humbles. But the language in others often has a certain suspicious lightness of touch – think of Scattergood, Spendlove and Drinkall – and capture rather too apt visual images, like Barrel or Hogg. We know people deal in irony and quite like laughing at their rulers through the arrogant Kings and Lords and Bishops and Friars who are gluttons and lechers. So we wonder whether all those Humbles and Rounds, Angels and Wises might not just be a joke for people who are the very opposite.

Sometimes the humour is visual and obvious – Knott is a thickset person, knotted together by ropes of muscle or fat; Waghorn, a musician who waves his horn hopefully, pretentiously and perhaps pathetically at the music. And sometimes it is ironic – calling a person Goodenough, or after a habitual expression, as Purdey captures *par Dieu*. More often the humour relies on contrast for a laugh so you do not know quite what a name means. Any surname for a body part or physical attribute risks being ironic. So Hand can mean someone with deft hands or clumsy ones, or even a maimed one; Foot and Legg suggest people who can run well, or not at all and who are slow instead of speedy. With joking opposites, the laugh depends on the contrast between the name and the person it is first given to. Dictionaries have some records of this, and we know from contemporary writing and art that this type of wit is pervasive, from Chaucer calling his unlucky courtier Absolon a 'joly lovere' to the giant Littlejohn in the legend of Robin Hood. The possibility of such reversal is part of the fun of surnames.

Ambiguity can run through many surnames. Forgetting for the moment those with different meanings from different derivations, even non-symbolic names can be nuanced. Black can mean black or shining (as in glossy), Sealey can be fortunate or simple-minded, and Scattergood spendthrift or generous. Surnames can carry other overtones. Reed, for example, means red and the first Reed may just have had red hair or a red face. But in medieval England red is also the colour of debauchery, often of clerics who are frequently painted with pink faces in medieval art. Chaucer's parish clerk in *The Canterbury Tales*, the prowling and womanizing Absolon, has a red complexion – as he stalks the pretty wife of the carpenter 'in red stockings ... [he] walked exquisitely'.[12] So the first Reed could have been some local lecherous priest. But the symbolic names have the most complex possibilities of definition, often starting with directly accessible physical images. The Hoggs, trotters in trough, can mean greedy, usually for ale. On another level, contemporary literature and art tell us Hoggs can symbolize lust, particularly of clerics. Ravens are sleek, shining and black, but symbols of ill-omen in Celtic and Christian tradition, and in Norse legend are an odd combination of intellect and of birds of death, feasting on corpses.

The Triumph of English

Surnames are an intricate mix in which Old English dominates, but which includes a substantial proportion of Old French and a smattering still of Norse and Celt. These linguistic roots reflect the language that most medieval English speak. They show the clash and settlement of cultures as English absorbs invaders and emerges victorious before this is apparent from the official language of the country.

Surnames develop when England is still ruled, administered and subject to moral guidance in French and Latin. After Harold II, no king of England is to use English as an official language until Henry IV at the end of the fourteenth century, when most surnames already exist. Language signals class. 'Unless a man knows French, he is thought of little account,' says Robert of Gloucester. But Robert of Gloucester is talking only of aristocrats like himself. English, the language of the vast majority of the people in England, emerged from the early settlements of Angles, Saxons and Jutes. In the ninth and tenth centuries, Old Norse arrived with the Vikings, and a century later came the Normans and their allies, with Old French and Latin, then a written language, and some Norse and Celt from their own roots.

Part of the reason for the dominance of English in surnames could simply be in the numbers. It is thought that the landlords who own more than 70 per cent of the land in the late fourteenth century are around 7,000 out of a population of up to 3 million, while the Normans who came at the Conquest were less than 5 per cent of the total population.[13] That this 5 per cent of the population could not impose their language on the surnames of the remaining 95 per cent might not seem surprising. But after the Conquest the English almost universally jettisoned their single Anglo-Saxon names in favour of a few Norman ones, demonstrating their engagement with the new culture. So why, three centuries

36

later, do they not take more French-based words as surnames?

Much of the explanation must be that there are English words available for what needs to be said. French has added value in occupational names and some nicknames, but not the English countryside, for example. But part of the reason too might be that people have become resistant to Norman-French culture and the culture itself has, perhaps, also become over time more anglicized. This is evident in the ironic surnames from the titles of the Norman elite and in the way those Norman first names are so massively splintered into English alternatives when surnames appear – for example, Robert becoming Dobb and Rabbett, Hugh becoming Howett and Hutchens. The unchanged Norman names are generally held by the Welsh, who adopt them two to three centuries after the English take surnames. It is more surprising, given this assertion of an English culture, that there are still so many surnames with Old French derivations, and so many that co-exist with an English translation. These suggest that medieval spoken English has become a true local mix, with people saying Bonally as readily as Farrell for farewell, and Purdey, or *par Dieu*, as easily as 'God save'.

The Absorption of Norman into English

The mix is a triumph of a self-confident people. The immediacy, colour, inventiveness and range of Old English surnames show the vigour of the native language. The large number of Old French names record the contribution of the invaders to economic and social life and are evidence of the capacity of English to absorb what is needed.

Derivations can identify social and economic divisions. English surnames often describe the toilers and hewers, the French the fine specialists and overseers. The French bring a more sophisticated concept of service and hierarchy to manorial households and estates. The general and more menial servants and traditional and subordinate activities on the land, like the Hines and the Manns, the Reeves and the Haywards, the Woodmen and Shepherds, are Old English, but the Butler and the Chamberlain at the hall and the Bailiff and Steward on the estate are Old French. Most of the less skilled occupational surnames are Old English, traditional functions that dig deep into the English way of life like Smith and Webber, Chapman (a trader), Baker and Miller, Stoneman and Pedler. But sophisticated craftsmen like Carpenters and Masons, large traders like Drapers and Merchants, and suppliers of quality products and fashion for fun like Officers, who do gilt embroidery, and Taylor, that alchemist, are Old French. The French dominate management and quality, bringing hierarchy to service and new skills to occupations. The Old English name for Taylor is Shearer, who also shears the nap from the woven cloth and has ended up attending to sheep instead.

These connotations of higher skills, scale or social class in French words could be the explanation why some Old French words have been absorbed into the language rather than their English translation – think of archer instead of bowman and porter rather than wain. Yet the surnames still co-exist. Wise and Sage, Woodward and Parker, Chapman and Marchant, are all English and French translations of each other that lock in different and finer distinctions in meaning.

There are two striking exceptions to this co-existence of French and English derivations. Surnames to do with the land that appear as occupational names, symbolic nicknames and, especially, topographical names – Fords, Greens, Lakes, Hills and Woods, Wares, Ways and Bridges – are Old English with a few Old Norse. French cannot improve on how the English know and record the countryside. Old English already has a word for everything that needs to be described. More potently, these Old English surnames may also show how far removed is the ruling elite from the land it owns and the people who work it.

At the same time, nicknames to do with the church and saints' names tend to be French or Norman versions of classical/blical names. The English are happy to cede religious dominance to the invaders. It is striking that despite the strength of Celtic Christianity and its missionary saints, its historical importance is not reflected in the few Celtic surnames that survive to record it. But the titles of the basic hierarchy of the church are Old English – surnames like Pope and Bishop, Abbot and Prior. The English church was already integrated in the continental before the Normans came. Only a few lower levels, like Frere and Parson, are French.

Languages Even More Ancient

Despite the eventual victory of the Anglo-Saxons, followed by the Conquest, sparse shadows of the Norse still fall in the sunlight. Norse names add ancient professions, pedlar, charcoal-burner, meat-flayer, basic activities that survive alongside more recent translations. The Old Norse derivation of Bates comes from *bati*, dweller by the fat pasture – one of the reasons those early Scandinavians come, one supposes; Crook, sly or crooked, is a nickname; and the wonderful Sprackling is the man with the creaking legs. Most of these surnames have other meanings, one reason they have survived. Many Norse first names survive in surnames – Gamble, Harald, Thurkell, Osborne. They revive memories of Viking myths and pagan beliefs. Remarkably, after the passage of some 400 years after the Vikings first appeared off the coast of England and the turbulent times since, these names emerge and still tend to be concentrated in the old Viking areas of the north and east.

There are relatively few Celtic surnames. The English names of those recorded as holding land in the Domesday Book for Celtic Cornwall show Cornish landowners with non-Celtic names, single then. Several Celtic surnames, like Brian and Neal, survive because they share roots with the Norse, and Allen, Joel and Griffin are brought by Bretons at the Conquest, while Howell and Griffith are Welsh. Welsh names tend to be from these first names rather than occupational names or nicknames, and this preference dominates when they choose surnames like Roberts and Jones in the sixteenth century.

Surnames that Capture Evolution

The language captured in the amber of our surnames can be a base from which to trace its evolution since the Middle Ages.

The names that seem so wonderfully direct today appeal to us because the words they come from still mean the same. Others, Goff (a smith), Mander (a basket-maker), Pinder (an impounder of stray animals), and Trinder (someone who braids or plaits), are incomprehensible, either because more popular synonyms have supplanted them, such as Smith, or because the function has gone from the language, as with Pinder and Trinder. The same goes for Alabaster, a maker of crossbows; Wigg, a beetle; and Cork, a maker or seller of purple dye. The words now mean something quite different to the dictionary definition of the name. Many English personal names bring back ancient words, as Quennell records *cwenhild*, or 'woman war'.

Time has added a fillip of humour to other names because of changes in meaning and usage. Hot and Hotter were basket-makers; Barkers were shepherds, all madly barking like their dogs? Cowards were cowherds, always running away? Cants were church singers who became hypocrites. Belcher was fair-faced, and Blank a blonde. Other names are amusing now because small changes in meaning add comment. So Larges were generous and are now just big; Pettys were small and have become small-minded; a Leach was just a doctor and is now a general bloodsucker; Sadd was serious and discreet; Bragger, not boastful, but a cloth-worker who sold wool to the staplers, always talking up its quality? Did the character or behaviour of early holders of the names lead to these adjustments in meaning?

Variations in the same surname show usage evolving as names from all over the country reflecting different dialects and clerks with different ears and attention spans come together. The spelling of Norman names is particularly variable. So we have people from Montbrai in La Manche who are recognizably Mowbrays in County Durham, but Membury in Somerset, Memory in next-door Devon and further north in Leicestershire, and Mummery in Kent. The first serious effort to rationalize how names are written is not attempted until the fifteenth century, and spelling is to remain fluid until compulsory education in the nineteenth century. So Brewer is written Brewere or Breuwer, Hand is Hond or Honde, Hammond is Haymund, and Hill is Hulle. Although we have no firm idea about medieval accents, you can hear a soft drawl in Whita for

White, Vyssher for Fisher, Yate for Gate, Pasemore, a sailor, from
the Old French *passe-mer*, and in Beera from Beer.

Names Illuminate Other Records

An understanding of the language in surnames can add a new
dimension to ancient records. Just the names on the sundial still
visible above a porch of the church at Kirkdale in Yorkshire,
shows the fading of paganism in this most Viking area. The
sundial reads, in translation:

> Orm, son of Gamal, bought St Gregory's church when it was
> all ruined and tumbled down and he caused it to be built afresh
> from the foundation [in honour of] Christ and St Gregory in
> the days of king Edward and in the days of earl Tosti. This is
> the day's sun-marking at every hour. And Haward made me,
> and Brand, priest [?][14]

All the names, bar those of king, saint and church are Norse. Tosti
was earl of Northumberland from 1055 to 1065, so the sundial
was inscribed just before the Conquest. Early records of Orm,
Gamal, Haward and Brand are in the Danelaw. Orm, in pagan
Viking legend, is the serpent/dragon destined to destroy the world;
here he buys and rebuilds a ruined church. The high chief warden,
Haward, becomes a mason, and the Brand who wielded a pagan
sword, a priest.

In 1030, just before the sundial was inscribed, an English missionary, Wilfred, was martyred by pagans in Sweden. At about
the same time, the namesakes of these Scandinavians in Yorkshire
were restoring a church that their own ancestors could have
destroyed.

Capturing Medieval English Culture

Our surnames, exploding into the records in the late fourteenth
century, represent the final triumph of English over French and

ground the culture of England. They crystallize our language and explore its opportunities before it develops into the King James Bible and Shakespeare. Ordinary medieval folk are bound to later wordsmiths through their directness of observation, a turn of epithet and image, and an ability to communicate ideas and wit. Names allow us to track the evolution of the language of ordinary people much further back than formal literacy would suggest. The variants of the Norman personal names show most emphatically how the English of ordinary people was bound to triumph over the Norman languages of their rulers. There is a gusto and a rhythm in the rhymes, alliterations and beat of all those Robins and Dobbins, Hicks and Dicks, Jans and Jankins that echo the sound and structure of the Anglo-Saxon past and tell of a sheer joy in using language.

Surnames confirm what medieval and pre-Conquest excavations and history tell us about medieval England – about the growth of industry and trade, the emergence of towns, the integration of England in continental Europe, the control of the land and the dominance of the aristocracy and the church. What they add is the dynamic of how the majority of the population is changing, grasping new opportunities, developing skills, travelling, investing in covetable possessions. They tell us about values and attitudes. Nicknames that criticize the church and the aristocracy and topographical names that show the distance of the ruling elite from the land they live off contain warnings that anticipate peasant revolts and the failure of feudalism. They show how English culture absorbs Norman language and ideals while maintaining a stronger and separate identity and world view. More than that, they tell us about the people – direct, observant, imaginative and, above all, realistic and humorous. Surnames put the people back into history. Understanding them brings these people back and sheds a new light on what we already know.

Over the 600 years since surnames were established in England, church, king and aristocracy have lost their menace and are no longer widespread targets for mockery. We no longer settle disputes using Champions, find pilgrims, pagans or wildmen in our midst, call our siblings Friend or Cousans, or know the habits of birds (or even our fellow men) as well as our medieval ancestors. Nature is no longer central to our world view, nor is its potential for violence, with its background in pagan cultures and their panoplies of malevolent predators and gods. With the change in the role of religion we are less concerned with the evils of greed, or vanity, we do not scorn gossiping because it makes enemies, notice speed, strength or dexterity in the same way, or believe stupidity will lead to a bad end. And the fascination and fear of deformity, the idea that physical and mental traits are linked, and, especially, the recognition of the savage potential of man and nature, show a different cultural attitude arising out of quite different experiences.

Yet much of the reality in these surnames is appealingly familiar. Many of the occupations they record still exist, as do many of the towns and even local villages. We still notice the blondes, the tall and the fat, the happy and the miserable, the flirtatious and the pious. We still, to a certain extent, engage in metaphor – calling a runner after his legs or a lecher a rabbit. And we still admire noble or selfless behaviour, notice human frailty and smirk at pretentiousness and hypocrisy; indeed, much of the humour in English sitcoms comes from such observation – from Captain Mainwaring in *Dad's Army* to Del Boy from *Only Fools and Horses*.

Investigating these possibilities in our surnames opens the gate on a winding path that takes us back over seven hundred years or more. It is not an orderly journey. Surnames are not tidy. Often hard to classify and difficult to interpret, tracking their story is like weaving with gossamer. Threads fail, patterns are faint and partial, and one is always at risk of breaking the thread by weighing it down with over-interpretation. But the fabric they weave documents something of what we were, and what we were is a part of what we are. That is the story that English surnames have given to England and the thousands of English who left our ports to find another home across the seas.

CHAPTER 2

CRAFTS, SERVICE AND FASHION: THE POPULAR OCCUPATIONS

SMITH AND CARPENTER, Butler and Falconer, Taylor and Hatter are all occupational surnames, and document a changing society in medieval England. In this chapter, the focus is on the most popular groups: names to do with crafts, service at the manor and the cloth and fashion industry.

Popularity records what is most valued. A few names dominate: Smith is 70 per cent more popular than Taylor, while the wool-tramplers – Fuller/Tucker/Walker – and weavers are way ahead of other specializations. For surnames recording those who work the land, the clerks and traders, the builders, musicians and soldiers, see Chapter 3.

On a straightforward level, understanding a single name can vastly expand what a record can tell us. Robert le Taylour from Shrewsbury, in 1309, has an impressive forty-shilling riding horse, sumptuous clothes and a stash of silver and jewellery. The date of his inventory suggests that he is the tailor who has acquired these status goods out of his own hard work. Just looking at his surname shows that the opportunities exist for someone in his profession to do quite astonishingly well at this time.

Groups of occupational surnames tell about society, how medieval people earn a living and where the country's productive wealth lies. Craftsmen in the villages and servants at the manor are still rooted in feudal life; Smiths and Stewards are ancient occupations. But alongside is the story of land as the primary source of wealth being challenged by the new rural industries and the increasing prosperity of an urban population – a story as much about consumption as work. Fashion brings in a new world, people with French names meeting sophisticated wants.

In England surnames emerge at a time of social and economic stress and show how people turn this into opportunity. Famines from 1315 to 1322 and plagues from 1348 first weaken, then empower, peasants, leading to greater opportunities for enrichment. As the population collapses, food prices fall, and diets improve. An acute shortage of labour betters its conditions. Landlords find it more and more difficult to hold onto their tenants and bonded labour. In the countryside, settlements are abandoned and less labour-intensive pasturing replaces arable land.

Towns proliferate, attracting those with skills as well as those with none. In 1100 there are some 100 towns in Britain and 830 towns by 1300, when almost a fifth of the population is urban.[1] More and more, people are called after what they do instead of their settlements of origin. Occupational names in one sample rise from about 16 per cent of the total in 1265 to some 26 per cent by 1377.[2] There are 175 occupations listed in London in about 1300.[3] Guilds encourage craftspeople to move to the towns; guild membership is the commonest way to get the freedom of a city or borough. Others become servants.

At the same time, England shifts from exporting wool to producing and exporting the more profitable finished product. The names of the cloth- and woolmen in this chapter, those of the merchants in Chapter 3 and those of the cities and fairs they build and the routes they travel in Chapter 4 show the organization and the reach of this key medieval trade. The value of foreign trade, most of it in wool and cloth, is believed to have risen some three times in real terms over the century before the peak for wool in 1304–5 and cloth exports alone are to rise twentyfold in the last half of the fourteenth century. This surge in cloth-making benefits the countryside: spinning, weaving and fulling to prepare the cloth are all rural activities. Poll tax returns show by the end of the fourteenth century about a third of the English population earn most of their living from wage work and up to two-thirds in the wealthy east.[4]

Shearer Rises to Taylor

Occupational surnames document the detail of this great dynamic. Groups of names record specialization as a scale of skills evolves within activities. Surnames to do with fashioning wood show a simple Sawyer or Hacker finding it worthwhile to invest in skills and possibly equipment to become a Turner or a Wright. The Shearers and Cisore who cut basic tunics can evolve into Taylors. And both traditional and new activities can be vertically integrated. From Scullion and Horseman to Chamberlain and Steward, the servants at the great hall build a hierarchy of responsibilities; from Tozer, who teases the raw wool, and Dyer to Packer the cloth industry is organized around interlocking specializations. Evidence of higher wages for skilled work shows one reason people may specialize. Another might be survival as famines and labour shortage force farmers to adapt and shift between crops and livestock, and out of them altogether into crafts and other occupations. The surnames recording the opportunities for Sawyers to become Wrights and Shearers to rise to Taylors reflect a social revolution as fundamental and significant as the political upheaval of the Peasants' Revolt of 1381.

Popular groups of names reflect a tension between needs and wants and record growing prosperity. The range and number of names of general servants show many ordinary families from across the country have at least one servant. The names of suppliers of clearly luxury goods are evidence that they are destined for a larger market than the small secular and religious elite. For subsistence, Smiths and Carpenters make the tools to grow the crops and the Carters take any surplus to market. But just as important are those who make the luxuries bought with the surplus. In the towns, Taylors, embroiderers, Hatters and cape-makers are supplying a new market of people like themselves working their way out of their feudal tunics and tabards.

There are attitudes and aspirations in these names. Even as it evolves away from feudalism, society is hypnotized by appearances and social rank. The titles of servants record status signals for the lord: high-ranking Stewards, Falconer and Marshall for hunting, Butler for the wine and Chamberlain to manage his private rooms. All those making the more sophisticated garments and luxury goods identify the signals by which the elite and aspiring classes define and recognize social standing. After Smith, Taylor is the second most popular occupational name; everyone wants to look like a lord. The survival of these names also suggest people like these titles and what they mean.

The surnames in records identify occupations that seem to be associated with success and show that it is often the people purveying exotica – the Taylors and Glovers – who do the best. Craftsmen with the first occupational names recorded in small concentrations in the larger settlements become the leading townsmen who compete in wealth with the aristocracy. But success also depends on opportunity, luck and the talent to use them. The goods in inventories show people with relatively lowly names acquiring status possessions. Among all the barbers, potters and hoopers assessed at the lowest tax rates in Shrewsbury in 1309, a barber, John le Barbour, has the brassware of the middle class and the relatively valuable clothes, the cup with silver fittings and the meat that signal prosperity.[5] Yet many struggle. Successive inventories show that one wheelwright fares reasonably well for a while, but then retreats to paying the lowest tax rate. When he has funds, he buys some brassware and clothes, but these have disappeared from his final inventory.

Language in Amber

Comparing the medieval and modern meanings of surnames can show how language has evolved. Many still mean the same. A Bowler would still make bowls; a Jewel, jewels; a Glover, gloves; and a Hall would work at the manor-house. Interestingly, the twin meanings of Ware – a weir or a nickname for wary – are still the same. For some names, the meaning has just shifted slightly.

Marshalls no longer look after horses, but Grooms, then general servants, do; Pages and Squires do not worry about knights; and Chandlers sell ships' stores instead of candles. But the meaning of other names has completely changed. How would you know that an Officer is actually an embroiderer in silver and silver-gilt thread, or that the Challinor makes blankets, and the Trist (both Middle English from French) looks after hounds? These are the names that identify lost activities.

The way language has changed can give unintended humour. A Coffin used to make baskets, as did the Hotts and Hotters. And there are good reasons to do with etymology and the phonetics of dialect for why the modern meanings of Berry (then a servant at the manor), Burrows or Bowers (one at a bower house), Leach (a doctor), Clout (a cobbler), and Lavender (a washerwoman) are so different. But rosy-cheeked help, doctors who bleed you to bankruptcy, thumping cobblers, and sweetly-smelling washing are vivid images. The surnames mark the evolution of language, but the bonus of time is that the changes can make you laugh.

The linguistic roots of these surnames document what different cultures contribute to English occupations. Most names are English, mainly recording basic activities that dig deep down into English history. The fewer French names identify the exotic. When it comes to naming occupations to do with crafts and essential clothes, our ancestors generally find an appropriate English word. But when they need to identify fashion for fun or the sophisticated management of personal service, they turn to French. The few names with Old Norse roots keep alive memories of ancient activities: Swain and Gill both mean servants, Theaker is a thatcher and Skinner a butcher.

Medieval people love ambiguity. Even with names from the same root, classification is like corralling teenage girls in a shop; they sprawl out all over. There is a particular overlap between occupational and locational names. Many names based on Old English words can mean either that the person lives by a place or works there. Yate could live near the gate or be the gate-keeper; Miller could live at the mill or be the miller. Then many names have several meanings, only one of which is occupational. Gill could be a servant or dweller in a deep glen; Hyne, a servant or be called after a female deer; Master could be a schoolmaster, master of a farmhouse or building site or of an apprentice, or someone who lives at the master's house, when he could be a servant or indeed an apprentice himself. There are overlaps too among occupational names. Since craftsmen and fashion-workers could be makers or sellers, Glover could be here under fashion or in the next chapter under traders. Professionalization and scale also affect classification, so Smiths, Carpenters and Wrights could be craftsmen here if small scale or builders in the next chapter if bigger and more skilled.

There is a final, intriguing, aspect to these, as many other, names. Tucker, for example, that good old Devon name for a wool trampler, is still far more popular there than Walker or Fuller, the names for the same occupation elsewhere; Trinder, a rare name for a braider, is still around in Oxfordshire; and Angove, from the Old Cornish word for smith, is still mainly in Cornwall.[6] These names were local 700 years ago and are still local today, despite migration, waves of lethal plagues, wars and the social vicissitudes that meant the population of England did not reach its mid-fourteenth century level again until the eighteenth century.

We can only guess why some activities lead to surnames and some do not. There is a theory that part-time occupations, which most are (at least, initially), do not, while full-time ones do. But most glovers and cap-makers, spicers and falconers cannot, even in towns, be full-time. And from records that show unlicensed brewers keeping the courts going in medieval England, we know that brewing is a very common part-time occupation. Yet Brewer is a common surname. So being part-time does not seem to preclude naming. But being full-time can. In Chapter 3 there are very few names for ploughmen, reapers or gleaners, yet there is a multitude of Smiths when there are no more than one or two in most rural hamlets. So scarce and valued skills seem to explain more surnames than whether the activity is full-time or not.

Country Craftsmen

This is about daily essentials, the craftsmen working in metal, wood and clay. Many names show specialization: Hoopers who make hoops; Wheelwrights who make wheels; Roopes who do ropes. Tax records show they invest to do their jobs and that few are seriously wealthy. Smiths and Carters nevertheless support technological innovations that vastly increase farm and transport productivity and go on to facilitate the great cathedral building of the Middle Ages discussed in the next chapter.

The Dominating Smith

The popularity of Smith is one of the main reasons crafts are the top occupation. It records a highly valued, essential and ancient craft still hammering away today. Smith, Ferrer or Ferrar, who produce the place name of Ferrieres (or iron works) dotted all over France, Faber, Goff and Angove are all smiths, and Marshall, a groom, can also be a farrier. Including the rarer names does not add many numbers, but the alternatives show the activity is important across the cultures making up medieval England.

In early times, according to the *Oxford English Dictionary*, smiths were general craftsmen or skilled workers in metal, wood and other materials. Some, working for kings or nobles, may have specialized in fine inlaid work on armour and sword hilts. English metalwork was prized in continental Europe in Anglo-Saxon times. By the Middle Ages, smiths are workers in iron and other metals, forgers and hammermen who make basic inputs into other crafts essential to farming, building and transport. Excavations of medieval sites record they made metal necessities for the home and for hunting – buckles and candleholders, chest keys and padlocks, window and door pivots, knives, arrowheads and spurs, harness parts and horseshoes as well as farming tools.

Smith is so common today it is hard to grasp how important and innovative the function is in the Middle Ages. At this time, most tools have not changed much since Roman times but the smiths contribute to new harnesses, equipment and better-designed vehicles that allow teams of six to eight oxen draw the heavier 'mouldboard' plough and teams of horses, 50 per cent faster and with greater stamina than oxen, to carry heavier loads. With faster ploughing and transport, farm productivity rises. On large building sites smiths are involved in making the innovative hoists to lift stones to great heights and the new stone-cutting chisels so masons can dress and fit stones so precisely that the joints are almost invisible.

The name carries with it the magic of smiths in many of the traditions that feed medieval culture. In a society where the powerful are those successful in battle, the forgers of weapons and the weapons themselves take on an importance that verges on the mythical. The smiths are the dwarves who protect, transferring knowledge and making magical weapons. The smith Sithchen in Irish Gaelic legend is a magician and a seer; Reginn, the wonder-smith of Norse legend, gives the hero Sigurd/Siegfried instruction in the mysteries of runes and teaches him different languages. Reginn forges the sword Gramr for Sigurd from a fragment of one his father had from the chief god Odin; in the *Chanson de Roland*, Charlemagne has the sword Joyeuse, his:

> ... peerless blade,
> That changes colour full thirty times a day[7]

Roland has Durendal; Oliver has Hauteclaire; and the feisty Archbishop Turpin has Almace. The Norse Dvalin makes the spear Gungnir, which never misses its mark, and the god Thor's hammer is Mjölnir, forged by the dark elves, a symbol of his energy and power. In Beowulf's final battle with the monster Grendel's mother, he grabs a sword 'an ancient heirloom/from the days of the giants', which strikes off her head, after which:

> ... the sword
> began to wilt into gory icicles,
> to slather and thaw ...[8]

The wonder of ordinary people for these hammerers of iron and creators of beauty out of fire comes down to us in Viking legend, whose dark elves are the craftsmen who make the bindings for the powerful wolf Fenrir 'from the sound of a cat's footsteps, a woman's beard, the spittle of birds and the longing of the bear.'[9] Reginn crafts the ship Skiobladur, which always finds a following wind and can sail across air as well as water carrying an army in full armour, yet can be folded up and packed away in a purse. He also makes the delicate golden tresses of Sif, Thor's wife, after hers have been cut and stolen by the evil Loki.

The Smith invests in his own skills as a specialist metal-worker and has capital investment in a forge and tools and operational costs for his inputs of charcoal and wood. In an inventory from 1391, John Smyth from Long Marston in Oxfordshire has an anvil, a hammer, tongs, bellows and a grindstone.[10] Smiths can be high-status craftsmen, often owning more land than others, but the William Smith from Ingatestone who joins the Peasants' Revolt in 1381 shows all the signs of a frustrated rebel. He is a serf and an ale taster, owning cattle, calves and pigs. Despite his march to Mile End with Wat Tyler, his landlord seems to have been unable to get rid of him, and he is back tasting ale in his village by 1386, still recalcitrant and refusing to pay a fine and a year later being bound over to be well-behaved towards the bailiff.[11]

Shrewsbury, around the turn of the thirteenth century, has few Smiths but quite a number of Marechals. These are farriers, taxed on their trade equipment – iron, coal, charcoal and firewood for the forge and sometimes horseshoes and nails too. All but one have low tax assessments, although several are doing well enough to be eligible for tax over a decade or more. The exception, one Thomas le Marechal, in 1309, is assessed on a number of status goods, cash, valuable clothes, silver and meat as well as quite a volume of malt, so he (or more probably his wife) may be brewing as well. He no longer has the equipment of his trade and has obviously found a way to join the wealthy of the town.[12]

Woodworking

Woodworkers also make essentials. Some invest in skills and equipment, creating a professional hierarchy from Sawyer, Hacker and Carpenter to Turner and Wright. Wright is a joiner and the Turner fashions wood, metal or bone on a wheel or a lathe. The Hooper makes or fits hoops or staves; the Cooper, wooden casks or buckets; the Wheeler and the Cartwright make what the names suggest; as do Barrell and Bowler, while the Busse make barrels and casks. Bowler is a tippler as well as a bowl-maker, a glimpse of typical medieval metaphor and humour; people drink their ale from wooden receptacles for most of the Middle Ages. Mander, Coffin, Bushel, and Hotter make baskets of willow. And the Collier, or charcoal-burner, supplies the Smiths or the fires of the wealthy.

Woodworkers use local materials. Most people have rights to take timber from local woods, supervised by a manorial official, usually the Wodeward. The right is called *housebote* if the wood is taken for house-building, and *ploughbote* if it is for agricultural tools. (Dead wood is paid for in hens and called *henbote*.) Colliers use oak, beech and birch, and Coopers beech and ash for cups, bowls and buckets because beech sap does not leach.

Not everyone will be able to invest in specialist skills and equipment so the names of the few who can record their scarcity and their value. The Sawyers, Hackers, Carpenters, Turners and Wrights are generalists, but these names still show an evolution of skills. A Hacker makes simple tools like mattocks; a Sawyers would do basic carpentry; and a Carpenter would work on buildings and even boats. Most houses have stone foundations but are still primarily made of wood, even in the towns, with a typical house needing twenty trees. Carpenters use oak, particularly for shingles and framing buildings, and the oaks grown on steep, exposed land in western England produce the crucks, or curved timbers, in medieval framing. Beech is used for boat-building. Turners and Wrights would have done the more sophisticated joinery on doors and roof-work needed by richer clients. Chaucer's reeve in the Prologue of *The Canterbury Tales* is also a 'wel good wrighte, a carpenter', turning to woodwork when his other duties allow.

Tylers – Slaters, Tilers, Helliers and all its variants – reflect a change in roofing as towns discourage flammable thatch roofs. They are an example of a craft in which the major investment is skill, tilers needing only an auger to make the holes to fit the tiles in place.

More skills and equipment seem to have meant higher incomes, although the scarcity or otherwise of the specialist will also have contributed to what they could earn. Information on wages shows a hierarchy. In the mid-fourteenth century, tilers earn some 45 per cent more than carpenters, who earn more than twice the wages of an unskilled labourer.[13]

Other Crafts

The popularity of surnames records which occupations are valued across the country. But less common surnames show important activities. Still around, although with very few numbers against them, are Lockyers, some of whom make locks, and Kays, who could, among other meanings, make keys. Security is important. Excavations show doors and chests have keys, windows have shutters and homes are surrounded by hedges and ditches. Cutlers, Cottles and Nasmyths make knives (Sheffield is already specializing in metalwork in 1379)[14]; Spooners spoons or, in the south, roof shingles; Ropers and Roopes, ropes; Maletts, hammers; and Corders, cord. The Tanners and Barkers tan leather, the Barkers stripping tree-bark. The inputs for tanning are costly – the oak bark for the tannin, pits lined with timber – and hides take a long time to treat. All of these supply needs.

The Potters and Crockers record the many rural kilns scattered across the country and the new glazes developed in the late thirteenth century. Crockerton in Wiltshire and Marston in Leicestershire both have a reputation for pottery. Their functions differ. Crocker is from the Old English *croc(c)*, or earthen pot, and Potter from the late Old English *pottere,* who makes metal pots as well as earthenware vessels. Shrewsbury potters are assessed for tax on the brass sheets they melt down for their metalwork and their clay moulds. Potters are also sometimes bell-founders, using the same technology.

While inventories of craftsmen can show people with quite humble names buying expensive clothes and brassware, they can also show the struggle to find a niche. Just sometimes, records give an insight into the lives of ordinary people, and William le Whelwruhte from Shrewsbury seems to be a good example of the unexceptional life of the urban craftsman. He appears in tax assessments from 1297 to 1316. Doing well enough to be assessed, his ratings rise to two shillings and over in successive assessments until 1313. Throughout he is assessed on his equipment; he remains a wheelwright. His team of carthorses starts at one, rises to four, plus cart and harness but falls back to one. As his income rises, his other possessions include some modest clothes and brassware, but never the silver or jewellery of the wealthy. His last assessment falls to a low twelve pence (12d) when brassware and clothes have disappeared from his possessions.[15]

Service

The popularity of surnames recording domestic service shows how common it is. There are two types: general and specialized.

There are quite a number of names for general, 'do-everything' servants. Records show that 20–30 per cent of urban poll-taxpayers are servants.[16] So we have surnames like Mann and associated names Berryman (a lovely one from the Old English *burgh* for fortified residence), Yeoman (who could also be a farmer), Youngman, Monksman or Harriman. There is Groom (*not* a stable boy), Gill, Hine or Hyne, which all just mean servant, while Swain is a boy servant and Hall, a popular name, works there.

The number of names for general servants suggests that hiring servants is a reasonably widespread practice. Court rolls from the thirteenth to the fifteenth centuries in one community west of Birmingham show that at least 43 per cent of families have servants for some time before the Black Death and that even after it 20 per cent do.[17] For a landless farmer with no skills, becoming a servant is a good way to get off the manor. General names also suggest servants have little status in this rank-conscious society. This is confirmed in contemporary records where servants are simply recorded as 'servant of', and in the many names ending in '-s', such as Parsons or Vickers, that can also mean a servant at that house (as well as anyone else living there). The forms of the names show servants are usually men, although Hine, because its other meaning is hind, could denote a woman. Other records show that in towns many are women. Between 1373 and 1393 in

Exeter, 37 per cent of known female inhabitants are servants who have no byname (an as yet not inherited surname).[18]

My Servant, My Rank

The status of the servant is carried in his or her name, but, by implication, the number and type of servant on a manor also signals an employer's social standing.

There is a vast number of specialized sub-activities. They record a vertically integrated consumer business, with a structure of managers and specialists designed to meet the needs and wants of the employer. A parallel structure of occupations peoples the oversight and production of estates and is discussed in Chapter 3. Some positions, like Steward, Chamberlain or Sargent, could belong either to the manor or the estate.

There is, of course, a hierarchy. Senior retainers, who could be relatives of the lord or gentry themselves, include the Chaplins, Cappels and Caples for religious and secretarial services; the Stewards or Stewarts who oversee the household or the estate (the Scottish Stewarts were originally hereditary stewards of the Scottish kings); the Chamberlain or Chambers who manage the lord's private rooms and the finances of the household or estate; the Wardropes, in charge of bulk purchases; and the Ushers and Sargents, who are middle-level managers (the latter has several other meanings, including a lawyer). Large households would have the Leaches and Barbers as physicians and dentists, and Harpers, Luters and Pipers for entertainment. Among the better-born retainers are the Batchelors, or young knights, the Squires and the Pages who attend to the lord and his knights here as well as on the battlefield.

More menial posts include the Butler or Spencer for the wine; the Cook, Kitchen, Kitchiners, Kitcheners and Scullions in the kitchen; the Lander or Lavender for the laundry; the Napiers and Nappers in charge of the table linen (from which we get napkin); and the Norris or nurse for the baby. Outside are the gatekeepers, with three names for them: Yates, Porter and Usher. The Days are in the dairy or the bakery, and the Marshalls, Horsemans, Capelmans, Amblers or Palfreys look after the horses. (Palfrey could also be the saddle horse.) The Falconers and Hawks with all their variants attend to the falcons and hawks and the Trists care for the hounds. Then the Burroughes and Bowers are servants at the bower-house or sleeping quarters, the Gardeners and their variants tend the gardens and the Galpins are the messengers.

Large households spawn villages of suppliers: Poulters, Bakers, Brewers, Chandlers (the candlemakers) and Smiths, the Skinners who flay the meat and the Saddlers who make the harnesses. We cover some of these under traders in Chapter 3.

The sheer number of servants boosts an employer's rank. Dukes and earls, bishops and rich abbots keep 40–160 servants, rich knights 12–30. In 1384 John of Gaunt, the richest man in England, has 115 retainers, excluding 150 soldiers.[19] The Redvers family, Earls of Devon in the thirteenth century and considerably wealthy with major estates in Hampshire and Dorset and on the Isle of Wight as well as in Devon, has 135 retainers in 1384. Records of Redvers property transfers and gifts refer to chaplains and clerks, some of whom are attorneys, and stewards who have responsibilities across the Redvers estates. Household staff include chamberlains and butlers, a cook called Hamelin and Kenebold, the minstrel, as well as other servants. Records give glimpses of the symbols of the mutual obligations of feudal patriarchy. John, servant to the family's private sheriff, is given land in return for two arrows a year and the gift of a little knife.[20]

The number of specialists and what they do reflects the lord's social heft. Senior retainers – especially when they have servants of their own, like Ushers – are valued as much for being there as for meeting a need for efficiency and privacy.

Service for Display

The names of the specialists signal what lends status. Hospitality does. A separate functionary to manage bulk buying gives an insight into the sheer scale of wealthy living. A Lincoln draper, Stephen of Stanham, provides the king's 'wardrobe' with spices, wax and cloth in London in the early fourteenth century.[21] Good food is part of it, hence a separate cook, with Kitchins and

Scullions to help him. William of Malmesbury, writing in about 1125, has a nicely nuanced comment on the invaders and their food, saying: 'The Normans were and still are ... delicate about their food, though not excessively'.[22] Even Chaucer's group of guildsmen, craftsmen all, take their cook with them as they travel together on a pilgrimage to make, among other dishes, stews, pies and blancmange. Towns have many community cooks, witnessing charters and appearing in court. Assizes or statutes regulate the quality of their food; they have to sell fish and meat, all to be wholesome and nothing cooked twice.[23]

Wine is important; two names have to do with dispensing it. Wine is the premier import into Exeter in the thirteenth and early fourteenth centuries, and imports 'for drink' by the gentry and the clergy are exempt from customs duty. Wine consumption rises with income. At Beaulieu Abbey, abbots, priors and other dignitaries are offered wine, but most knights and parish clerks get good ale.[24] In 1345–6 a rich baron, Thomas de Berkeley, spends 6 per cent of his food budget on wine – £46.[25]

Hunting is a noble sport and horses, falcons, hawks and hounds are symbols of rank. The lord has special management for these; falconers and hawkers have several variants and there are five names for grooms. Horses are expensive to buy and to keep. A warhorse costs £80 and a good riding horse £10 in the thirteenth century, when a knight's landed income is £10 or so. Keeping the Earl of Cornwall's warhorse for eighty-two days in the summer of 1297 costs 36s 9½d when an agricultural labourer is paid only a penny (1d) a day.[26] Large households keep thirty to forty horses. For Thomas de Berkeley, 57 per cent of all expenditure in 1345–6 is on food and 13 per cent on keeping and buying horses and falcons.[27] Among all the status goods in the tax inventories for Shrewsbury in the early fourteenth century, expensive riding horses identify the truly wealthy.

Menial specialisms are intriguing. A Norris is obvious; a general servant cannot be a wet nurse and a wet nurse is essential if a mother has died in childbirth or can or will not feed her infant. But why the specialist launderers when there are plenty of names for general servants? Do they have skills that general servants lack? Does laundry take too much time? Is it taken away to be done, so managed differently? The Landers seem to reflect the same importance of clothes that makes fashion one of the most popular occupations. Gardeners supply many of the needs of a household for vegetables and fruit. The gardens of Glastonbury Abbey in 1333–4 grow 8,000 heads of garlic and 3 quarters of onions.[28] Small gardens grow leeks and fruit-like apples and pears as well.[29]

Time Edits Meaning

The surnames of some servants seem to have survived by evolving. After his start at the manor, Steward takes on college catering, ships' stores, and race tracks and has moved on from cabin steward and deck steward to Lord Steward of the Sovereign's Household. Marshalls go from looking after the lord's horses, shoeing them and treating their diseases to being field marshals, marshals in courts of law and Marshall of the Ceremonies in the Lord Chamberlain's Department. Chamberlain begins managing the lord's private rooms and then takes on royal duties as Lord Chamberlain of the Household and even Lord Chamberlain of England. Squires move from serving knights to being ladies' escorts and then become country gentlemen. Others do less well. Pages go from being lads training for knighthood to checking the door and running errands in hotels, clubs and shops and holding up the bride's train at weddings. Other names have become dehumanized. Wardrope shifts across from managing clothes to being the furniture that stores them. Spencer goes from being in charge of wine, to being a kind of wig, a short or double-breasted overcoat for men, or a fitted bodice for women and children in the early nineteenth century, and a fore and aft sail set with a gaff on a yacht.

Other names seem to have stayed as they were, and are hardly surviving. Palfreyman, which still records a groom for saddle horses, is a only little more specialized than Marshall, but is much less widespread. Day, the dairymaid, dairyman or kneader of dough, is still with us in goodly numbers, yet the name has not taken on a more general meaning.

Records show how some of these servants fare. In the Shrewsbury tax assessment for 1306, Adam le Grom, once a serving-man, possesses the silks and muslins and gloves that suggest he has become a small-time mercer, and has invested in some fine clothes and household brassware.[30] The date of this assessment means he has moved out of his servile status within a generation. A Richard Gillot, his name a diminutive of Gill, a menial servant, is the master of *le Cog Seynt Jake* from Dartmouth docking in Exmouth in the nasty month of January in 1318 with a sunny cargo of figs, raisins and oil.[31] Despite expectations, the Middle Ages gives the humble space for social advancement.

Fashion

Feudalism is all about appearances. King, courtier, landlord and churchman use them to advertise and consolidate power and to impress. We have seen the role played by retainers – all those stewards and cup-bearers, grooms and falconers. Clothes and jewellery also signal rank. The survival, range and popularity of the fashion surnames record the social and economic value of the industry.

The Sumptuary Laws of 1363 show the hierarchy of the new social order of the landed aristocracy, the church and urban society scaled according to the clothes they can wear.[32] Knights with lands worth 200 marks a year (a mark is worth 13s 4d) and their families cannot wear cloth of gold and the women can only wear jewels in their hair, but lords with lands worth £1,000 annually have no restrictions.[33] These laws are an attempt to regulate dress to keep people in their place and perhaps also to minimize spending on foreign textiles, the velvets and damasks that still have to be imported.

The Sumptuary Laws are not enforceable and everyone joins in according to their means. A late fifteenth-century entry at the Mayors' Courts records from Dartmouth runs:

William Skynner in Court received from William Wode '1 Tawny Gown, 1 Spaynysh Cote of violett, ii dobeletts, 1 per of Blewe cote ... furred ...'[34]

Wode has an ancestor from a wood, Skynner from a meat flayer.

They are exchanging clothing valuable enough to be the subject of court proceedings and described in detail – a gown, coats, doublets. The colours are expensive and fashionable: tawny, violet and blue. One has a fur lining. This brief reference encapsulates the importance of fine clothes for ordinary medieval people.

The wealthy buy the jewelled and ermine-lined robes we see in contemporary paintings and liveries for their servants. (Elizabeth de Burgh, Lady of Clare, clothes more than 260 people.) Unsurprisingly, the rich spend a lower proportion of their income on clothes. Thomas de Berkeley allocates 11 per cent of his identified expenditures on them, excluding boots and shoes, in 1345–6. John Catesby, a well-off squire, spends 16 per cent at the end of the fourteenth century. A relatively well-off peasant reeve, Robert Oldman, spends 29 per cent of the value of his grain and stock on them in 1349–52.[35] But the absolute amounts spent by de Berkeley and Catesby, £142 and £18, compared with Oldman's 33 shillings show the enormous differences in spending power not only between peasant and gentry but between the lower and upper aristocracy as well.

The Mighty Clothmen

Cloth production surges during the surname period. Exports rise from an estimated 2,000 pieces (each about 25 yards) in 1348–9 to some 40,000 in the 1390s; overall cloth output including production for the domestic market is thought to be four times this volume.[36] Many thousands of sheep are farmed by Cistercian abbeys, but most landowners and even very small tenant farmers keep some. Exports are boosted by the king's embargoes and taxation on wool, innovations in fulling making cloth production more efficient, and the decline of the Flemish cloth industry. Cloth exports, worsteds from East Anglia, fine Lincoln scarlets and Bristol red broadcloths, rival wool by the end of the fourteenth century. Chaucer's Wife of Bath encapsulates the transition:

> Of clooth-making she hadde swiche an haunt [knack],
> She passed hem of Ypres and of Gaunt [Ghent].[37]

Records show that medieval women entrepreneurs are successful in the cloth industry. Emma Erle is a major cloth dealer in Wakefield, Yorkshire, at the end of the fourteenth century.[38] Ypres, Ghent and Bruges, the cloth-making cities in Flanders, are eventually to be ruined by English manufacturing.

Surnames record the specializations that each produce an input into the next. So the Tozers tease or comb the raw wool, and the Carders comb it. The Spindlers make the spindles and the spinners, who have come down to us as Spinsters or Rocks (from the Middle English word for a distaff), spin it. Women and children spin and card in their cottages. Dying is by the Dyers in the southwest and the Listers in the north, particularly Lancashire and the West Riding of Yorkshire. (There are still six times as many Dyers as Listers in Devon.) The still popular Webbers, Webbs, Websters and Weavers weave the wool into cloth. Webster records a female weaver. Female forms of names are never common in medieval records; nor are they today. The Slays and Slaymakers (Slay is also a nickname for cunning) make the shuttles for the looms. Next come the wool tramplers at the fulling mills, who trample the raw cloth to scour and thicken it – three names for them: the Fullers in the south and east of England, the Tuckers in the west and the Walkers in the north. This distribution still largely exists today. The Shearers and Sharmans, once tailors themselves, cut the nap; it is the quality of shearing that makes Lincoln scarlet such a highly coveted export.

The Packers ferry the wool from spinners to weavers and then pack up the cloth and take it away to be dyed and then again to be sold. Packman means a pedlar or hawker, and this may have been how cloth was first distributed. Woollers record the men who collect the wool from the farms and estates to sell first to Italian buyers at the fairs in Boston, Lincoln and Ludlow, and, after 1303 when foreigners have to pay export taxes, increasingly to English Merchants. Finally, the Taylors and their namesakes make the cloth up into garments for wear.

Fullers are at the forefront of one of the main stimuli to the growth of the cloth industry: the mechanization of fulling.[39] Their job had been to take the carded, combed and hand-woven wool and trample it underfoot in a trough of water combined with fuller's earth to shrink, strengthen and then purify it. Water-powered fulling mills instead use a drum attached to a water wheel to beat the cloth with wooden hammers. This innovation saves on labour, important in post-plague England, but it also encourages merchants to take cloth production into the countryside to avoid the guilds of the Fullers, Weavers, Shearmen and Dyers who try to enforce higher wages and shorter working hours. The popularity of the Fullers and Webbers reflects how widespread cloth production is. In the mid-fourteenth century, most communities have a mill that has become the centre for villages of weavers and associated artisans, bringing some prosperity back to a countryside deserted by the plagues, although the real profits are made by the merchants.

Weaving is a cottage industry; even in cloth-making villages, weavers usually work at home. But in the later Middle Ages some clothiers are setting up several looms in their own houses to establish a little cottage industry of weavers; 19 per cent of the freemen of Wells are textile workers in the late fourteenth century.[40] Weavers have been around since prehistoric times. A weaver, Gilbert Textor, is recorded in the *Chronicle of Battle Abbey*, written in about 1180, as one of the peasants given a house and land to commemorate the Battle of Hastings.

The Listers and Dyers prefer imports. There are local dyes – greenweed for green, seeds of weld or sweet gale leaves for yellow, roots of madder for red and pod of woad for blue. But 10 per cent of imports through Topsham in Devon into Exeter are dyes for the cloth industry, the third largest import from 1302 to 1321, only supplanted by wheat imports in the peak famine years of 1319 and 1320. Red and blue are popular colours; thus the fine doctor in *The Canterbury Tales*: 'In sangwin (blood red) and in pers (sky blue) he clad was al'.[41] Our Scarletts deal in fine reds from Bristol and Lincoln, popular on the continent of Europe (or wear them, or are red-faced – you are never far from alternative meanings with these names). Half of the dye imports is woad, mostly from Picardy until the Hundred Years' War when it becomes enemy territory, but archil is also imported, as are copperas, ochre, weld, and mordants like alum and potash. Exeter traders have a grip on dye sales. Importers who are not freemen of Exeter have to offer their woad for sale to Exeter merchants forty days before it is offered to others. If it is then sold outside Exeter, customs duty has to be paid on it. Cities also try to control quality. From 1399 to 1407, when Bristol's cloth exports are falling, the mayor appoints two Masters to inspect all dyed cloth and dismiss dyers without the right skills.[42]

When Celia Fiennes goes to Exeter in 1698 the cloth trade is still important:

> As Norwitch is for coapes calamanco and damaske soe this [Exeter] is for Serges – there is an increadible quantety of them made and sold in the town ... the whole town and country is employ'd for at least 20 mile round in spinning, weaveing, dressing, and scouring, fulling and drying of the serges, it turns the most money in a weeke of anything in England ...

Celia uses the general English name for fulling because she comes from near Salisbury, but she later refers to tuckers working the wool in the fulling mill.[43]

Fashion for Fun

Fashion is the rendezvous for needs and wants. Even as the artisans are weaving a new society, old and new wealth stretch out their fingers to grasp the goods that signal rank. Tailors dominate, but then there are makers of hats and caps, gloves, wigs, bags and shoes, fashionable beads, gold embroidery, and those who put jewels on bishops' copes.

Some surnames record the supply of goods that are clearly luxuries. To a degree, the distinction could be hard to make; a bowl from a Bowler might be a necessity for some and a luxury for others. But the output of the Amblers, who are enamellers, as well as the Furrs, Codners (shoe-makers) and Setters (discussed on page 66), will have been luxuries for most. The Sumptuary Laws help by identifying which goods are luxuries under the law. They require all working on the land with less than 40 shillings of goods to wear blankets and russet. Lords with lands worth

£1,000 annually have no restrictions, but lower beings are graded according to whether or not they can wear luxury furs, cloth of gold and jewels and where they can wear their jewels. Merchants, citizens and burgesses with goods worth £1,000 can wear the same as gentry with land and rent that brings in £200 a year: cloth of silk and silver and anything decorated with silver, but no gold or jewels.

These laws are unworkable and are quickly repealed, but they reflect both the importance of rank and of fashion as a signal of rank as well as the social mobility that brings the newly rich into competition with the old. Fourteen per cent of London merchants dying between 1350 and 1497 have estates of £1,000.[44] They set a standard: everyone wants to look like a lord. People everywhere, in town or countryside, wear the best they can, as the court reference to William Skynner's award on page 60 shows. After the Black Death, when landlords are having difficulty keeping their workers, there are records of a ploughman being given 'a brightly coloured doublet and gown' to keep him happy.

The makers of the final product have overwhelming importance. Taylor is the second most popular occupational name and the fourth most popular name overall. The less common Parmenter and ancient Shearer and Cisore are also tailors. They are successful, their names prominent in lists of town and city magnates. 'Gods certainly ye are' sings an anonymous satirist of the Taylors in a medieval record, 'Who can transform an old garment into the shape of a new one.'[45] The quotation in its mocking reference records the social standing of the tailor and at the same time tells us why it is merited – because he can make new fashion out of old. Clothes are valuable. People have few; a medieval coffer would hold them. A tax assessment for 1285–90 in King's Lynn records that a merchant, Simon de Leverington, has two suits of clothes for men and three for women and one cloak, while a barber, Richard le Barbur, whose wife is a spinner, has just one supertunic and a tabard.[46] They are assets to be passed down. A Vice Archdeacon of Cornwall in 1190 leaves, among goods and chattels, gold and silver, 'one new cloak of burnet, to the use of a certain niece of his ...'.[47]

Supplying All Sorts

Some names of these fashion-workers record a range of quality. Cappers make ordinary caps, Hatters hats, while Hodders and Hoods make hoods but Caprons make the hoods or caps worn by nobles. People who do not wear headgear are unusual enough to be named – Hoodless. Codner, a variant of the medieval Cordwainer and the French *cordoarnier*, Clouter, and Souter from the Latin *sutor* all mean shoemaker. The Codner makes fine shoes from soft goatskin imported from Cordoba in Spain, the origin of the name. Clouter, which comes from the Old English word for rag or patch, suggests lower quality and that tailors and their namesakes could also have made shoes.

Other fashion-workers clearly produce luxuries. The Burnet makes burnet, a dark-brown cloth fashionable in the twelfth century and valuable enough to be bequeathed by a Vice-Archdeacon. Wiggs could make wigs or small fashionable beads (it might also be a nickname for a beetle). For the relatively prosperous, the Furr makes fur-linings and edgings, the Officer (from the French word *orfroisier*) embroiders in silver gilt and silver, while the Setter sets the precious or semi-precious stones in embroidered garments like bishops' copes. An Alexander de Settere who embroiders a cope for William Testor, Archdeacon of Lichfield and Coventry in 1307, has taken, or inherited, the name of his craft.[48] (Setters can also work on stone buildings.)

Others probably produce a range of quality goods, too. These include the Capes and Copes who make capes, the Trinders, a rare surname, who braid or plait thread, and the Glovers who make gloves. For those working on the land, the Burrels make the coarse, undyed cloth of russet or grey for the tunics you see peasants wearing in paintings or tapestries, the Corders, their belts of linen, and the Challinors make their blankets, often for linings. The name comes from the Middle English *chaloun*, or blanket, from Chalons-sur-Marne, where they are made.

Medieval people are hat people; contemporary art shows them wearing a great variety. A painting in the Bedford Hours of a wooden house being built shows a wonderful collection of hats on the carpenters' heads: a skull cap, a stocking hat close to the head with a long droopy top, brimmed hats, and hats going down over the ears and draping the shoulders.[49] Patrons and architects wear more fitted, structured and higher hats. Coventry is briefly a centre for cap- and hat-making in the later fourteenth century.[50]

Tax lists for rural areas show very few Sutores or dedicated cobblers. Medieval paintings of men in shoes show them looking soft, often the colour of the leggings, so they could have been made by the Taylor (although the artist might just have decided that colour coordination worked better aesthetically). Shoes clearly signal rank; the courtier's massively long and pointed, while men working on building sites and servants serving at table have much foreshortened versions. Soft leather shoes cannot have been practical, and one painting shows workers in neatly fitted boots that could have been of leather. The overseer in the same painting has large soft boots turned over at the ankle; rank is important on a building site. Shoes are typically 6d a pair in the earlier fourteenth century, when an unskilled agricultural worker is earning 1d a day. According to a 1364 ordinance of Bristol shoemakers, workers are to be paid 6d per dozen for finished shoes, but it anticipates that this is likely to be too low, because it also forbids poaching workers. We have delightful insights from the records; the accounts of Beaulieu Abbey tell that its shoemaker greases his shoes with herring drippings from the kitchen.[51] There are few Shoemakers and Cobblers, although both names exist in medieval England.

Dedicated to Luxury

Our Furrs record intense social competition. Exotic furs are imported from Scandinavia and the Baltic. The Sumptuary Laws specify weasel and ermine linings and edgings for lords, pure miniver for wealthier knights and above, and lamb, rabbit, cat and fox for yeomen. Squirrel furs are imported by the thousand from the Baltic for linings. After the Black Death the wives of craftsmen take to using squirrel linings, so their betters turn to marten. Squirrel linings can add £2–£3 to the cost of a garment when the cloth itself costs 2–3 shillings a yard.[52] English furriers are prized even in Anglo-Saxon times. Eleventh-century Italian records of customs paid by English traders on Alpine passes include fifty pounds of pure silver plus two greyhounds and two fur coats for the customs official.[53]

Embroidered clothes identify the elite. Thus the Squire, the Knight's son, in *The Canterbury Tales*:

> Embrouded was he, as it were a mede [meadow]
> Al ful of fresshe floures, whyte and rede
> ... Short was his goune, with sleves longe and wyde.[54]

Embroidery could be done by nuns or high-born women or men as well as professional Officers or Setters, men and women who serve seven-year apprenticeships at guilds, mainly in London. Garments and even shoes and leggings are embroidered with silver-gilt and silver thread, and encrusted with jewels. Alice Perrers, mistress of Edward III, who dies in about 1400, is recorded as having 22,000 jewels with 30 oz of pearls, many of low value and probably meant for embroidery.[55]

Medieval inventories and wills record hangings for beds and for walls, banners and blazons for battle, jupons to go over armour and horse trappers, chasubles and copes for the bishops; all could be ornamented by these magicians. From the mid-thirteenth century to the mid-fourteenth century and the advent of the Black Death when it dies out, English embroidery (*opus anglicanum*) is the finest in Europe. Pope Innocent IV, 1243–54, preferred it 'above all others'. The embroiderers are often important enough to be named in records: Dendenall de Deek, embroiderer for Edward III, Stephen Vigner for Richard II, Mabel of Bury St Edmunds for Henry III.

The Glovers are interesting because gloves, as well as being used for warmth, riding and falconry, have a symbolic value. If somebody sends a messenger, he adds his glove as a token of authority or perhaps to prove he really is the sender. Gloves seem to carry the personal responsibility of the giver and the trust of the receiver. *Beowulf* refers to Charlemagne using gloves to transmit messages. You see them being used as a token in business transactions, usually at Easter – did people always need new gloves then? Rent for a farm on the edge of Dartmoor in about 1249 is reduced to a pair of white gloves or ½ penny to be paid at Easter each year. In Dartmouth records a pair of gloves, or white gloves, given at Easter again, is used as a token to seal land transactions throughout the thirteenth century. Gloves are also a symbol of fairs, and are always displayed then. Shakespeare's father was a glover.

The survival and prevalence of the names of these luxury workers epitomize the style and priorities of the medieval world. The prime market is the wealthy merchant, the master craftsman, the aristocracy, the monarch and the church. But fashion creates wants in everyone.

Medieval art shows the difference in clothing between lord and peasant to be in the fabric. For peasants there are no fine details: no patterns or embroidery; no fur, no lining, or edging; and no fashionable designs; they wear longer tunics, baggier hats and no mile-long shoes. Overseers and patrons on building sites wear long, loose robes in rich fabrics with sumptuous linings and edgings. Peasants, builders and carpenters wear belted tunics, often with slits up the side, with matching leggings that are less fitted than the courtiers' (think of the skill in making tight leggings from hand-woven cloth). In the early Middle Ages old people, according to maintenance agreements, wear linen underclothes, leather shoes and loose tunics. After the Black Death they wear a doublet of russet with a blanket lining and a lined hood from the Burrels and the Challinors, hose and shoes.[56]

Fashion is for men as well as women. In the Paston letters, written in the mid-fifteenth century, only forty years after the surname period ended, John Paston writes to his wife:

... please send me two ells of worstead to make doublets to wrap me up in this cold winter, and ask where William Paston bought his tippet of fine worstead which is almost like silk.

Not to be outdone, Margaret Paston writes that she wants:

some grey woollen gown cloth, to make me a gown ... for I have no gown to wear this winter except my black and green one with tapes, and that is so cumbersome that I am tired of wearing it.[57]

Her reasoning is entirely modern.

Luxury clothes come in for contemporary criticism. Extravagant dress is associated with vanity, a sin in the eyes of the church. The fashion industry panders to it. In St Laurence's Church, Ludlow, there is an early fifteenth-century misericord of a woman in a fashionable horned headdress with an horrifically ugly face, a criticism of vanity.[58] Chaucer admires modesty in dress. In *The Canterbury Tales* his chivalrous knight wears a doublet of 'fustian', or coarse cloth, when he could afford better, and the unworldly clerk has a 'ful threadbar' cloak. The showy are the worldly who come in for mockery. The merchant is 'in mottelee', a gaudy outfit, while the worldly friar has a cape of double worsted, a finely woven fabric. Critics even blame the Black Death on extravagant clothing. An anonymous chronicler is quoted as saying that God had been offended by the extravagant and unseemly dress of the courtiers and the nobility who, instead of the old long garments wear short tight clothes.[59]

Surnames in medieval records show many of these fashion-workers do well. If you compare the tax assessments for Shrewsbury, a wool town, from 1297 to 1322, the Tailors or Parminters have strikingly higher assessments than groups such as smiths, with Parminters due to pay up to fifty shillings in contrast to the smiths' maximum of two shillings.

The inventory of Nicholas le Dyer in the assessment of 1309 shows he has woad, so is still in the same business, but has done well enough to have a twenty-shilling riding horse, a mazer cup, silver, jewellery and meat – all status goods. Richard le Glovere, three years earlier, is assessed on his mazer cup and his jewellery, as well as costly clothes. His possession of a cart, harness, mules and grains as well suggests he is already a merchant. Robert le Taylour in 1309 has done even better. He has a forty-shilling horse, a more valuable mazer, and more silver, jewellery and meat. His possessions do not include any that suggest what he does, so he is likely to have been a larger merchant with goods held outside his home. A tailor among the very wealthy of Shrewsbury – William le Parmunter – was assessed in 1306 on an expensive horse and clothes, a mazer cup and quite a bit of cash, so he too is probably a merchant.[60] William le Parmunter is an interesting example because his inventories show fewer status goods such as jewellery, wall-hangings and silver than others, but he is listed among the super-rich. Either he is more austere, or simply better at hiding his taxable goods.

The Revelations of Etymology

The derivations of these surnames show, first, the dominance of Old English roots; at least for craft and fashion names when our ancestors need the right word to describe an occupation, they generally have an English one to hand.

The different derivations show what the English, Norman and Norse cultures bring to medieval society. Important names and types of names are French, particularly names to do with management, speciality service and fashion goods, suggesting that they probably add new skills and/or tools to create popular specializations. Some of these French surnames drive out their English counterparts. Some co-exist with the English and both translations survive today, often with one still much more numerous than the other, suggesting one culture has the edge in that activity. Names representing distinctions within an occupation can trace an evolution. Some French names will have come with the invading Normans, but others (Chamberlain, Butler) are used by the Anglo-Saxons, showing England is linked to continental culture well before the Conquest.

Names from Craft and Fashion

Almost two-thirds of surnames based on crafts are from Old or Middle English words. Wood and metal workers can be French or English. The French bring the cask-makers – the Busses and Barrels – the basket-makers, the Manders, Hotters, Bushels and Coffins, and the Tanners, while the Bowlers, Coopers and Hoopers are English. For some occupations, both Old English and Old French words exist, with one much more popular than the other. Ferrer (French), Faber (Latin), Goff (Welsh/Breton/Cornish), and

Angove (Cornish), all mean smith but the English Smith is by far the most numerous. The French Cutlers are vastly more popular than the English Nasmyths; the French Carpenters three times as popular as the English Sawyers, while the English Hackers are hardly here at all. The implication is that smithing is being pursued adequately by the Anglo-Saxons and that there is no reason to change the name, while Cutlers and Carpenters bring new knowledge and/or implements that they apply to better effect than the English Nasmyths and Sawyers.

Almost three-quarters of names deriving from fashion are Old English. Here, there is a clear pattern. Most of the ladder of surnames that produce cloth at the end are English, from the Tozer to the Weaver and the Lister. Nice derivations exist: Tucker is from *tucian*, originally meaning to torment, which gives a vivid picture of what the western tramplers do to that wet wool. Webb and Webber come from *web* or *webba*, which also means a web. It's good to think our ancestors imagining themselves creating a web rather than plain old weaving. Where there are synonyms, the French name records the more sophisticated product.

The fashion surnames with French derivations are mostly producers of final or more sophisticated goods. The French Capron (or hood-maker) makes hats for the noble, for instance, while Old English Capper, Hatter and Hood supply the rest. The Codner of the classy footwear is French while the rag Clouter is English. Producers of final goods include Taylor, the most popular and important name of all, Burrell and Burnet, and the gold embroiderer, Officer – all Old French. Without the *tailleur*, Norman fashion would not exist. Like designers today, Taylors and the less common Parmenters facilitate social position and are highly valued. The Old English names for the person who cuts and sews clothes are Shearer or Cisore. Cisore has gone. You can see their passing in the records. In Dartmouth, Devon, Randolph cissore witnesses a land grant in about 1210; in 1235 he is recorded in a similar transaction as 'Randolph the tailor (cissore)'. Thereafter, records have only Taylors and variants. A few Shearers still exist, but their occupation has changed. The need for new skills that ousted the Cisore sent the Shearers downwards until they came to a rest shearing the nap of the wool and then sheep snipping.

Service Names

Servants are a different breed. About 80 per cent of the management job names come from the Old French – Chaplain, Chamberlain, Wardrope, Usher (Middle English as well), Sargent – as do the majority of the names of the more specialized menial jobs, like Butler, Spencer, Lander, Napier, Barber, Norris, and Marshall. Few of the names for general and menial servants are French. Mann, Berryman, Yeoman, Hall, Hine, Groom, Cook and the outside workers, the Days and the Yates, are Old English. The Steward is the only Old English management position, and could be a manager of a household or of an estate for a lord or a king, which is where the title Lord High Steward of Scotland comes from, naming the first officer of the Scottish king. And Scullion, the lowly kitchen serf, is one of the few Old French menials. The names suggest that the Normans had a much more sophisticated hierarchy of personal service than the Anglo-Saxons.

Ancient names survive. Both Gill and Swain mean a general servant in Old Norse. Goff and Angove are both smiths in Cornish/Celt. Jewell could be Breton or Celt. These names co-exist with English and French translations, suggesting that in some places they are important to the medieval namers. This could be because of language loyalties; early records of the Norse names are in the Danelaw and of Celtic names in Wales or Cornwall. Or they may represented a unique skill in the occupation. Yet some with humble names can do well. A simple cordwainer with a Celtic name, Walsh, is said to be the best mayor London has had in the fifteenth century.[61]

So the majority of these, our most popular, occupational surnames, are Old English – identifying activities that often existed well before the Normans came. French names add scale, quality and hierarchy. The few Norse names show memories of earlier invaders hang on. The combination reflects an inclusive world of English Webbers weaving the cloth that the French Taylor cuts for the Norse Gill, or servant. Surnames show how the English finally absorbed the Normans.

CHAPTER 3

FARMING, BUILDING AND
OTHER OCCUPATIONS

THE OCCUPATIONAL SURNAMES in this chapter include the agricultural workers and the clerks, the traders and builders, the musicians and the military. These document feudal structures, recording responsibilities for a landlord's assets and economic and social change in the opportunities open to ordinary people. Some names identify long-forgotten activities – Pinder, who impounds stray animals, and Price, who sets prices in markets and elsewhere. Other surnames document surprisingly modern jobs, like Judge and Lawman. Like the surnames in Chapter 2, they tell a rich story about feudal structures and how people are moving away into a new place.

The agricultural workers belong to the old world; most existed in Anglo-Saxon England. Their names record how the feudal system's main source of wealth and power – land – is enjoyed by the few and farmed by the many. The names of many micro-managers show how these are co-opted into making the system work through the same complex hierarchy of devolved management as servants, from the Herd responsible for his flocks up to the Bailiff who oversees the manor. The range and popularity of these names show how the many accept a fine title for their efforts. The mill race still turns the great wheel of feudal society through the force of the farmers channelled by king and church.

But there is leakage. Individuals find their way like trickles of fresh water through crumbling banks. Labourers diversify into trade and unprecedented specializations and scale; masons and carpenters celebrate their world with soaring cathedrals that create a new one for the future; archers march off to win victories for a distant king in far-off places. Over the thirteenth century, England's trade, exports plus imports, rises from £55,000–£75,000 to some £500,000 – threefold in real terms, accounting for inflation.[1] Names record economic mobility. Masters of ships using the Exeter port of Topsham between 1266 and 1321 include Cooks, Webbes, Spicers, Bakers and Pypers.[2] Names in inventories document peasants and craftsmen joining the wealthy, often within a generation. When they have money, people with quite lowly names buy meat and silver, jewellery, brassware and clothes. The surnames of the traders, builders, musicians, and soldiers record an assault on feudalism as people prise new wealth out of the fist of the past.

Names carry attitudes. The most popular show what people value. Clerks, the recorders of history, carry the third most popular occupational name; literacy is important and respected. Baileys and Parkers record the value of traditional functions close to the lord at the manor; Bakers and Millers, with their many variants, the importance of the food staple; and all the names for archers and the suppliers of archery equipment document the proud contribution of the peasantry to the great wars of the kings. But not much less popular are the names of the traders and builders, all the mercers and spicers, masons and tilers, the people no longer tied to the traditional way of life. People record their dislike of trade in names; Barratt means both trader and cheat.

Old English dominates the roots of these names. Those relating to the land are virtually all from native words; the countryside belongs to the English. But other derivations reflecting the different cultures in medieval England show similar patterns to those in Chapter 2. Surnames to do with the church are largely Old French, as are those of senior overseers, larger traders, the better-skilled builders and suppliers of quality products. The surnames for subordinate activities on the land and in the building trade and for smaller traders supplying everyday needs are English. Where Old French and Old English translations co-exist, often the French word has cachet and is adopted. So we talk about archers rather than bowmen, masons instead of stonemen, butchers not shinners. Some Old Norse names recall ancient occupations: Skinner, a meat flayer; Ashburner and Coleman, charcoal-burners; Milner, a miller; and Grave, a reeve. These are often first recorded in the old Norse Danelaw shires. The co-existence of names with different roots can show the evolution of an occupation; Theaker, for instance, is Old Norse, and Thatcher, the later Old English name. But here the English word stays in the language; Theaker, the surname, is the only relic of the Old Norse word.

Names can show how language has evolved in the gloss time has added to their meanings. Fishers still fish and drapers sell cloth, but Corks have nothing to do with purple dye, Neate is not a cowherd, Alabaster not a crossbowman; nor is Bacchus a baker. Some changes produce new jokes. Cowards are cowherds – always running away? Barker is a shepherd – acting like his dog? Camp is a warrior or an athlete; is the Hundred Years' War only an act? Grieve or Grief, the reeve from the north; always making everyone, and perhaps himself, miserable. Cant, the churchly chanter, is pious – and hypocritical? And Miles, the soldier, walks and walks and walks.

These classifications have the usual overlaps. Some of the craftspeople, servants and fashion-workers in Chapter 2 will also be traders. As a general principle where the selling is more important than other functions, the name is here. So Smiths, Taylors and Webbers are in Chapter 2, but Drapers, the makers but more often sellers of woollen cloth, are here. Many names could be occupational and fit here or be a resident in Chapter 4, as Ware could be the weir keeper or simply live near it. And many names have two very different meanings; Boutle could be a sifter of meal, from the Old French word for a meal sieve, or a maker of bolts from the Old English word. Looking at groups of names, about one-third of military, church and musical names have at least two completely different meanings. As usual, overlapping meanings have probably helped some of these names to survive.

Maintaining the Manor

Land-based surnames show the feudal system operates through devolved management. Only a handful of surnames record ploughing and sowing, weeding and reaping. Farmers, Fielders and Georges are all 'farmers'. But Farmer can also mean bailiff or tax collector and the name has come to straddle quite a wide social spectrum by about 1400. The virtual absence of 'farmers' means that most do something else. Where everyone reaps, but one is also a shepherd or a reeve, their names, if occupational, are likely to be Shepherd and Reeve. These names describe a system of guardianship of important assets – people, land, animals, trees, parks and water. Strikingly, they are about responsibilities rather than skills.

Below the top managers, the Bailiffs and Stewards, swings the rope ladder of peasants with the Reeves, part-time supervisors of their peers, at the top – positions that are uncomfortable but give opportunities for enrichment. Below and alongside the reeves are those with more and more restricted responsibilities: the whole raft of foresters, the keepers of the locks and weirs, down through the various animal herders to the Hayman. The survival and popularity of many of these surnames, such as Bailey, Parker and Shepherd, show how widespread the system is. Co-option into the system is how the tiny fraction of overlords manage the rest. Management names might also record that people may not want to be called a ploughman or a reaper. These names not only describe the system, but imply that people buy into it.

Cascading Responsibilities

At the top, the landlords appoint bailiffs and/or stewards to manage their estates. They are often gentry and relatives of the lords. Our Bailiffs and Baileys also, in principle, have public functions, and are salaried; responsible for the affairs of the Hundred (the medieval district) and particularly the Hundred court. It is the bailiff who seizes the security, usually the land, of debtors in the courts. There are urban bailiffs as well, a leading position with the mayor and the sheriff, controlling the economic and political life of the town. The Stewarts, Stewards and Steuarts, a name later belonging to the royal house of Scotland, could also preside over the courts and manor and keep the manorial officials, the demesne farm and tenants in good order, setting fines, determining inheritance and resolving disputes. Bailiffs and stewards are responsible positions and the people in them have a great deal of power.

Management functions cascade down to the reeve on the manor, and down from him. If you are called Prater, Reeve, Grave, Graves, Grieve or Grief (or one of its many alternatives), the feudal system pivots around you. Grave and its variants are Old Norse and come mainly from the Danelaw counties in the north and east. A peasant, often unfree and perhaps a craftsman too, reeves are appointed by the landlord or his bailiff to protect their interests.

The functions arise out of the interdependence between landlord and farmer and the nature of farming. People live mostly in small hamlets or villages, with arable lands nearby and common pastures and woods beyond. They till usually long strips in open fields so everyone benefits or suffers from the same soil conditions. Therefore, farming depends on keeping the separation between the strips, maintaining hedges and ditches and protecting crops from animals; pasturing means ensuring the commons are not overstocked or encroached upon; and communal grazing and woodlands means rights to them have to be protected.

As the lord's man, the reeve ensures his demesne is well farmed, collects his rents and dues and even sells the produce. It is the reeve who collects from the peasant the horse or the oxen as death duty to the lord; summons the tenants to harvest the lord's crops; sells pasture rights and offers wages for field labour. Chaucer's reeve keeps the granaries and predicts yields; manages the lord's stock, cattle, sheep, dairy, pigs, horses, poultry; submits the accounts and knows all the tenants and servants.[3] Towns have reeves, too: port-reeves, the highest elected officials of the borough. In Tavistock the port-reeve collects the abbot's rents and fines and tolls from the Friday market, and from the mill and the fairs. Reeves pay heavy fines if they resign.

Yet despite the power, people do not like being reeves; it is an uncomfortable function. In medieval Tavistock it is rarely held more than once by the same person.[4] There are more explicit records of underlying tensions. A reeve of Bourton-on-the-Hill and Todenham in Gloucestershire in 1315, Henry Melksop 'of fair face but an ugly snout' enrages his landlord, the abbot of Westminster Abbey, by refusing to show any gratitude for the cancellation of a debt owed by his fellow tenants because he thinks the debt is unfair in the first place.[5]

Depending on the size and prosperity of the estate and the personal involvement of the landlord, the reeve is supported by a scaffold of others. Haywards and some Howards (originally Haywards) prevent cattle from breaking into the enclosures. People have rights to graze cattle or horses on hayfields once the hay is cut. Hayman and variants and some Hammonds also have some responsibility for monitoring these, securing enclosures and selling the hay. Ward and Warden are general guardians or watchmen.

The many names and variants of names for herders reflect the rise in herding after the Black Death when scarce labour forces landlords to put much arable land into pasture. Herd is a general herdsman. Booth, Byrom, Coward and Neate watch the cows. Hogg, Hogger and Hogarth, some of the Swans and Foreman are swineherds. And Shepherd, Weatherhead, Lamb, Lambert, Ewart, some Grooms and Barker (or Tanner) are shepherds. A master shepherd is responsible for moving flocks to fresh pastures and arranging centralized shearing and the sale of wool.

Fertilization is important: the Marler digs the marl pits to fertilize fallow land, especially cleared woodland (marl being a loose mixture of clay and carbonate of lime). And Ashburner, Collier and Coleman are charcoal-burners, producing charcoal for the wealthy and the all-important smiths.

Watching the Woods

Woods are a scarce and valuable resource. In 1204, the men of Devon buy a charter for disafforestation of the county for 5,000 marks (about £1,800 in those days) at a time when an unskilled labourer earns less than 2 pence a day (1d is a penny).[6] At Domesday about 15 per cent of the country is thought to have been wooded; by 1350 woods are down to 10 per cent at most.[7] They are status assets for the owner, a place for hunting and a source of income, but peasants have rights in them that have to be managed. Ownership can be private; private but where others have rights; or common. Common woodland tends to be over-grazed and to disappear into rough pasture or arable. Hunting wild animals is a privilege of the elite and there are also restrictions on hunting woodland birds.

The managers are Forrester, Foster (some genuine foster parents or siblings), Forster and Forrest, and then Woodward. Foresters can be gentry and have nothing to do with hands-on work. Forester to the king is a position of privilege. But most are peasants and in the same ambivalent social position as the reeves, peasants monitoring and regulating their peers but representing the landlord. People pay to be foresters, suggesting the position holds rewards. Like Chaucer's Yeoman, who is a forester, they would often, like Robin Hood and his band, be:

> ... clad in cote and hood of grene;
> A sheef of pecok-arwes brighte and kene
> Under his belt he bar ...[8]

with their uniform marking them out, giving them status.

Peoples' rights in private woods generally include grazing along the edges or in clearings, allowing pigs to forage, and taking wood for heating and carpentry. Foresters monitor these rights, collect dues in cash or kind for the landlord, and protect against poaching to keep the woods clear for hunting. They coppice and pollard to protect new growth. They or the landlords would fell and often sell the timber: oak, beech, and birch are best for smelting, oak for building, and its bark for tanning, ash for tools, beech for boat-building; and hazel for thatching.

Park- and River-Keepers

Parks and Parkers manage a grander status asset. Like Foresters, Parkers can be gentry and their position one of privilege. The king's park-keeper in North Worcestershire in 1300 has his own small manor.[9] Originally royal preserves, parks are usually a mix of grass and woodland around castles or the houses of the wealthy, and hold roe and fallow deer for the noble sport of hunting. Deer are owned by the king and can only be hunted with a licence. Parks are a Norman innovation (the surname is Old French), but they caught on; thirty-five at the time of the Domesday Book, there are 3,200 by the early fourteenth century but they become less profitable after the Black Death. They tend to be surrounded by tremendous fences or earthworks and ditches, and parkers often live inside the park to police them better – poachers are punished by death.

Game is a source of fees and protein. There are some general names for hunters, Hunt and Hunter, quite popular names, Chase and Venner, and some specialists, the Hawks, or hawkers, Partridges, or partridge hunters, Fowlers, or bird-catchers and Falconers or Faulkners (some are symbolical nicknames). Private forests are often called chases from the French word *chasser* (to hunt). These names could record servants, legitimate hunters on common or waste ground, or poachers, and document which birds are set against birds and which are hunted. Excavations show that people in Exeter eat rabbits, game birds and scavengers, woodcock, ravens and crows as well as a host of smaller birds.[10] Rabbits, a Norman introduction, are bred in warrens in parks, but presumably escape, because records show some tithes paid in rabbits.[11] Warren could be a name for someone who raises them (or who is someone from la Varenne in France). These are ancient pastimes. On the eighth-century Bewcastle Cross in Cumberland, beneath the figure of Christ and its runic inscription, is a falconer, a falcon on the heavy gauntlet on his left arm.

Many surnames record occupations around water to do with subsistence and taking dues. Our Bridges, Bridgemans and Bridgers keep the bridges and Wares, Locks and Lockes manage the weirs and locks set up to handle shipping, mills, freshwater fish farming and salmon fishing. (All could record people who just live there.) There are more than 10,000 watermills and some wind-powered mills in England by the end of the thirteenth century.[12] Fishers provide a major source of protein for farmers and revenues for landlords. Fisheries are listed meticulously in the Domesday Book. Records relating to salmon fishing show its importance. The rights of the Abbot of Tavistock on the Tamar are jealously protected and an agreement at the end of the twelfth century defines his and those of the lord of the opposite bank. Subsequent disputes over weirs (one involving the Black Prince) and fish-traps only end when Henry VIII orders the destruction of all weirs in 1535.[13]

Life and wealth come from the land. If the landlord's properties are not productive, country and king grow poorer. Manorial accounts document the importance of these micro-overseers for the functioning of the feudal firm. Those of the Redvers family, Earls of Devon, show that the sale of grain alone in the early thirteenth century accounts for 10–12 per cent of revenues, and rents 30 per cent, with significant income from mills, fisheries and salt.[14] Honest millers, weir-keepers, shepherds, reeves and bailiffs are of vital interest to the landlord.

Managers and overseers have leverage and can be rich, and even weir-keepers, Foresters and, particularly, Parkers, stand to gain. Chaucer's reeve is a careful, clever old man, 'With grene trees shadwed was his place ... ' and, dressed in fashionable Persian blue, 'Ful riche he was astored prively [privately]'.[15] Yet John le Reve, in the hamlet of Soutton outside Shrewsbury, although sufficiently affluent to be assessed for tax in 1309, has animals and grains in his tax inventory, but no extra status goods such as meat or brassware.[16]

The Free and the Bonded

A few generic names fit here. There are several surnames for freemen: Freeman, Free, Fry, Franklin, and Yeoman, a small freeholder. Freemen would have been unusual at the beginning of the naming period, but later some Franklins, Freemans and Yeomans are beginning to join the ranks of the gentry. The Tennants and their variants are just that.

Bond is one of the few names for a bondsman; Villain and its variants another. Perhaps bondsmen are so widespread that the name is useless for identification or perhaps, during the fourteenth century when surnames are establishing, bondsmen are dying out. After the plagues of 1348, serfs who are subject to manor courts and harassed by landowners for fines are buying their freedom for £5 to £10, or simply leaving their customary land to join rural cloth industries or to go to the towns. During the period 1370–1500 more than 2,000 villages and many thousands of hamlets and farms in England are abandoned. Although towns are hard hit in the plagues, there are massive migrations into them from the countryside. The bondsmen who remain can be obstreperous. The William Smith from Ingatestone mentioned in Chapter 2 is taken back by his landlord after participating in the Peasants' Revolt, but is recorded as refusing to pay a fine and a year later being bound over to behave better towards the bailiff.[17] It is significant that the lord not only accepts him back, but keeps him and that he continues to rebel.

Bondage has nothing to do with wealth. As early as 1238, Geoffrey de Leya in Devon is buying his freedom and that of his two sisters for sixty marks of silver from the Lord of Kingskerswell and Diptford, and a week later he buys two estates in South Milton for another twenty marks of silver.[18] A mark is worth about 13s 4d (there are 20 shillings to £1), and Geoffrey is making these sumptuous payments at a time when agricultural labour is earning 1d a day, and customary tenants like him are paying between 1d and 4d rent a year. This is an example of how frustrating records can be; we have no idea of how Geoffrey raises this sort of money, or what happens to him and his sisters later.

Surnames in medieval tax records show peasants moving out of the feudal system through the inventories of their goods. Some are hesitant. To be listed at all puts people among the wealthiest 20–30 per cent of the town's population. Richard le Villeyn, a serf, and Roger Atteschupene, a shepherd, assessed for tax in Shrewsbury in 1313, have a few possessions of the wealthy. Villeyn has three wall-hangings and some brassware and Atteschupene has the sheep of his profession, but also meat, brassware and two wall-hangings. Neither Villeyn's widow, Alice, nor Atteschupene have the brassware or hangings three years later.[19] Yet some peasants show extraordinary social mobility. In the early 1500s, Richard Marler from Coventry is among the wealthiest merchants in England.[20] His name records that his forebear is a peasant who digs and spreads marl fertilizer on the land. The date of the record shows he is only a few generations removed from this ancestor.

The Great Recorders of the Middle Ages

Medieval England hosts an explosion of written records. Numerous Clerks and their variants record their value. It is the third most popular occupational name, after Smith and Taylor. They are the great recorders of history, particularly from the early fourteenth century; virtually everything we know about medieval times is due in some way to them. They are essential to the functioning of the courts and the administration, and their written records supply precedents that protect ordinary people from the untramelled power of the elite.[21]

Clerks tend to be well respected. Some of Aethelstan's tenth-century charters are first drawn up by royal clerks, and later by the beneficiaries, putting the clerks, early on, on a social par with the elite.[22] King Henry I is called Henry Beauclerc because of his learned ways. The twelfth- and thirteenth-century Redvers charters name their clerks, who are often linked with families connected with them in Normandy. Chaucer, who pokes fun at most of his merry pilgrims, admires the lean and sober clerk, who wears a 'ful thredbar' cloak and loves books 'yet hadde he but litel gold in cofre'.[23] In medieval Dartmouth, clerks are mayors and members of Parliament. In 1213, King John sends letters patent to all steersmen and masters of ships from Bristol, Wales and Ireland moored at Dartmouth, stating that 'they are to do as Philipp the Clerk tells them'.[24]

Clerks are not part of the ecclesiastical hierarchy, but education is a monopoly of the church, and clerks are almost always educated clerics. The *Oxford English Dictionary* definition of clerk is 'man in a religious order, cleric, clergyman'.

It is hard for an ordinary person to become a clerk. Schools are small and rare.[25] In 1540 there are only 26,000 pupils out of a population of 5 million.[26] Peasants have to pay a levy to the lord when a son goes to school, because it reduces the labour force in the fields. Before the Black Death, teaching is in Latin, translated into French, then English. Most learning must have been by rote; in 1357 Bishop de Grandisson of Exeter orders his archdeacons not to teach grammar boys to learn by heart but to understand their prayers.[27]

But some ordinary people do become clerks. An analysis of the surnames of clergy from Devon graduating from Exeter College, Oxford, between the early fourteenth century and 1530 shows they broadly match the classifications in the wider Devon community and so the clergy must have been drawn from all social groups.[28] A few peasant-born clerics become distinguished. William of Wykeham, born of peasants in 1324, finds a patron and his education opens the way for him to become Chancellor of England as well as Bishop of Winchester.

The educated, often less wealthy knights, younger sons or other gentry who also work for magnates as the bailiffs and stewards, can be government clerks, officials or lawyers. Surnames show England was a legalistic nation early on. These are Judges and Lawmans, Sergeants and Pledgers, who stand bail, as well as our Deacons and Clerks trained in the law. Law becomes increasingly professional from the twelfth century, based on local and royal courts. Some Sergeants, also servants, are sergeants-at-law, top lawyers working in the royal courts. In the mid-fifteenth century a sergeant-at-law is earning £300 a year and a part-time local lawyer £26. The lawyer Thomas Kebell dies in 1500 with many estates in Leicestershire. In 1345–6 Thomas de Berkeley allocates 1 per cent of his expenditures to legal fees (£11), more than half his expenditure on building.[29]

The Ever-present Traders

Combine the skills of those working the land, a desire to move and a need for money and you get specialization and trade.

The surge in prosperity from the wool and cloth business and improvements in markets and communications encourage trade. The fourteenth century is a time of road- and bridge-building, while humble innovations in vehicles and harnesses facilitating and improving the use of horse-power make transport twice as efficient.[30] The Carters, Wainers, and some of our Porters taking produce to the markets spearhead modernization. Markets and fairs are everywhere. The number of towns, as noted earlier, increases sevenfold over the thirteenth century and many have fairs, with charters granted by the king, for a price, but many without. The tolls, dues and fines from fairs are an important source of revenue for the owner, usually the local aristocrat or abbot.

There is an enormous number of names for traders. Many deal in staples – bread, flour, fish, ale – but many in the spices, meat, linens and jewellery for the more affluent. At the same time, pedlars function alongside substantial merchants with international connections. Surnames in medieval tax lists record how well some do and that scale and specialization in luxuries make men rich, sometimes within a generation. Most of those with occupational names from the food business pay the lowest tax rates, but spice-sellers, millers, butchers, and, particularly, Mercers and Merchants can be wealthy.

Selling the Basics

The food and drink business employs more people than any other trade.[31] Almost a quarter of the occupational names in the 1377 Poll Tax records for Dartmouth are to do with food and by-products.

The Millers, Milners, Millmans, Mellers and Milnes grind the grain and sell the flour; the Bakers, Backhouses, Backmans, Baxters, and Pesters sell the bread; Fishers, Fishermans, Herrings and some of the Miles (also soldiers), are fishers and fishmongers; the Taverners and Tappers sell ale, with the Brewers and Browers, Brewsters (a name for a woman brewer) and Goodalls. The Cheeseman and his variants deal in cheese (monasteries are big producers and eaters of cheese). The Pease and the Poulters sell them.

The number of names for millers and bakers record the importance of bread. Rural Bakers would bake for a village, while manors and urban households would do their own baking.

Bread is some 26 per cent of the food budget of chantry priests at Bridport in the mid-fifteenth century who have a total annual income of less than £20.[32]

There are eight millers in Winchester in about 1300 for a population of some 10,000.[33] Most manors have one oven and one mill, generally owned by the landlord who charges for their use. The Redvers charters show that in 1224–5 about one-eighth of the total income from their Devon estates comes from mill tolls paid by tenants. One of the primary causes of a bondsmen's revolt at St Alban's Abbey in the fourteenth century is compulsory milling at the abbey mill. Mills are tightly controlled to ensure quality, minimize leakage and raise money for the owner. The Dartmouth Assize sets out the weights to be used (the king's) and limits the livestock kept at the mill to three hens and a cock, specifying no hogs, geese or ducks, presumably because they would have eaten too much grain.

The names for our millers give nice examples of regional variants. Millers come from all over, but especially the south-east and the far north; Milners, from the Old English or the Old Norse, are strong in the Norse counties of the north and east, especially the West Riding; Millward is from the Midlands; and Millmans are from Devon.

The several surnames for fishermen and fishmongers record their importance. The church bans most meat-eating for up to three days a week – Friday, Saturday and Wednesday – throughout Lent and the nights before important feasts. Excavations at Exeter show the bones of twenty-four marine species. Herring for the wealthy is traded up and down the coast, particularly from Yarmouth and East Anglia, whence it comes from the rich herring waters of the North Sea, and is salted or smoked. Fresh-water fish, bream and pike for the luxury market, are stocked in ponds and rivers. In two months in the 1380s, the household of the Bishop of Ely consumes 2,000 fresh-water fish.[34]

All the brewers record that people like their ale, like bread a staple part of the medieval diet. In 1311 at Colchester there is a brewer for every thirty people, and the Bridport priests spend as much on ale as they do on bread.[35] A gallon of ale in 1320 costs ¾d–1d according to quality, compared with 3d–4d for a gallon of wine. Most is home-brewed from barley malt in pewter-lined vats. Brewers are often women – as suggested by the name Brewster – and part-time. Beer, introduced from the Low Countries at the end of the fourteenth century, is made from hops, a preservative, so lasts longer than ale, which has to be drunk within a few days of brewing. Court rolls show the brewing and selling of ale is regulated and customary tenants at manors elect ale tasters to monitor the quality. Ale brewing is the grist that puts bread on many tables, particularly of the landless and during famines, and it also turns the wheels of the courts; rolls from Halesowen, west of Birmingham, for 1270–1349 show that 5,476 cases out of a total 6,639 are about brewing and selling ale against regulations.[36]

Supplying Conspicuous Consumers

Spicers, Butchers and Vinters, the Corks selling purple dye, and the Goldbeaters, Amblers or enamellers, Jewells and Pearls, all show growing demand for expensive things. Merchants often sell a range of goods, but the Mercers and Drapers usually specialize in linen, costly silks and velvets and woollen cloth, respectively. Expensive fabrics and goldwork are probably sold in the towns, with the church, the aristocracy and the richer merchants as the main customers. Most of the cogs ('cog' being the general word for a ship) docking at the Exeter outports in the thirteenth and fourteenth centuries bring wine and in among the onions, salt and herring in other ships come spices, figs and raisins, rabbit skins and bishops' copes.

The Goldsmiths and Goldbeaters who sell plate and jewellery are certainly meeting high-end demand. (Golds could sell it or have blond hair or be wealthy.) Much will have come from the elite. An inventory of the goods of the wealthy Thomas Woodstock, Duke of Gloucester, at the end of the fourteenth century shows he has silver plate worth 10 per cent of the value of his goods in his castle and 45 per cent of those in his London house, while his clothes are worth only 7 per cent.[37] Demand also comes from the church, for copes and other vestments as well as altars and books for the monasteries and new cathedrals. A superb example of what medieval

Goldsmiths and Amblers can do is William of Wykeham's bishop's crozier with its enamelled plaques on silver gilt portraying saints, angels and seraphs playing musical instruments, with precise and elegant detailing showing facial expressions, each tress of golden hair, each feather on an angel's wing and fold of a robe.

But the newly wealthy also aspire to luxuries. In 1501, in the Dartmouth Mayors' Court, a dispute is recorded over:

> ii ear-rings ... of gold garnished with precious stones of which one ... has v dyamons and vii perilos [pearls] and the other ... has iii rubies and one dyamonnt with vii perilis.[38]

Records tell us that even successful suppliers of staples can accumulate status goods. In 1297 in Shrewsbury, Richard de Stretton, baker, has an eight-shilling riding horse, meat and some brassware. On the other hand, while city Goldsmiths can be wealthy, early fourteenth century records from Shrewsbury also show le Goldsmiths assessed at low tax rates with inventories of brooches and rings worth ten shillings or less.[39]

The spicers are the Salters (who could be psaltery players, too) and the Spices, Spicers, Garlicks, and Peppers. Spicers are specialists and spices are used in medicines as well as in cooking and preserving food. Many are expensive and imported, bought by the relatively prosperous to liven up meat – dried fruit, cinammon, cloves, ginger and so on to saffron, which sells for twelve to fifteen shillings a pound. Many ships coming to the Exeter outports and to Dartmouth carry imports of garlic, anise, cumin, pepper and saffron. As early as 1186, a Robert of London is recorded buying £183-worth of pepper in Genoa; at least some of this luxury trade is in English hands.[40]

Ordinary people use substitutes for imported spices that seem to be anything hot. When in *Piers Plowman*, Glutton asks 'Have you got any hot spices?' Betty the Brewer answers that she has pepper, peony seeds, garlic and fennel seeds, which she puts in the beer to make her drinkers thirsty.[41] Salt-making is an ancient activity in England, but by the later Middle Ages it is in decline because of imports from France. But spices can be status foods. Chaucer's hospitable Franklin has sauces that are 'Poynaunt and sharp'. Saffron is the costliest; the Duke of Buckingham's household uses almost 2 lb of it a day in 1452–3.[42] Thomas de Berkeley, a rich baron, in 1345–6 spends 3 per cent of his food budget on spices, half the proportion he spends on wine. And when Edmund Stonor gives a dinner in August 1378 for the judiciaries in Oxfordshire he spends 10s 6½d on spices.[43]

Butchers or Bowkers, Skinners and Shinners flay and sell meat. Associated traders are the Fells who sell the hides; the Tanners and Skinners the leather; and the Saddlers the saddles. The popularity of butchers suggests that meat is widely eaten, despite the church's limits. Traditionally, animals are slaughtered at Martinmas (11 November), when there is feasting and meat is salted to keep until the following year. But many households do keep animals through the winter. Butchers sell beef – about half the meat consumed – as well as pork and mutton. Game is an aristocratic food, poached and widely eaten, but rarely sold. Animal bones from the twelfth to fifteenth centuries excavated from village sites show the predominance of sheep, followed by cattle and pigs.[44]

Wine sold by Vinters is produced in the south and west of England until the marriage of Henry II with Eleanor of Aquitaine, when imports from La Rochelle and Bordeaux begin to make the southern ports of Devon prosperous. At its 1308 peak, 20,000 tuns, or five million gallons, of wine is imported into England, almost a gallon per person.[45] It comes mainly from Gascony (Bordeaux stays English until 1431) and from northern France and the Rhône. Contemporary morality is against alcohol. Even Chaucer says, in the Pardoner's Tale:

> A lecherous thing is wyn; and dronkenesse
> Is ful of stryving and of wrecchednesse.
> O dronke man, disfigured is thy face,
> Sour is thy breeth, foul artow to embrace ...
> In whom that drinke hath dominacioun,
> He kan no conseil kepe.[46]

As usual, Chaucer gets up really close to his man.

The Generalists

The names for more general retailers range from traditional suppliers to large entrepreneurs. The Huckers, Peddars and Pedlers, Farman, Jaggers and some of the Chapmans and Copemans hawk small goods from hamlet to hamlet and market to market. Many dealing in garden produce are women. Fourteen women pay half a penny each to sell beans, peas and apples in Bristol in 1282–4.[47]

But Marchants, Mercers, Drapers and some Chapmans can be large-scale entrepreneurs, particularly those in the wool and wine businesses as well as the herring and grain trade. Chaucer's Merchant is prosperous:

> ... hye on horse he sat,
> Up-on his heed a Flaundrish bever hat[48]

and worries about French pirates capturing his ships taking his goods from East Anglia to the staple towns of Flanders to be sold. These merchants become the elite of their towns, their wealth from trade and property. As much as 14 per cent of merchants dying in London between 1350 and 1497 have estates worth £1,000 or more, the equivalent of rich knights and barons. In 1392–4, Richard Whittington sells £34,750-worth of luxury fabrics to royalty.[49] Large merchants generally deal in wool and cloth, but they diversify. Associations like the Wool Staplers and Merchant Adventurers, who handle cloth exports, are advisers and creditors to royalty (Staples and Venters could be their namesakes). The international reach of their travels and their networks are discussed in Chapter 4.

Traders and Trust

Surnames tell us that medieval people do not always trust traders. Barratt means commerce or fraud and Tranter, a carrier or hawker, can be associated with *trant,* a tricky person. Merchant may also be pejorative. Medieval art and writing frequently show merchants symbolizing the sin of greed. In *Piers Plowman,* merchants dress Guile up as an apprentice to get him to display and sell their wares; being a Merchant is to be a cheat – merchants do not follow the church's rules and they swear – a serious transgression. If they want to save themselves, Truth tells them to put their profits to helping the sick and orphan girls, feeding the poor, putting boys through school and endowing religious orders.[50]

If the mistrust is directed at the larger and wealthier town merchants, people seem to have a point. Exeter's records show that the large importers, a tiny fraction of the population, all of them guildsmen, supply the office bearers and control the town in the thirteenth and fourteenth centuries. The emerging trade and craft guilds (Lancashire's Preston Guild was established in about 1179)[51] connect with the church, protect their members and regulate trade. They have monopoly power in the towns and exclude non-guild traders except at fairs. Apprenticeship is a requirement for membership; only guildsmen can be aldermen, sheriffs and mayors and have the freedom of the city. Nobles and clerics are co-opted by being made honorary members. Such power leads to abuses and is exclusive. In East Anglia and the west of England clothiers avoid the guilds by putting weaving, fulling and dying out to workers in the countryside.[52]

Monopoly power over prices is resisted. The surname Price records the person who monitors or fixes prices at fairs and elsewhere. Statutes, or assizes, regulate all weights and the prices of basic goods relative to the costs of their main inputs, so that the price of bread is fixed in relation to the cost of wheat, ale relative to barley malt and candles to tallow. There are penalties for 'regratting', or buying up goods, particularly food, to resell at a profit. Ale and wine tasters monitor the quality of these. The church dislikes trade, partly because it encourages excess, vanity and greed for money, and the assizes incorporate the idea of a just price that rewards labour, but not by too much.

Inventories in medieval tax records give a picture of which traders do well. Obviously, enrichment will also depend on factors such as individual talent and opportunity, but there is nevertheless a pattern that shows which activities are remunerative. The Shrewsbury tax assessment of the early fourteenth century shows clearly trade to be a major source of the town's wealth. Besides the tailors mentioned in Chapter 2 who become wealthy merchants, a spicer has risen; in 1309, Robert le Espycer has not only the spices of his occupation, but also a twenty-shilling horse, a mazer cup and a great deal of silver, linen, jewellery and wall-hangings.[53] Reginald Perle, pearl seller, moves from being a mercer in 1297, with an inventory of silk, muslin, girdles and hose, to become one of the wealthiest merchants in the town in 1312, with assets of £30.[54] William Moleyns, in 1400 to the following year, has £357 in income and spends £539, mostly on luxuries – horses, clothes and wine. The not-too-distant ancestor of this spendthrift came from a mill and he, or one in between, made a fortune.[55] One day his capital or his creditors will put an end to it and he will slip back down from his gentry status.

Not all do so well. Sellers of staples, like Bakers, regularly appear among the lowest tax-payers. Although Edward le Mustarder, or mustard-maker, copes sufficiently to be eligible for tax in Shrewsbury, his inventories show the values of his goods oscillating at a very low level. Mustard seed occurs only once in the four years he appears in the lists, and the tallow and candles of Paris in each suggest he is trying to be a chandler. The last two entries include iron and steel and nails too, evidence of a foray into ironmongery. But none includes any brassware or clothes.[56]

Musicians

New College, Oxford, has a remarkable piece of medieval craftsmanship, described as 'incomparably the finest example of English goldsmith's work of the Gothic style which has come down to us from the Middle Ages'.[57] This is the crozier of William of Wykeham, Bishop of Winchester and Chancellor of England from 1367 until, with interruptions, his death in 1404. Up and around the head and crook of this beautifully worked two-metre silver-gilt crozier are tiny blue- and green-enamelled and silver panels showing angels playing musical instruments.[58] The head of the crozier is about ear-level for a tallish man and William would have processed with it down his medieval aisles cocking his ear to the music of these angels walking with him.

This crozier gives a context for the musicians recorded in our names. They tell us the instruments that are played: the flute and the bagpipe, the fiddle, the harp and the psaltery for the melody; the trumpet, the tabor (drums are not common before the six-teenth century) and the organ for rhythm; and the voice, the plain singers and the churchly chanters. So for the rhythm of dancing, we have the Organers, the Tabers and the Horns and Hornblowers. For the tunes and poetry, we have the Players, the Pipers (usually bagpipe players) and Trumps (or jew's harp players), Fiddlers and Crowthers (a medieval stringed instrument), Harpers and Salters (psaltery players as well as sellers of salt). And for meditation and devotion, there are the Singers, Caunters, Chants and Chantrells as well as the poets themselves, the Rimmers (a rare name from south Lancashire).

Music belongs to everyone – those in ale houses, at fairs and in great halls, at the king's court and in the cathedrals, abbeys and churches. It is studied with arithmetic and astronomy in mon-asteries and cathedrals during the twelfth century. The youth of the elite are taught music and dancing; Chaucer's admired young squire in *The Canterbury Tales* 'coulde songes make'.[59] There are itinerant minstrels who play and sing for their bread and royal minstrels who are well-paid professionals, often of noble birth. The Anglo-Saxon St Adhelm is a renowned harpist. Wealthy houses have their minstrels; an early Redvers charter refers to Kenebald the Citharista, or minstrel, distinguished enough to be recorded by name.[60] Musicians have a sort of trade guild called the Court of Minstrels granted by Richard II in 1380–1.[61]

A minstrel, Gleeman, keeps oral culture and history alive. Roman historian and senator Tacitus, writing in the second century, refers to the ancient songs of the Germans as the only historic traditions they had. It is likely that the Anglo-Saxons brought this oral culture to Britain in the fifth century. *Beowulf* records the tradition of minstrels being either professionals or aristocrats. Describing the feast after he had killed the monster Grendel and its mother, the hero remembers:

> ... an old reciter,
> a carrier of stories, recalled the early days.

At times some hero made the timbered harp
tremble with sweetness, or related true
and tragic happenings.[62]

Harpists are particularly admired. Among all the musicians in Celtic Ireland only they can become freemen, although only if accompanied by nobility. When troubadours become fashionable with Eleanor of Aquitaine in the twelfth century the ideas of a courtly life of knightly courtesy, honour and romance invade England and its songs.[63]

Music and the Church

But the church has issues. Some music is important to ritual, but other music is thought to incite lust and lechery. In *The Canterbury Tales*, the Pardoner describes young people who 'with harpes, lutes and giternes,/They daunce and pleye at dees, bothe day and night'. A gittern is a sort of lute, from the French for guitar. They are a debauched bunch: '... it is grisly for to here hem swere'.[64] In the eleventh century priests are forbidden to be 'ale minstrels'.[65] Medieval art, some of it in churches, drums in the association. On a misericord at a church in Lavenham in Suffolk a man plays a pig as if it were a bagpipe.[66] Interpretation might take us a moment, but medieval people would have recognized the joke immediately; pigs are symbols of lust and the bagpipes a common symbol of depravity. Music leads to sin.

In the Miller's Tale, Chaucer's two jolly wooers of the old carpenter's wife both play music. The clerk Nicolas has a 'gay sautrye [psaltery],/On which he made a nightes melodye/So swetely, that al the chambre rong', and the unfortunate Absolon woos with a small rebeck and a gittern. The debauched friar in Chaucer's Prologue 'Wel coude he singe and pleyen on a rote' a rote being a fiddle.[67] Courtly troubadours also annoy the church for their emphasis on the pleasures of this world. William IX, Duke of Aquitaine, who died in 1127, is a troubadour who sings of his joy in earthly things – horses and furs as well as love and the changing seasons. 'Can a minstrel be saved?' asked Honarius of Augsburg

'They are ministers of Satan; they laugh in this world; God shall laugh at them in the last day.'[68]

Yet music is important to the church, as our Caunters, Cants and Chantrells show. The psaltery and gittern engaged in wooing the miller's wife and the fiddle deployed by Chaucer's lecherous friar are all on William of Wykeham's crozier. Even the low-class bagpipes are there, the bag under the arm of a fair-haired angel with bright brown and green wings and purple, bright blue, purple and green robes, playing beneath dark brown and grey clouds.[69] Together with the Tabers we have what we need for dancing. With the crozier, William of Wykeham left something else to New College, which he founded – his sandals. Our music is still in his footfall.

Inventories for tax assessments show a William le Trumpour had done well in Shrewsbury. In 1313, his cart and harness and team of three packhorses suggest he is now (or also) in trade, and his twenty-shilling horse, clothes, jewellery, meat and brassware show he makes enough profit to display his affluence.[70]

Builders

If the minstrels are the entertainers, the builders are the creators of medieval times at a period when building is at the forefront of international innovation. Their hands stretch into the future with new and growing cities, castles, houses great and small, roads and bridges. Normans, ironically for warlords, are already ambitious builders in Normandy before the Conquest and great builders in England afterwards. The Middle Ages sees active road- and bridge-building by landlords and town and village communities; by the early fourteenth century eight bridges are built on the Severn below Montford Bridge and only ten are added over the next four hundred years.[71] The peak of the construction of great buildings is 1210–1350 when the church builds monasteries, churches and magnificent cathedrals – visual evidence of the Norman triumph.

The culmination of this triumph is the soaring Gothic cathedral that seems to defy gravity and incorporate the aspirations of the time. 'The vault seems to converse with the winged birds' writes a contemporary poet of the new Lincoln Cathedral in about 1220.[72] These builders leave the highlights of a visual world that has lasted over 700 years, a glory of cathedrals. Castles and monasteries have not lasted as well, but royal palaces and even everyday houses survive.

Great buildings cost a fortune. In 1376 an aisle of Gloucester Abbey costs £781, when a skilled building worker is earning 4d a day (1d is one penny).[73] Only the church and the wealthiest aristocracy can afford such work. Patrons are usually abbots and bishops, deans and chapters, kings and dukes, and even monks. They can get closely involved. A contemporary poem describes Bishop – later Saint – Hugh at Lincoln who 'carried the hewn stones in a kind of hod, and the lime mortar also'. Contemporary documents, like the contract for building the nave of Fotheringay Church in Northamptonshire in 1435, show that the patron supplies the transport, materials – stone, lime, sand, ropes, bolts, ladders, timber, scaffolds – and machines. By implication the workmen bring their own tools. A boss in the cloister of Norwich Cathedral shows a deeply serious mason in tan stocking hat and matching leather apron holding an enormous set square. Clerks become clerks of works who administer and run the finances, ensuring supplies are delivered, workmen come and are paid. The contract to build Fotheringay Church specifies the clerk can even stop payment to the Master if he does not pay his workmen.[74]

The Masterly Masons

Large projects would have overall site directors. Contemporary documents call them Masters or Masons, or even Jenners (military engineers). Master seems to have been a catch-all surname, covering masters of schools, farms and apprentices. The contract for Fotheringay is between the Duke of York and 'William Horwood, free-mason'. William Wynford, working on New College Oxford and Winchester College is another Mason who becomes an 'architect'. The text on the rebuilding of Canterbury after a fire in *The Chronicle of Gervase of Canterbury* describes William of Sens as

Master, but his successor, William the Englishman, as Master and 'our mason'.

These Masters have to understand the new materials and techniques as well as how to deal successfully with the patron. Gervase records the monks' choice at Canterbury: 'William de Sens, a man active and ready, and as a workman most skilful in both wood and stone'. This William turns out to have crucial skills of persuasion, convincing the doubtful monks to take down much more of the damaged building than planned (which 'excruciated the monks with grief'). He goes on to demonstrate an ability to innovate, constructing 'ingenious machines for loading and unloading ships and for drawing cement and stone' and sending moulds for shaping stones to the quarries in Caen to save on transport costs. He leaves in 1178, five years into the project, after a crippling fall. His successor, William the Englishman, 'our mason', is described as 'William by name, English by nation, small in body, but in workmanship of many kinds acute and honest'.[75] William has no falls and finishes the project in 1184.

Some of these Masters do not turn out so well. Master Simon, directing the fortification of Ardres:

> had houses and barns demolished; he cut down orchards ... pulled down many buildings ... broke up gardens ... beat down the fields.... He did not bother about those who became angry and cried out aloud, nor about those who grumbled silently about him.[76]

The Jenners' knowledge of military technology is key. The colossal Gothic stone cathedrals stimulate the invention of the cranes with counterweights and pulleys powered by windlasses and treadwheels in medieval paintings, adaptations of such war machines as the twelfth-century *trébuchet*, used for hurling stones. Skills developed for war are applied to reversing its destruction.[77] A crane for a new church at a Dominican convent in Arles has to be able to lift some 10 metric tonnes of stone and to be 44 yards high.[78]

Contemporary contracts between patrons and these Masters and Jenners signal issues. Finishing the building seems to be one.

Canterbury goes fast, but many do not; rebuilding Exeter begins in the 1270s and the west front is only finished in the fifteenth century.[79] So Masters' fees may be paid retroactively and in stages.[80] Absenteeism is another issue, suggesting good Masters are much in demand and hard to keep. When the bishop, dean and chapter of Meaux contract with Master Gautier de Varinfroy to build a cathedral for ten livres a year, they offer an additional three sous a day when he works on site or runs errands, insist he lives in Meaux and does not go to any other site, particularly Evreux (where another building must be going up) for more than two months without permission, and works faithfully and loyally for the project.

Masons, as their wages suggest, are the heroes. Stone is the new material for cathedrals, monasteries and castles. After the Conquest, England imports millions of tonnes from Caen, William the Conqueror's home town. Local quarries are developed over time but as late as the 1320s, when Exeter Cathedral is being rebuilt, a quarry in Caen is still being used alongside eight in Devon and one in Somerset.[81]

Masons' names suggest a developing profession in which wages vary according to skills. Masons, Setters, Wallers, Stonemans and Stoniers all represent differences in training, tools and skills. Masons work on the dressed stone with the tiny vertical and horizontal joints for the visible parts of the building, the facings, jambs and tracery. Setters are the specialists who lay the stones in place and Wallers the basic workmen. Stoniers are the quarriers who could do some roughing out and cutting of the stone on site to save on transport costs. In the twelfth century a specialized iron stone hammer is developed in northern France that revolutionizes the accuracy and finish of dressed stone; perhaps this turns the English Stoneman into the French Mason. Describing the new choir at Canterbury, Gervase talks about the old arches 'sculptured with an axe and not with a chisel', comparing them with the new arch-ribs and keystones.[82]

These workers in stone produce marvels, the scale and design of much of the building leading to innovations that cross frontiers. The William of Sens engaged to rebuild Canterbury comes from being the master architect for the first Gothic cathedral at Sens and brings the Gothic style and innovations in building techniques, transport and associated crafts.[83] English masons under Richard Ely invent the flat-arched fan vaulting in King's College, Cambridge, in the mid-fifteenth century that is copied in Germany and France. The wonderful rayonnant rose windows of St Denis in Paris travel to Westminster Abbey and as far as Famagusta Cathedral in Cyprus. Exeter Cathedral's traceries have elements of those at Westminster Abbey, Sainte Chapelle and Notre Dame and its vaulting patterns are reminiscent of St Paul's Cathedral, although they are richer.[84] Masons are artists with brands, and bishops with building programs fight to get them.

Crafty Carpentry and Glass

Although wood is replaced by stone as the main building material on large sites from the eleventh century, Carpenters, Sawyers, Hackers, Wrights, and Turners are no less important than the stoneworkers. Finding nearby wood in deforested countries is an issue in many contemporary documents. Almost 4,000 trees are felled to build Windsor Castle in the mid-fourteenth century. A simple house takes 20 trees.[85] A painting of the Grand Master of the Hospitallers in Rhodes, when his city is being besieged by the Turks and he has rebuilding in mind, shows him welcoming the carpenters first, before the masons.[86] As craftspeople in Chapter 2, here they are at the more complex and larger-scale end of the business, making sophisticated skeletons for stone exteriors and, with the Smiths, the ingenious machines to transport and lift heavy stones and the scaffolding to raise them to unprecedented heights.

Although mostly invisible today, carpenters build amazing structures inside the stone vaulting under roofs and spires, the most spectacular being the spire of Salisbury Cathedral, which can still be seen from the inside. William Hurley makes the outstanding timber octagon over the crossing of Ely Cathedral after 1322 that creates the illusion of stone vaulting, an example of the old technology staying modern by mimicking the new.[87] Carpenters also produce the rich wood carving in the churches, particularly the rood screens and the apparently more personal work like misericords and vivid oak bosses. Some of this must be from models because the scenes are repeated across churches – a fox stealing a goose – but many are unique and tied to their context, like the tiny man trying to squeeze out of a small opening in the pulpit of the fourteenth-century Southwell Minster.[88]

Carpenters still build urban housing, although there are references to stone houses in Portsmouth.[89] Even everyday buildings could be done to a high enough standard to survive more than seven centuries, as buildings for merchants and artisans in Ludlow and Lady Row in Goodramgate, York, attest. Most medieval housing is timber-framing on stone foundations with wattle and daub or cob walls and thatch on timber frames. The carpenters' *pièce de résistance* is the roof – the marvellous soaring jointed oak cruck roofs with their massive paired beams that often rise in single timbers from the foundations.

Stained and painted glass is found in medieval churches and rich mens' houses, only affordable by others towards the end of the sixteenth century.[90] Ecclesiastical glass is instructive, with figures of saints and biblical scenes painted by our Glass, Glasses, Glaziers and Painters. For example, Thomas Glazier of Oxford who works as a glass painter for William of Wykeham from about 1386. There is a possible self-portrait of him in the east window of Winchester Cathedral choir, a man praying in monks' robes with a sensitive, worried face turned toward the viewer. The antechapel to New College chapel still has his glass, some of the best surviving from the fourteenth century, in wonderfully subtle olive greens, aubergines, soft pinks and umbers. Thomas is recorded as dining in Hall with the Fellows at New College for twelve years from 1388, showing the respect distinguished artisans commanded and the importance of his craft.[91]

Other Crafts Scale Up

Smiths, Ferrers, Fabers, Goffs and Angoves from manor and town turn their hand to the metalwork for tools and machines, like the treadwheels with their weights and pulleys. It must have been expensive; the contract for the crane at Arles specifies that the prior is to supply and repair the ironwork for it.[92] The quality of masonry depends on the resistance of the tools to wear. Metal is used as an architectural support. Rayonnant architecture depends on the iron reinforcement of tie-rods and tensioning connectors, chains and bars.[93] Medieval tie-rods to contain the thrust of the vaults arguably saved the vault ribs in the apse of St Quentin when it was bombed in World War I.

Craftsmen from the countryside work on these projects and the names tell us which specializations are needed. Roofwork is done by the Slaters, Tylers, and Helyers, Helliers and Hilliers and its other variants, all of which mean tiler; Thatchers and Thackers who thatch; Spooners who make the shingles in the south of England; and the Theakers from the Old Norse, who simply roof.[94] Leadbeaters and Plummers do lead roof work and make the gutters and water pipes in large buildings. At the construction of Noyers Castle in the twelfth century, Hugues de Noyers combines a fortified castle with a 'palace of great beauty' below it, with sub-terranean passages from the wine cellar beneath the tower down to the palace with 'cleverly fashioned' lead pipes for wine and water.[95]

Others adapt to new demands. The mixers of mortar, an important function, carry the names of the baskets they mix it in – Coffin, Mander and so on. Carters, Wainers and Porters are essential. Stone and timber are carried in barges by water or on land by horses and especially oxen, using the new equipment that allows heavier loads to be carried further and faster. Transport is costly; stone from Caen costs four times its quarry price in Norwich.

Data on wage rates at building sites show a clear hierarchy, from experienced masons at the top down to unskilled labour. At Caernarvon Castle in 1316 maximum rates for a middle-ranking mason are £5 1s 4d for 286 days' work, £4 1s for a carpenter working at most 262 days, £2 1s 4d for a quarryman, and £1 11s 8d for an unskilled labourer for 243 days. The vast majority of workers on a site are low paid. The high-paid masons have several rates, thirteen at Caernarvon, according to differences in experi-ence and skills.[96] Contemporary paintings of large building sites show patrons and Masters watching scenes aswarm with Masons and Carpenters, Smiths and Wallers, men mixing the mortar and workmen humping stone, working cranes, climbing scaffolding and ladders.

The east window of Winchester College chapel has a nineteenth-century copy of a fourteenth-century glass showing three men, a carpenter, a mason, and a clerk of works. Thomas Glazier of Oxford is elsewhere in the same window. These are the men who create our visual medieval world and our surnames record them.

The Military

There are many names for archers and the archery industry in this time of incessant wars. Archers, Bowmen, some Butts, from the archery target, and Armstrongs (also nicknames) and Alabasters, who are crossbowmen, are the archers. Arrowsmiths and Fletchers make the iron-tipped arrows; Stringers string the bows; and Bowyers and Bowers make them, although the latter could include chamber-servants and people from minor places. Then we have Miles, who are soldiers and probably archers as well, and Riders, who are mounted soldiers. Darts could be makers of small pointed arrows, or the soldiers or hunters who use them (or, indeed, someone from a river called Dart). We have warriors: the Warriors themselves, Harmans and all their variants, the Kemps and the Camps, who could also be athletes or wrestlers, and the Duncans, or brown warriors, from the Gaelic or Old Irish. And then we have the Knights, the Squires and Pages who attend the knights, whether at home or on the battlefield, and the Bachelers or Batchelors, the knights-in-waiting (all also servants in Chapter 2). Dukes, Earls and Barons, and, indeed, Kings, will have been on the battlefield too, but those names are given in irony and are discussed at length in Chapter 6.

Finally, we have the Homers who make helmets, the Cottells and Cottles who make armour or daggers, or who could have been cutlers, the Spurrs and Spears who make spurs, the Sworders, and those smiths who still make armour. London spur-makers make a small piece of history in 1381 when they are discovered to have been fixing profits on spurs. Seen as a sinister threat to the public, they have to disband, more because as unskilled workers they are not allowed to form an association than from concern about price-fixing, which is common.[97]

These military names tell a clear story; most people are archers; half of the names are of archers, ordinary soldiers, also probably archers, and their suppliers. Foresters and parkers, woodwards and poachers all use arrows, which must have boosted the popularity of the Arrowsmiths, Fletchers, Bowyers and Stringers. On the battlefield, there are commonly 10–20 footmen, usually archers, per knight.[98] The secret of the archers' success is the six-foot bow of oak or yew, which could cut through armour almost 400 yards away. People will have been proud to be archers; they are the heroes of the Hundred Years' War. English archers under Edward III ensure control of the Channel when they almost eradicate the French and Genoese fleet at Sluys in 1340, where 'a shower of arrows out of long wooden bows so poured down on the Frenchman that thousands were slain'.[99] They are the deciding factor in victory at Crécy six years later, at Maupertuis near Poitiers in 1356, and again at Agincourt in 1415. In 1337, Edward III forbids anyone to engage in any other sport or pastime, on pain of death; archers practise in churchyards across England after Sunday service.

Financing the Military

War is part of English medieval culture as the nation consolidates within its shores but loses its first empire abroad when France expands at last to its western seaboard. Wars are continuous from the 1290s; between 1294 and 1340 England has armies in Scotland, Wales, Gascony and Flanders. In the Falkirk campaign in the 1290s, 25,700 infantry are raised out of a population of some 2–4.5 million (population estimates are notoriously uncertain). There is neither a standing navy, nor a standing army. Conscripts could be any age between sixteen and sixty. This is a time when an unskilled labourer earns 1.5–1.9d a day, and a carpenter 2.8d, a footsoldier earns 2d and a mounted archer 6d. So if pay alone is the criterion, the labourer (if he had the choice) would go to war as a footsoldier and the carpenter would not. Equipment for a mounted archer costs about £2, the price of four oxen.[100] A knight bachelor, an inexperienced knight, would get from the king 2 shillings a day; a bannaret, a knight or baron with experience and wealth, would get 6 shillings; an earl 8 shillings; a duke 13 shillings 4d. Wage hierarchy and social hierarchy are two fingers of the same feudal hand.

The cost is shared between king and country. Knights pay for their own warhorses (£40–£80) and equipment; the king pays for the horse if it is killed. War is a burden on local communities. From 1307, local communities pay for the equipment and wages of local soldiers serving outside the country (mounted archers are more expensive) and suffer the losses. Coastal towns also have to pay for coastal protection.[101] The king also taxes the population to pay for his share. The Foreman could be a tax collector as well as a swineherd and the Farmer could be a tax collector too. Between 1293 and 1306 there are six levies to pay for the wars; between 1294 and 1334 there are sixteen and they become more onerous as the century proceeds. These are the Lay Subsidies, the 1332 one specifically to provide funds for 'great and arduous affairs in Ireland and elsewhere'. Exclusions of goods and people favour the wealthy and the church; land and buildings are excluded, as are jewels and precious metals belonging to country knights and their wives. The minimum taxable rate in the country is the cost of one cow or four-six sheep in 1332.[102]

Taxation, as ever, drives behaviour, and stories of people deserting their land rather than pay show how great the burden is. It contributes to the abandonment of the countryside that accelerates after the Black Death to produce an almighty shift of power towards the peasants and the slow death of feudalism. The 1380 Poll Tax, three times higher than the 1377 tax, is the trigger for the Peasant's Revolt of 1381, when rebels march on London under the leadership of Wat Tyler, sacking religious establishments on the way, including the archbishop's palace in Canterbury, going after John of Gaunt, the warmonger regent of the young King Richard II. The rebellion fails, but its targeting of the church and the warring baronies is a warning that the peasantry can no longer be relied on to be submissive and blind. The reaction to the way our Archers are financed is to lead to massive social change.

The Knights

There are two types of Knight: the knight-bachelor, inexperienced and generally poor; and the bannaret, experienced and wealthy and classed with the barons. Knights are not necessarily nobles; initially, it is a military rank for mounted soldiers. They hold land called a knight's fee from a more important lord, to whom they owe military service. The Abbot of Tavistock has to contribute 15 men-at-arms to the king in times of war; to get them, he creates tenancies by allocating land as 'knights' fees' to 16–17 military tenants, 15 plus a couple for insurance since if not all respond to a call, the abbot is responsible.[103] There are a few civil knights, such as the Lord Mayors of London. In 1301, about 900 knights serve in the Caerlaverock campaign.[104]

Knight is a tricky name to classify. The name could mean a feudal knight, or servant, after the Old English word, or a common soldier. In 1353 all those holding land valued at £15 or over could be knights. At about the same time the Pardoner in Chaucer's *The Canterbury Tales* was earning £60 a year. Often knights are mercenaries, selling their military service to a lord, holding their knight's fee in lieu of payment. Sometimes it can be descriptive of the lesser country gentry that most knights become in the later Middle Ages. But it could be a nickname, perhaps descriptive of gentility, from the knights who become the heroes of courtly romances, or ironic for pretension, for labourers with attitudes, as noted in Chapter 6. Knight could also record someone who plays a knight in a mumming play, pageant or game, such as bowling. Knights of the Green are recorded in the eighteenth century as the winners of bowling matches and the title could have been part of oral tradition much earlier.[105] These different meanings are part of the untidiness of classification, but contribute to its richness.

Skills and Scale Differentiated in Derivations

Out of all these names that give an overview of the feudal world at a time when the administration of the country is in Latin and French, Old and Middle English surnames dominate, particularly names to do with work on the land. People mostly think of themselves as English and in English. But not always. The names to do with education and the church – Clerk, Judge, Sergeant – tend to be French or French/English, recalling common Latin roots. None is solely English.

But look a little closer and patterns emerge. As with the occupations in Chapter 2, the Normans bring with them the words for new skills and a dominance over management, scale and quality. As with servants and craftsmen, names for traditional and subordinate activities tend to be Old English – Shepherd and Coward, Ward and Reeve, Hellier and Stoneman. Names for the overseers closer to power tend to be Old French – Bailiff, Forrester, Park and Mason. English trade consists of basic activities; Saddler and Brewer, Baker and Backhouse, Taverner and Tapster. But the purveyors of exotica, the Spicers, and the Vinters and the Mercers who deal in costly fabrics, are Old French. The differences are striking in the names to do with music and the military. More than half of the Old English names in the latter group have to do with archers and reflect pride in the name. The Old French names are more varied, with suppliers of helmets, armour and daggers. Our musicians are Fiddlers, Pipers and Harpers; the French are more sophisticated with Salters, and Luters, Tabers and Trumpers. There is a similar pattern with scale. Names for the larger traders are Old French – Merchant and Draper; smaller traders are Old English – Chapman, Pedler.

Surnames that are Old French and Old English translations of each other tell us something about which skills and activities the Normans have an edge in. So the Old French Carpenter can do more than the Old English Sawyer and the Old French Porter more than the Old English Wain or Carter; the Farmer, Butcher, Mason and Plummer have more sophisticated skills than the Fielder and the Shinner, the Stoneman and the Leadbeater. The French roots of Mason and Plummer carry echoes of the international context of these callings.

While both the Old English and French translations survive, it is often the Old French word that has been taken on in English. So the Old French Archer has become our word for the occupation, instead of Bowman; we have the Old French farmer instead of fielder; porter instead of wain or wainer; bailiff instead of reeve; parker instead of woodward; merchant instead of chapman; butcher in place of shinner; mason instead of stoneman; and plumber instead of leadbeater. The Old English names still exist, but the word is not used for the occupation, so we do not always know what it means. The striking exceptions to this patterns are shepherd, baker and hunter – all Old English. The Old French equivalents are Barker for the shepherd, Pistor for the baker and Chase or Venner for hunter, not immediately comprehensible today.

The survival of these translations record the mix of languages that ordinary people speak. And for some callings, etymology might give a timeline for an activity from pre-Conquest times until the fourteenth century, marking improvements in skills from the Norse to the French. The pattern could apply to the Old Norse Farman, Old English Pedler and Old French Tranter, who are all hawkers; the merchants – the Old Norse Copeman, the English Chapman and the French Merchant; and the roofers – the Norse Theakers, Old English Thatchers and Thackers and the Middle English/Old French Tylers and Slaters.

These few Old Norse names that co-exist with other names broadly meaning the same thing show how occupations that had existed for centuries are evolving quite rapidly during the naming period. Although analysis of distribution is very dependent on which records survive, it is very striking that first records of Norse names over the eleventh to the fourteenth centuries are in the Danelaw. Most – names like Theaker, Farman, Copeman and Milner – are both in East Anglia and the north. But Ashburner is only in Lancashire, Yorkshire and Cumbria.

Surviving occupational names give us the highlights of the time. Medieval England is on the road. Its builders are creating a new architectural landscape, its artisans and patrons exchanging concepts and technologies with the European continent and beyond. Its traders hawk their goods from village to village, town to town, and across the seas to foreign fairs. Its archers and soldiers go by the thousand to distant wars. Change is in the wind. Flayers of meat are becoming proper butchers, Stonemans with axes are becoming Masons who wield chisels, skilled Wallers rise to become Setters. Traders, once pedlars, can be large-scale Merchants or specialist Mercers; flour and bread are still sold, but so are imported velvets, spices and wine. People are doing what they can with what they have. Surnames show the feudal system surviving by co-opting peasants to manage their peers in every conceivable activity. They show diversification; few farmers, many managers and craftsmen. The names of the clerics record the explosive entry of written records into ordinary life and recorded history. The musicians tell of the music of the bawds and the pious. These people think of themselves mostly in English, but say Merchant (French) as readily as Chapman (English). It no longer matters that Bailiff is a French word and Swain Norse; bailiffs, masons and merchants are English now, too.

CHAPTER 4

PLACE NAMES: LANDSCAPES AND TRAVELLERS

ABOUT HALF THE surnames the English carry today are topographical or locational. The topographical ones tell us about people who live near some feature of the landscape – a hill or a ridge, a valley or a marsh. Locational names record those coming from a place with a proper name, London, York or places in continental Europe. Of the ten most popular names in this group, all but one – Scott – is topographical.

Very English and on the Move

Topographical names are virtually all Old English or Old Norse. It is thought that the francophone elite – the earls, barons and wealthier knights (some 234 people), the gentry, the church and the king – own some 90–95 per cent of the land in medieval England.[1] These surnames show how far they are removed from it and the people who work it. Not only do English words exist for the names people want to use, but, since French words are integral to everyday language, people must also choose not to use them. French culture invades occupational surnames and nicknames, but not these names.

They record earthy English briars and swamps when

110

contemporary tapestries and miniatures in illuminated manuscripts show idealized French or Italian landscapes. These names record a rural, pragmatic people, unsentimental about the nature around them. Groves, mounds and waterfalls are sacred to Celts and Vikings. English names from across the country tell of sources of subsistence and income, streams and weirs for fishing, woods and trees for timber, pastures and farms recording land clearances and enclosures, and the tracks and ridges, fords and bridges that document travel and transport.

Locational surnames in medieval records show that up to one-third of the population in a given place comes from somewhere else; feudalism is not as binding as commonly imagined. They show the sheer distances people travel, living sometimes hundreds of miles from their origins. They record economic highlights. Some names preserve the memory of eleventh-century invaders; others the later traders and migrants snapping at their heels, the sea a highway, not a frontier. They show how English commerce happens. Many document wool and cloth markets in Flanders, Brabant and Holland, cloth dyes from Picardy, and wine from Gascony and Burgundy. Others tell of the great English wool and cloth cities of the east and the north, the Welsh Marches and the Lake District. Names tell us that some of this trade is in the hands of the English and some belongs to foreigners, many of whom stay as immigrants, becoming shipmasters, farm labourers or craftsmen. We know from occupational names that England imports spices, silks and other exotica; locational names record the local foreign and English ports where most imports are transhipped. There are few names from distant places. A solid group of Welsh travel here, as do the Scots and a few Irish, and names from many small places, often keeping alive names of deserted settlements, tell us that people move around all over medieval England. But still there is, as always, a local footnote to our story; many of the surnames in a given area in medieval times, often from very local places, are there today.

The trade routes documented in our surnames also have sinister overtones. The Black Death, in Constantinople in early 1347, is in Sicily in October, Marseilles in November and Genoa by December. During 1348 it is working its way overland from Venice into southern France. At the same time it is travelling the much speedier sea routes of our spices and silks through Bordeaux and the coastal ports of Normandy, reaching them and Weymouth on our southern coast in August or September 1348. It is not to reach northern France, the Low Countries and Scandinavia overland until 1349, long after it has devastated much of England.[2] Its coastal route is in our locational names. Status and travel are evident from the records.

Medieval records of people with topographical names describe society. They document social mobility. One record shows that after the Black Death at the end of the fourteenth century Henry Bramley, a baker's apprentice, is able to negotiate higher wages by offering his services to two bakers. His name shows he comes from a difficult brambly clearing, so he is likely to be one of the poorest villagers. Thomas Fartheyn has risen to become a steward of Exeter between 1315 and 1321. His name records that his ancestors owned a tiny plot or paid a miniscule rent. At about the same time, Richard Whittington, the lowly third son of a country knight, becomes a purveyor of luxuries to royalty, leaving a fortune when he dies. Records also tell of the limits to power. The Dean and Chapter of Exeter cannot get rid of a serf, Joel bysouthecolm (called after his south-facing plot), who fells their trees. Records of other names tell how far ordinary people travel. Tax records from Shrewsbury at the turn of the fourteenth century include people called de London and de Grimesby – places over 150 miles away to the south and the east.

And people wave to us from these snippets of information. Henry Bramley, cocky and self-confident, getting two bakers to fight over his services. Joel Bysouthecolm, serf, who reckons his lord's oaks are his to cut.

As always, there are overlaps. The main one is between topographical and occupational names. Names like Forrest and Bridge, Mills and Milne could mean you live near the places or you work there and could be classified here or among occupational names. Other names have two meanings, one of which could be classified here. Moor could mean a moor, or a Moor, a nickname for a swarthy-skinned person; Lobb could be a spider or from places in Devon or Oxfordshire; Wood or Wooding could be a dweller by or worker in a wood from the Old English, or a madman, from the Old or Middle English; Waller could be a dweller by a stream, a nickname for a happy fellow, or a wall builder; and a Rider could live near a clearing or be a soldier. Finally, there is overlap between locational and topographical names themselves, since many names of features like Leeds (a loud brook), Combe (a small valley), Bowden (a domed hill), and Hayes (an enclosure) are place names as well. Generally, we cannot tell which comes first.

Many of these names originally carried prepositions such as 'de', 'in', 'atte', 'by', 'up' and 'under'. Most of these are gone by 1400,[3] although there are regional variations and '-atte' appears in Devon records, for example, much later than that. This is why many of these names seem to name just a feature: for example, Hill when the original sense was atte Hill, meaning dweller by the hill. Many still carry the echo of these prefixes: Atwell, Nash or Noakes. Foreign names are often preceded by 'de', which is either dropped or, if the following word begins with a vowel, is absorbed, d'Aumale becoming Damerell, for instance.

Topographical surnames

Early records show that people all over England choose many of the same topographical surnames. These, like other surnames, tell us that their priorities, judgement and attitudes are similar. This would not be surprising if peoples' choices are only influenced by their physical lives, because feudalism produces broadly similar conditions wherever it operates. But the choice of name is also affected by social and moral attitudes, thoughts and culture. These names show how deeply rooted English people everywhere are in their land. But they do not show an aesthetic appreciation, just as nicknames and, particularly, symbolical names, hardly ever record the beauty of nature or the grace of animals. These names show our ancestors to be essentially practical. Instead of glorious valleys, glistening water or sacred trees, names document economic life. Varied names identify sources of income and subsistence – water, and its locks and weirs for trapping fish and establishing mills; woods and trees; valleys for farming and even the brambles and marshes that obstruct cultivation. They record the importance of communications in the names for hills, ridges, roads, lanes, fords and bridges. They document the effect of the golden years of population increase before the crop diseases and famines starting in 1315 in the names telling of land clearance; and they tell of later enclosures and outlying dairy farms near the pastures that spread after the decimation of the plagues. They record the prevalence of the church, the crosses, the chapels and that the important houses of the village are those of the parson, the vicar and the dean.

At first it seems odd that if surnames are to identify people, so many topographical names – Hill, Combe, Way – describe such common features. But in many parts of the country these features may not be common, hills in East Anglia, for instance. In other parts, there would not have been more than one or two hills, valleys or roads within a reasonable walking or riding radius.

Individually, these topographical surnames record people identified by a single feature; together these features jigsaw into an English landscape, each name bringing a slice of the view. Colours are infrequent; our ancestors use them mostly to describe people, not nature (although there are some red cliffs and green woods, hills and valleys). It is a wide landscape of hills, valleys and moors in the background with rivers and streams, farms and villages to the fore. Even though the Middle Ages has rapid urban growth, even though medieval records have some unquestionably urban names such as Dounintoune, de Northstret and de Cobblestrete, few modern surnames are definitely urban. Townsend is one, Spittle, someone living near a hospital, and Venelle, a dweller in an alley, are others. Cross, Rowe and Whitehouse could also be urban, although Rowe could refer to a village or live near some rough land instead. Perhaps people exchange their topographical for occupational names after they leave the countryside; data on names in Exeter over the thirteenth and fourteenth centuries show the shares there of occupational names rising.[4]

Communicating

Water is a source of subsistence and facilitates travel; many people live near it. Their surnames are highly differentiated. Apart from

River (also from la Rivière in Calvados) many names document people from streams: Beech (a stream as well as a beech tree); Bourne and Blackbourn; Brook and Brock; Carswell and Kerswell; Leed; Lake; Pool; and the Devonian or Cornish Yeo. Weldon comes from a stream near a hill and Winch, when not a nickname, from a bend in a stream. All these streams are different. Bourne, still an ordinary stream (burn) in Scotland and the north, is an intermittent stream elsewhere – storm-water running off the moor perhaps, so only good for seasonal fisheries. Brook is a stream or a water meadow, so slow and meandering. Pool is a pooling or tidal stream. Carswell is a stream where watercress grows. Leeds are the noisy ones, running over rocks. The Wells and Coldwells are from rivers and streams that give very important drinking water. Only Lake and Yeo mean just stream.

Waterways are communication routes. Related names include Ware, Lock, and Mill and Milne, and all the Fords – Forders, Radfords, Handfords and so forth as well as the Wades (which could be a personal name). These names are popular; in the rural Hay Tor Hundred in Devon in 1332, almost every hamlet has an atte Forde. Bridge, Bridgeman and other variants record the surge in bridge-building that occurred in the fourteenth century. (Bridges refers to someone from Bruges.)

Many surnames record other features important for travel. Hill, Knott (also a nickname) and Bowden, from the curved or bowed hills are from the high ground that is best for roads. Underhill show the underside of the outcroppings. The low, rolling uplands are given by Fell (a northern name) and Down (a small hill) and the hilltops by Knapp and Knowles. The rare Weedon records the hill with the heathen temple. Ridges, important routes from Roman times, are documented in Ridge, some of the Rudges (the rest are red-haired) and the Old Norse Orr (also meaning sallow from the Gaelic), while the Devon Bremridge comes from the brambly one. The windy pass over them comes from Wingate, the ravines from Clough and Gill (also servants).

Between the streams, pastures and villages run Lanes and Ways and Holloways where heavy loads dragged by oxen and horses have driven deep tracks into the soil. The clerk called William Holeway who wrote charters in Dartmouth in 1354 was called after these 'hollow ways'. The Twitchens come from the place where the roads meet.

Seeking the Shade

Woods are an important asset. All the names for woods and trees suggest the land is not densely wooded and there are not many single trees in or around medieval settlements, otherwise they would be useless for identification. Woods are home to Wood, Harwood and Horwood (the hares' woods and the muddy wood), Greenwood and Manley, or the common wood where people forage their pigs and cut firewood and timber. The alternative meaning of Wood is mad or wild, and in its sense of innocent it carries an echo of pagan veneration of trees and groves. Forrest and Park come from the larger private efforts enclosed for the nobility but full of rabbits and deer for poaching and where people may have rights and some employment. Hursts come from a wooded hill, Holt and Shaw live near a wood and Wotton comes from the farms close by. Kelly is from a small grove, perhaps recording a remnant of a larger forest. In 1286, a Robert Broun clears a quarter of an acre in Cannock Forest, Staffordshire, and encloses it with a ditch, sowing it 'twice with spring corn and twice with winter corn.'[5]

Individual trees are singled out. For Celts, trees embodied ancestral spirits and the birch, alder, willow, oak, rowan, hazel, apple, and ash were 'noble'. Our English names tend to identify trees useful for timber and recording boundaries. So we have the general Attree; for building, we have Pine, Holme (holm oaks or hollies), Oak, Noakes and Roke or Rook (the latter often meaning rook, but which can mean oak in Devon). People also live by ashes used by coopers, including Asher, Ash, Nash and Naish and ash trees by cottages and folds, Ashcroft and Ashfold. Ash trees are central to many pagan myths. Yggdrasil, the cosmic tree of the Norse, the centre and source of life for god, giant and man, is an ash. The chief Viking god, Odin, has a spear that never misses made of ash. An ancient charter referring to a boundary of Taunton, Devon, refers dismissively to an ash 'which the ignorant

116

call holy'.[6] There are Beeches for boat-building. Reinbald de Bece (or of the beech) is, according to the *Chronicle of Battle Abbey* of about 1180, a peasant picked to be allocated house and land to commemorate the Battle of Hastings.

Names record Thornes, Perriers and their variants that mean pear tree; Appletons and Applegarths are apple orchards. These are ancient trees; in the *Anglo-Saxon Chronicle* 'King Harold came against [William] at the hoary apple tree'. A Sir Edmund Appleby of Appleby Magna leaves an estate worth £200 in 1374, a modest working manor with an inventory of grain, animals and agricultural tools, with the status symbols of Sir Edmund's rank, armour and two horses.[7]

Farms

Many surnames tell of valleys where much of the farming went on. The Slacks (otherwise a nickname for a lazy or careless person) show us the shallow valleys; the Holdens and Holmans, the hollow part of the coomb or glaciated valley; while the Dales are the extended shallow ones. Widdicombe and its variants comes from the valley where the withies grow; Brimblecombe from the brambly one; and Luscombe from the valley with pigsties. Both these last two are good old Devon names. Slade simply means a dweller in a valley.

Population is thought to have more than trebled in England between Domesday and the crop failures and famines between 1315 and 1322. Surnames record how woods are cleared for farming as population increases. The most popular are Beer and Lea and their many variants (Lea can also be a wood). Beer is quintessentially from the south-west; there are thirty-five places called after a variant of Beer in Devon. Devonians paid 5,000 marks in 1204 for a charter of disafforestation of the county and Beer, from the Old English *bearu* or grove, must record clearings of these forests.[8] (Beer probably usually means a clearing because beer only replaces ale as a common drink after most surnames are fixed.) Reedland is also from a clearing. Barnett, from the Old English word for burning, refers to land first cleared by fire,

Riley is from a rye clearing, while Bottomley records a clearing in a valley.

Other names show how farming is done. Hay and all its variants including Hague and Hough, a name from the West Riding, Yorkshire, from Old English and Old Norse for hedge, come to mean land enclosed by one. The name often occurs at the limits of cultivated areas where people may be expanding fields as population increases before the Black Death.[9] The Woollards or Wolfords mean, when not a personal name, an enclosure to protect against wolves or a place with that name. The Balkhams are from land divided into strips by balks or ridges. Easter, a lovely appropriate metaphor, is from a sheepfold, and Field, Snape and Bates record pastures (Bates could also be a boatman). Thorpe is from a hamlet or a dairy farm on outlying pastures, where the Barnes and the Booths give shelter for animals and Norwich can also mean a dairy farm. Barton and variants identify the large farms (most of which date back at least to the Conquest). Garner is the keeper of the granary.

Surnames also identify features that are useless for farming. Mitchelmore comes from an extensive moor, while Broom and Heath record the vegetation. Hern and Hale come from nooks or corners; Blackhall from a dark nook; and Ratcliffe and their variants from the red cliffs. But Holme comes from land that stands clear of the fens and can be farmed (the name also refers to a holm oak). Marsh, Bogg (also a nickname, meaning bold or proud) and Moss record a morass, bog, or swamp or wet ground. Names preceded by Black, like Blackmore or Blackburn, relate to dark swampy land. Devonian place names give evidence of reclamation; Marsh Barton outside Exeter, cleared between 1170 and 1180, means farm on the marsh.[10] Carr from the Old Norse word for brush or wet ground records that some vegetation growing in marshes is useful. Rushes are a widely used floor covering.

Hamlets

Sutton, Milton and all the other names ending in '-ton' record more farms or villages. Richard Whittington, our successful third

118

son of a Gloucestershire knight mentioned earlier, comes from a little settlement to become a wealthy London merchant in the late fourteenth century and leaves jewels, silver plate and £5,000 in cash when he dies.[11]

Cross records the cross on the road where the pilgrims pass, at the village boundary or on the village green where the popular Greens come from. When Queen Eleanor, the wife of Edward I dies at Harby near Lincoln, her body is taken to Westminster Abbey and crosses are erected to her memory at each place her body rests, whence Waltham Cross. Workers stand by the village cross to be hired. Cross and Twitchen mean a crossroads. Our Woolriches have a namesake in a slave called Wulfric whose liberation was recorded by an Anglo-Saxon clerk and is one of the very few slaves we know today by a name. He was freed at a crossroads to symbolize his new ability to choose where to go.

Bell lives near the church bells and is responsible for ringing them; Butt from the archery targets; Yate for the gate he lives by and Chappel, Deans, Parsons and Vickers (the last three usually carry a final '-s') record the people living or working at the relevant houses. Rowe lives in a row of cottages. Each '-cott' – Northcott, Southcott and Westcott – show cottages with their tiny acreages. The Whitehouse is striking, perhaps limed stone when the others are cob. A lovely ancient name with Old English, Old Danish and Old Norse roots, Farthing, meaning a quarter measure of a virgate of land, so some seven acres, records someone from a little homestead. (Farthing can also mean a traveller.) The surname of Thomas Fartheyn, steward of Exeter from 1312 to 1321 shows he has come a long way.[12]

Many topographical names, like the '-cotts', and '-tons', follow the points of the compass, recording how natural it is to think in terms of the movement of the sun. So we have people named North, South, East and West, with suffixes for brooks, gates, wells, valleys, streams, woods and many other features recording people living in a given direction. The popular Normans and Norrises and their variants (the latter could also be wet-nurses from *nourrice*) are men from the north, and Norman often means a Viking from Scandinavia. There are Eastbrooks, Norgates, Southwells, Suttons, Westlakes and Westwoods; many of these could be place names as well. A nice Devon story about the name-sakes of the Southcombs shows how strong the customary rights of serfs are. The Joel Bysouthecolm mentioned earlier, who fells and sells forty of his landlord's oaks, is punished (he eventually admits that as a serf the oaks are not his) by being allowed back onto his land only for life. When he dies in 1307, his daughter Joan claims it. She is refused on the grounds that she had left the manor without a licence rather than her father's disinheritance.[13] So the Dean and Chapter finally rid themselves of a troublesome family, but the delay suggests that customary precedent supporting the rights of bonded tenants to their land mean the lords have to wait and think hard about how to do it.

A National Picture

Early records of these topographical surnames show they have come down to us from across the country. Hills and Combes, Woods and Lakes arise across England, from east to west, north to south; Bridges, Fords and Coldwells are just as widespread. The modern distribution of these names across England may differ, but early records show what is happening where. All the '-tons' – the Hortons and Miltons, Mortons, Burtons, Suttons and Woottons – tell us that the English are farmers and villagers everywhere. Farms and homesteads, names based on the Old English word *woro*, come from all over too, but the Worths and Worthys are more in the south, the Worthings and Worthingtons from further north. Land clearance goes on all over – Bradley, Buckley, Riley arise in counties from Yorkshire to Devon. Barnett, who lives near land cleared by burning, is more southern, from Hertfordshire, Middlesex and Surrey. Land is enclosed all over the country; Hay, Hayes and many other variants come from everywhere. Local dialect and spelling can produce deceptive variants. Brooks, now found mainly in the West Riding of Yorkshire, can be Broke or Bruck, Lane can be Loan or Lone, the latter recording West Midland dialects. The Oaks can be Rocks in Devon and Worcestershire, Rokes in Oxford and Rooks in Devon again, from 'atter oke'. All these variants can be confused with surnames that mean something quite different.

That so many of the same topographical names are found across England suggest both the landscape and the needs of the ordinary people who choose the names are similar. It is obvious that descriptive names based on general features like Hill and Combe, Brook and Wood can emerge spontaneously anywhere these features exist. But the prevalence of the other names show that the conditions faced by ordinary people are pretty homogeneous too: communication is important, with its fords, bridges and roads; woods are scarce and valued; the country has to be cleared for farming as populations grow; and farmland is enclosed for pasturing as agricultural labour becomes scarcer after the plagues.

English Names Record the English Scene

These practical, earthy topographical names almost universally have Old English or a few Old Norse roots from England's pre-Conquest past. They show the strength and endurance of an English culture and the language of ordinary people. Topographical surnames stay with the English words for woods of alder and ash, fords and bridges and valleys of brambles, rushes and pigsties.

We know from other surnames that the language of ordinary people includes many French words. Why are these not used here? Much of the reason must be that English words can say what is needed. That French has added value in occupational and some nicknames but not the names from the English countryside shows how distant are the ruling elites from the lands they own and the people who work them. It may also show resistance to Norman culture, evident in the ironic ecclesiastical surnames. People might just decide to use English even where a French word is available.

The meaning of most of these topographical names is clear today; country language has not changed that much. Others – Noak, Atwell, Nash – are fairly obvious when you factor in lost prepositions. Yet others are obscure because the word is obsolete: Beer, for a clearing; Easter, a sheepfold; Yate, a gate; Twitchen, a crossroads. Distinctions among other surnames are lost today too, see all the fine differences between the names for streams and woods.

Several of these obsolete words are in Norse surnames. So few have survived that it is worth spending a moment with them. Virtually all relate to basic topography, and three to water: Bourne, the dweller by the stream; Carr, by the fens; and Holme, who lives on the flat land in the fen. Three describe basic cattle farming: Farthing, the tiny homestead, Booth, the cow-house, and Bate, the dweller by the pasture. Most of the first records of these names are north of the Danelaw line.

English Locational Names

Surnames from specific places are, by definition, names of travellers – people identified by where they come from. Freemen can always move, for a fee, but landlords restrict the bonded majority. Yet the growth of towns and evidence of trade tell us that these restrictions are not binding. In 1100 there are some 100 towns in Britain; by 1300, when about 20 per cent of the English population is estimated to live in urban areas, there are 830.[14] Foreign trade is believed to have tripled in real terms over the thirteenth century.[15] Individual surnames echo the same mobility. The share of locational surnames in medieval records in some counties like Devon for dates when holders are likely to be the first generation with the name show that about a third of the population at a given place, and more in the towns, come from somewhere else.[16] Shares may fall later, but by then people will have held surnames for more than one generation and may not have been the generation that moved.

Professionals like clerics and builders move with their work; others move before the Black Death because of land shortage and afterwards to seek new opportunities in growing rural craft centres and towns. Earlier we saw how the surnames of shipmasters docking at Topsham, near Exeter, at a time when surnames are stabilizing over the turn of the fourteenth century, reveal the distances people travel. They carry surnames from ports along the south and eastern coasts – Winchelsea, Weymouth, Yarmouth and Dunwich (which the sea is already beginning to claim back)

– from inland places even further away, like Coventry, Chester and Kent, but also from Burgundy, Toulouse, Spain, Gascony and Picardy over the seas.

The Londons

To focus first on English travel, surnames show people moving from east to west, north to south, from tiny country places and from great cities. People with locational names tend to be among the wealthy, as if those who are ready to travel also make a success of other opportunities. In Shrewsbury, 44 per cent of those rich enough to qualify for taxation have locational names, compared with 24 per cent with nicknames and 17 per cent with occupational names. They own status goods – meat, riding horses, silver, jewellery and wall-hangings. Almost a third of the super-rich have locational names: John de Lodelowe (or Ludlow) is a wool exporter with an average assessment of over £43; Hugh de Wygan, an apothecary and wool exporter, has acquired a twenty-shilling riding horse by 1316 as well as still holding the goods of his trade, spices, ointments and a brass mortar.[17]

Some migration will have been transient and much quite local, but some documents travel over quite long distances. Records show that in late thirteenth-century York, for example, 42 per cent of migrants come from more than twenty miles away.[18] London draws from further afield. When John de Bois is killed in Cheapside in November 1300 (a piece of wood used to dry saddles falls on him) his death is witnessed by people from Middlesex, Essex, Suffolk, Kent, and Nottinghamshire, so from up to 100 miles away.[19]

Surnames in local records give a remarkably comprehensive picture of this travel. When the taxman comes calling in Shrewsbury in the years between 1297 and 1322, almost a third of the names of those assessed come from other places. Some are close by: Staunton, Shoplatch (then Scheteplache) are now in the city and Wenlock is remembered now in the name of a road some 3 miles from the centre. But others have really travelled: from the south 63 miles from Upton down the Severn, 85 miles from Stratford, 161 miles from London. From up to 120 miles to the north come people from Astley, Otley and Wigan, and from the east come those from Stafford, Derby, Coventry, Caldwell and even Grimsby, 165 miles away. A Nicholas de Grimesby is assessed on his dried fish and herring and carthorses to transport them in 1313.[20] Many come from the unsettled west, from places like Stowe.

Tracking the Great Trade

Locational names show economic activity, documenting the English towns and ports built on the wealth of English wool and textiles. When surnames are being established, England is emerging as a major exporter of cloth as well as wool, with cloth exports growing some twentyfold over the last half of the fourteenth century. Overall cloth production including domestic demand is thought to be four times exports, bringing great wealth to English towns.[21]

From the north, on the tide of this trade, come people with names that identify the sources of wool and cloth and their ports. From Cumbria come Lancaster and Kendal, to become the largest town in the north-west by the early sixteenth century. We have York, soon to be ousted by the emerging cloth towns of the West Riding recorded in names like Leeds and Bradford, which handles the trade from the extraordinarily productive Cistercian monasteries such as Rievaulx and Fountains.[22] We have Sheffield, already beginning to specialize in metalworking, and its ports of Hull, founded in the twelfth century by Edward I, or just Humber; and Lincoln, famous for 'Lincoln scarlets' and the high quality of their finish, popular on the European continent. From central England come people from Leicester, Derby, Coventry (specializing in caps as well as textiles), Chester and Warwick and Northampton, whose cloth is recorded in Portugal in 1253.

From the wealthy east come the Bostons and Lynns from King's Lynn. Boston is a major port of some 5,000 people in 1300, serving Lincoln and Stamford, which exports relatively expensive cloth as early as the thirteenth century. Boston later declines because of competition from London. King's Lynn is a port of about the same size as Boston, and serves Norfolk and Cambridgeshire. Three of the great thirteenth-century wool fairs are held in this area – in Stamford at Lent, Boston in July, and Northampton in November. We have the Norfolks and Norwiches, whose merchants specialize in linens and worsteds (from Worsted and Aylsham), and the Berrys, from Bury St Edmunds (among other Burys), whose goods also go to King's Lynn.

Going west and south, many folk have surnames from the Welsh Marches that record their prosperity founded on sheep – from Ludlow, Hereford, Gloucester, an inland port for wine, and the growing Worcester. From the south and west come the Winchesters (which hosts another thirteenth-century wool fair in September), the Salsburys, the Wells and the Hamptons from Southampton and other places, the main centre for the Genoese traders from the mid-fourteenth century. From further west come the Tauntons, the Combes from Castle Combe (among other places) and the Bristows from Bristol. Bristol, close to Cotswold wool and the cloth manufacturing of the West Country, is a major port by the mid-fourteenth century. It produces its own high-quality 'Bristol red' as well as handling the trade for the West Midlands and the south-west, is a third the size of London in 1300, and is to oust York as the second English city by the mid-fifteenth century.

The Combes, like the Wiltons, the Bradfords and the Berrys among others could come from many different places. There are nine places called Coombe in Somerset, six in Devon and six elsewhere. But those that come from Castle Combe in Wiltshire record how an imaginative and energetic entrepreneur creates a successful brand that builds a new cloth centre in what seems to be an overcrowded sector. Sir John Fastolf, a brilliantly successful soldier who makes a fortune out of the French wars under Henry VI, obtains the manor in 1409. It already has a fulling mill, but not much else. Sir John expands the village into a thriving town, attracting artisans, and from 1415 to the 1440s he clothes his soldiers in 'Castle Combs' – uniforms made out of the special red and white cloth developed there. By 1457 Castle Combs have become a trade name in London for fine reds.[23]

Finally, the Lundons remind us of the city's firm place as the country's largest commercial centre, with a population of 80,000 in 1300, three times the size of York, Norwich and Bristol. Other surnames remind us of the great centres of learning as well as industry. Oxford is the first university in the English-speaking world, first recorded in 1096. The University of Cambridge is founded in 1209, when scholars banned from Oxford for the manslaughter of an Oxford woman settle there.[24]

Small Links in a Chain

Surnames from smaller coastal places reflect the pattern of transhipment of goods from large ports like King's Lynn, Southampton or Bristol. This pattern explains why, when inventories, paintings and other records show the English enjoying foods from central Asia and silks from India, we have few names recording these far-off places. These are the Shirbons from Sherborne, the Dovers, Hastings, and the Wights and the Weights from the Isle of Wight, and even a number from Snape, now a tiny hamlet on the Alde in Suffolk but once an important trading centre for herring from the North Sea. Wine from Gascony and dyes from Picardy, all the spices and silks, figs and grapes from the Far East and southern Europe come to English towns and villages via the great fairs in northern Europe and thence by stages through these little English ports.

The locational names of shipmasters arriving at the Exeter outports over the turn of the fourteenth century give a more specific idea of how trade is managed. On the assumption that at that early date ships' captains come from the place of their names, they show sea transport of goods to the West Country concentrated in English hands. Almost three-quarters of the shipping berthing at the Exeter outports between 1266 and 1321 comes from English ports, and over half from Devon ports, carried in vessels of less than fifty tuns.[25]

The surnames also tell us that the shipmasters are largely from Devon and Cornwall, from inland places and from fairly local southern ports as country people move towards jobs and income. Most of those who bring in wine – the premier import into Exeter – have names from places close to home like Fowey, Powderham, Topsham, Weymouth and Lyme for Lyme Regis although some carry names from further afield like Winchelsea, Sandwich and the Isle of Wight and even Yarmouth on the east coast. William de Wyght brings in exotica like archil (red dye), almonds and wine. Woad from Picardy, scarlet dyes from Spain and wheat from East Anglia or France are brought in by masters with names from Teignmouth, while figs and raisins from Spain come with a ship-master called Winchelsea. Herring from East Anglia brought in by John de Donewych, or Dunwich on the east coast could have come directly from ports like Yarmouth or have been transhipped from places like Hastings or Winchelsea.

Local travel from smaller places, much of which must have been for work, is hard to capture. Many places – Bradford, for instance – have the same name. It is thought that only some 40 per cent of towns and villages in medieval England have unique names.[26] Some topographical surnames will be from lost hamlets that are impossible to trace today. It is thought that over 2,000 plus villages and many more hamlets and farms are deserted between 1370 and 1500, as population shrinks after the 1315–22 famines and the episodes of plague beginning in 1348. Many place names are indistinguishable from topographical because so many places are called after local features. Snape means a pasture and Norwich a dairy farm, so any Snapes and Norwiches with first records some distance from East Anglia, where the places are, could well be called after pastures or farms and not be from the actual towns at all.

Yet genealogists have had some success tracing families with surnames from small places. It is telling that Old Norse names like Fell, Carr, Appleby, Ashby and Bates can be broadly traced to individual northern counties, but Old English names in Norse areas can be tracked more specifically. So David Hey's work shows that Airey, Old Norse for a dweller by a gravel bank, can be broadly traced to Lancashire, Cumbria and Yorkshire. But the Old English Ackroyd probably comes from Akroyd near Heptonstall, west of Halifax; Huntbach from what is now Humbage Green, near Eccleshall, Staffordshire; and Broadhurst from south Lancashire and around Macclesfield in Cheshire. Easter could be from one of only two places in Essex; and Kippen, if not fat, probably comes from Kippen, near Stirling.[27] The Ardens, a dwelling place in Old English, come from places in Warwickshire and the North Riding.

A branch of Ardens can, with the Berkeleys, be traced back to pre-Conquest England. Ardens go back to Aelfwine, Sheriff of Warwickshire before the Conquest, and the name survives because his son Thurkill seems to come to an understanding with the Normans and keeps his lands, so his family's record can be documented.[28]

Other surnames are less specific, but useful as evidence of travel. We have people called after their counties – Cornwall (the Cornwalls and Cornishes), Devon and Dorset, Norfolk and Essex, Derbyshire, Lancashire and Westmoreland.

Because place names usually predate surnames, sometimes by two to three centuries, some carry information on pre-medieval settlements that enriches the locational surnames recording them. Surnames from the names for settlements ending in '-by' (Ingoldsby, Ashby, Appleby) are Norse. Most are in Lincolnshire and the north, the Danelaw shires, although there are a few outside, even including a clutch in South Hams in Devon (Bovey is one, from a personal name).[29] There is a chronological sequence of Saxon names for places meaning farms or homesteads. Names ending in '-ing', like Gilpin or Gilping and Billing came first, in the fifth and sixth centuries; those ending in '-ham', such as Bickham, Wakeham, South Hams, came next; while those ending in '-ton', such as Barton, Walton, Sutton, came last, and are still being created in medieval days – think of all the Newtons emerging. The '-ing' names tend to come from Sussex and Essex, *ingas* being Old English for 'people of'. The '-ham' names come from the east, with most in Norfolk, Surrey, Sussex, Cambridge and Essex, while '-ton' seems to concentrate in Cheshire, Shropshire, Staffordshire, Herefordshire, and so on.[30] Cornish and Welsh place names preceded by 'Tre-', the Celtic homesteads, like Tregelles or Tredennick, can predate them all.

Locational Names from Abroad

An air-traffic chart of surnames recording foreign nationality, towns and districts shows the foreign places that people come from to medieval England. They are concentrated across northern

Europe and down the west coast of France. The range of these names tells us how closely the island is linked with the coast of continental Europe. Together with the English locational names they record how trade is managed, with goods taken the shortest distances from markets in northern Europe across the Channel to be transhipped and carried on via small coastal ports. The excavation of a rubbish pit in Southampton shows that a merchant, Richard of Southwick, has, in the late thirteenth century, jugs from southern France, lustreware from Spain, figs, grapes and a little African monkey – all probably via a merchant in Normandy.[31] These might have come from the Mediterranean in a Venetian galley to Brabant and from there to Southampton and his house in Cuckoo Lane.

Contemporary writing on English trade sets the context for these surnames recording our medieval commerce in which the English exchange their wool and cloth for covetable foreign goods. A script written in the mid-fifteenth century describes how 'wolle ... and wollen cloth of ours of colours all', fells and tin are exchanged in Flanders and Calais. English earnings drive these markets:

> And here I say that we bye,
> [In] Flanders and Zeland more of marchandy
> In common use than done all other nations.[32]

The goods the English buy in exchange are wine, honey, soft leathers and dates from Spain and Portugal; luxuries from Genoa that arrive in:

> ... sundry wises
> Into this land with divers marchandises
> In great Caracks ...
> With cloth of gold, silke, and pepper blacke
> ... cotton ... good gold of Genne[33]

and from the 'great Galees' of Venice and Florence 'well laden with things of complacency,/all spicery' sweet wines, apes, japes, marmosets and '... things not induring that we bye'.[34] There are records of Flanders galleys sailing from Venice with goods from the Levant, Asia and Africa via Gibraltar to Southampton and Bruges every year after 1308.[35] This is how Richard of Southwick gets his 'things not induring' like his pottery, figs and grapes and his little African monkey, where our Spicers, Pepperers, Goldsmiths and Officers get their spices, gold and cloth of gold, our Mercers their silks and our great Merchants their living.

The Norman Invaders

The largest group of foreign locational names is Norman. Most of the followers of William the Conqueror came from Seine, Maritime, Calvados, La Manche, and further south from Eure and Orne.[36] By Domesday, incomers included Bretons, Flemmings and people from Anjou and Poitou. Later immigration came with the Plantaganets from Burgundy, Gascony and Anjou. People holding these surnames now may or, more probably, may not be descendants of the original families. Many names are not unique; Beaumont, for instance, or Cowdray, could come from different places in France, or even England.[37] Then an aristocratic Norman name could be taken in England by retainers or tenants, or even villagers, if the name is given to a village, as it frequently is. There are records of Londoners holding aristocratic Norman names – John de Maundeville, brewer, and William de Furnival, tailor – who could not possibly have belonged to the ruling elite.[38] Finally, some apparently Norman surnames, Dubarry, Duhamel, Dupuy, are not there in the Middle Ages at all, but arrive with later immigrants, like the Huguenots in the fifteenth century.[39]

Norman aristocratic surnames that come with the invaders include the Boons, originally the Bohuns from La Manche, who go to Norfolk; the Bruces, also from La Manche, who go to Yorkshire; the Furneaux, who go from many places in France to Somerset and Hertfordshire; the Mountfords and Mumfords, also from all over France, who go to Kent and Gloucestershire; the Percys, from Calvados and La Manche, who go to Yorkshire; the Sessions from Soissons in Aisne have early records in Cambridgeshire and Berkshire; the Warrens from La Varenne in

Seine-Inférieure, who go to Lincolnshire; and the Mortimores from Seine-Inférieure, who go to the Welsh Marches. According to first records identified by Reaney and Wilson, all of these families are around at Domesday. Less than a century later we have records of others arriving, such as the Tremletts, from les Trois Minettes in Calvados, who go to Devon and Staffordshire; and the Vallances from Drome, who go to London.

For some of these foreign surnames, there is no doubt about their derivation because the modern versions are still close to the original, such as Courtenay and Pomeroy. But as names anglicize, they change. For some just the 'de' has been dropped, while for others the present name is still recognizably what it was; you can see how Beauchamp became Beecham, for example. And a few, like Pine and Moyne, have conveniently morphed into similar-sounding English names. But others have completely altered. Many now have a very large number of variants as the English tongue tried to find some way around French vowels. How did the d'Aunays become Dando, for instance? Or Ouilly from Calvados become Doyley, Doley, Dolley, Duly, Dulley, Dayley or Ollie? The range of these variants encourages speculation; is our Dalby the Norman D'Aubigny?

The Foreign Traders

The names of the traders can record the foreign staging posts of trade. These people might be agents for English merchants or control the trade themselves. Italian merchants handle most English wool exports to Flanders and Italy until the end of the thirteenth century, when the roles subsequently reversed.[40] But many will have come along trade routes as economic migrants. Many of these surnames record town, district, or nationality. These people are not associated with grand estates. Tax returns show many a French, France, Frenchman and de Franse in remote country villages and hamlets, mostly labourers and farmers, assessed at the lowest rates, from Lancashire, Hereford and Derby to Dorset and Essex.[41]

Recording the places where the English exchange their cloth

and their wool, we still have the people from the great markets in northern Europe. These are the Callises from Calais, where the wool staple finally settles in 1392; the Bridges and Brugess from Bruges and the Brabons and Brabsons from the Duchy of Brabant, both early wool staples. Representing the Flemish markets, we have many Flemmings and variants from what is now Holland, Belgium and northern France and Hollands from the area around Dordrecht, the nucleus of modern Holland (Hollands could have come from towns in Essex and Lincolnshire as well), Flanders from the countship of the same name, the Gants from Ghent from where fine cloth comes, and the Bullens from Boulogne. Franks also come from northern France (the name can also mean a freeman).

From further afield are the Pickards from Picardy, connected with imports of woad dyes for the cloth industry until war disrupted trade in the late fourteenth century. It will have been an obvious step for someone engaged in one trade like dyes to become a more general trader, like the John Pykard, shipmaster from Dartmouth, who docks in Exmouth in 1317 in *Le Cog Seynt John* with a cargo of wheat and rabbit skins.[42] We have Janaways from Genoa, a reminder that the Italians handle most of our wool exports to Flanders and Italy through Southampton, buying their fine Tintern wool direct from the growers. In the late thirteenth century, two-thirds of Cistercian houses in England sell their wool direct to Italian merchants.[43] Later these Genoese might have come anyway in connection with the spices, silks and cloth of gold they sell in exchange for our wool and cloth.

There are the people from the wine trade – the Gaskens from Gascony, Champness from Champagne, and the Bourgoynes from Burgundy. Wine imports from Gascony begin in 1204 when it is the main English possession on the European continent until it is lost in 1453. They peak at five million gallons in 1308, about a gallon per person, depending on which population estimates you believe.[44] Wine consumption is high even in relatively poor Devon, where almost all the ships docking at the Exeter ports in the late thirteenth and early fourteenth centuries carry it. The clergy and gentry get wine 'for drink' duty free.

From Town and Country

We also have Paris and Parish from Paris, Charteris from Chartres, the Germans, Jarmans and Dennises and Danes (alternatively, these last two could come from a first-name related to Dionysius). There is one exotic name, Prettyjohn, a scarce Devon surname, but still here. It is thought to derive from Prester John, Hakluyt's king of a 'Christian Kingdom in Africa'.[45] Tales about him and his incredible empire are current in twelfth-century Europe and there are early records of Prestrejohans in England in the Middle Ages who become our Prettyjohns.

Then we have the Normans and some of the Norrises from Normandy. The people from Brittany are Brittons, Brittains and Bretts and their variants. It is not always easy to differentiate Bretons from Celts or Britons, because the names are so similar, but the context of a name in a record can help. Relations with the Bretons are complex; Breton in early records can mean someone boastful and/or stupid, as mentioned in Chapter 5. The Bretons are traders, selling us salt, wine and cloth in the Flemish markets. But local records from southern English ports show constant low-level warfare over who is to benefit from the lucrative trade from the Mediterranean that passes the Breton and Devon coasts as it comes down the Channel to Flanders. The contemporary (English) source quoted above calls them:

> ... the greatest rovers and the greatest theeves,
> That have bene in the sea many one yeere[46]

Records from Dartmouth, geographically opposite Brittany, tell of a succession of attacks and counterattacks as Breton and Devonian pirates compete for spoils from sea trade.

While some Normans or French have specific surnames, others are just called French or its variants, such as Francis or France or even Franks. The general name may have been given because their villages are unpronounceable to the English, or impossible to anglicize, or it may also reflect lack of distinction; in the Domesday Book the Norman followers of a baron are often called French. A John FrFrauncnceys is a tanner in Shrewsbury in 1306, assessed at 7d tax, and in 1313 a William le Frensche is a miller who owns a horse worth a mark, or 13s 4d, and owes a farthing on a tax assessment of 18d. (1d is a penny.) Neither is wealthy.

Foreigners in the Records

Names in medieval records tell stories about these foreigners. Coastal places attract foreign neighbours; the Channel is a highway, not a frontier. Mid-fifteenth century tax records show 45 per cent of foreigners in Devon are from Normandy, 15 per cent French, 6 per cent Dutch and 4 per cent Flemish and Breton largely concentrated in trading communities in the east and the south.[47] Those in the southern port of Dartmouth reflect the dominant trades. Although English names confirm that most trade is in English hands, a few foreign shipmasters have a hand in the wine trade, with names like de Gascoyng, de Bayonne and de Bourgoyne. Pycard tells of the woad imports; Spaygnel of Spanish wine and figs (although he may be a Breton from Espinay); and in 1306 a Mathew de Brussele is bringing in fine quality cloth. Other names can illuminate specific episodes; during the famine and diseases of 1315–22, Geoffrey de Bailloul, or Bayeux, brings in wheat.

Records show many foreigners becoming integrated. Apart from the Frenchs who are tanners and millers, there are Brabants, Flemings (primarily in Essex), Burgoyns, Gascoignes, Champeneys and Parises assessed for tax across England. Many Normands and Bretons and people with French, Breton or Norman surnames – the Jewells with their various spellings from the Breton Judhael, the Prydeaux and the Montforts, the Moubrays, the Bachelers, and the Pompelons – are in Dartmouth between 1385 and 1394, as are people with names from Gascony, Picardy, Artois, Flanders and Holland. Flemings, also particularly strong in Norfolk, Suffolk and Essex, especially Colchester, become prominent – in 1201 Richard the Fleming is Sheriff of Cornwall and owns Launceston Castle.[48] Flemmings in London are massacred in the anarchy of the Peasants' Revolt because of the jealousy of artisans convinced they were stealing employment. There is warming evidence of

Devon/Breton hostility thawing into friendship; in 1435 'a Breton' in Dartmouth gives 12d towards a church fund, a small amount from a poor person showing a big commitment. And in 1347, a Ralph Bryt has become Sheriff of Devon.

Fellow Islanders

After the Normans and the French, the next most popular groups of foreign locational names are the Welsh, Scots and Irish. Among names for the Welsh are Wallis, Wallace (the Scottish form), Welsh, Welshman and Welchman. Walsh generally means a foreigner; pre-Norman invaders called the Celts *wealas*, which meant foreigner or slave. Indigenous Welsh surnames are settled much later than the English, in the sixteenth century and later, so these names, first recorded in the thirteenth century, are used by the Welsh living in England well before then. Although there are always Welsh in the west (over 100 Walensis and Waleis are recorded in the Domesday Book), the Welsh wars of Edward I in the later thirteenth century will have caused more migration. Other names taken by the medieval Welsh, like Gough, Howell and Lloyd, are discussed in the chapter on personal names.

The next group is the Scots, travellers even then; there are Scots in the Domesday Book and they are still with us as Scott, Scotts and Scutt. Scott, a very popular name, originally means an Irishman, but comes to denote a Gael from Scotland. Like the Welsh, they are called after their country; in the eleventh century King Malcolm is called King of Scotia. Scotland is also in intermittent wars with the English over this period, but many of these families could have been in England in Anglo-Saxon times. Compared with the Scots and the Welsh, there are relatively few Irish, called either Irish or Ireland, who tend to go to Scotland or Wales in this period.

Most holders of the names today will find a medieval counterpart. The mayors' court records of Dartmouth in Devon cite several Welshmen, including a Simona Walshe who is a gossip and is imprisoned in 1498 as a common scold.[49] And a Welsh esquire is captured by the King's men in 1404 and taken to the King so the latter can 'learn the secrets of his enemies'.[50] This is the bonus of research into names; you learn how things actually work in the Middle Ages. Who would have guessed that Henry IV would know that a Welshman operating out of the far south-west could tell him about a local Breton assault?

The surnames England and its variants English and Angliss or Inglis are a puzzle. Perhaps they record the English who are given the names abroad and come back with them. That the names are in English is odd, but could be consistent with the English calling foreigners Gascon and Pykard, rather than English versions of the places. There are early records of le Engleis and variants in Leicestershire, Cumbria, Oxfordshire and Essex (the names are now strong in the West Riding), so they could possibly be the result of people differentiating their English neighbours from the Scots and the Welsh in border counties.

Local Persistence

A surprising number of modern surnames have local medieval matches. This seems unlikely, since so many identify widely found features of the landscape and cities or countries, but local medieval records can supply useful results.

A few locational names, according to first records, only seem to occur in Devon in the Middle Ages. And these surnames are in Devon today. Take the Kingdoms or Kingdons, the Bidlakes, Fursdons, Pidsleys, Blacklers or Blackallers, Brimblecombes, and Honeywells. There is patchy information on some of these names, more for the gentry than the others. So the Fursdons, from Fursdon in the parish of Cadbury, have a namesake in Walter de Fursdon, who had a small estate there above 800 ft, which presumably is covered in furze. Fursdons have lived at Fursdon House since the thirteenth century. There is a first record for a Bidlake at Combe Bridestowe in the mid-thirteenth century, if not earlier, and a Henry Bidlake's estates are sequestered after he supported the Royalist cause in the Civil War. The Pidsley of Douglas, Pidsley and Roberts, solicitors in Newton Abbot, might be interested to know that a Walter de Pideneslegh from

Pidsley, Sandford, near Cadbury, is in Devon in 1274, an Isabel Pyddeslegh in 1524 and a John Pidsleigh in 1642. The Blackallers and Blacklers first occur in 1333. One hamlet with the name must have been in the Totnes–Dartmouth area, because a carpenter called John Blackalre received an inheritance in Dartmouth in 1391 from Richard Henry of the same town and Margareta, his wife. St David's Church, Ashprington, has a monument to Henry Blackhaller of Sharpham who died in 1684.[51]

The local medieval matches of these modern names in Devon are consistent with research in Lancashire, the West Riding of Yorkshire and elsewhere, which finds that at the end of the twentieth century a large percentage of surnames are still recorded close to their medieval origins.[52]

*　*　*　*

This chapter has told of landscapes and voyages. From Hill and Holloway, Ridge and Combe, Reedland and Ford, surnames construct a picture of the medieval English countryside. Across this restless scene trade and work bring people from Lundon, York and Lincoln, Wells and Bristow, now tiny places like Snape, as well as Flemmings and Hollands, Janaways from Genoa, Gaskins from Gascony, Pickards from Picardy, and many others. These names carry the story of how the English are unpicking the ties of feudalism and how integrated they are with lands across the Channel. The next two chapters will enrich this picture of physical and economic life by investigating how surnames from nicknames add a diverse crowd of people, with all their humour, their ideals and their failings, their hopes and fears, and their beliefs.

CHAPTER 5

NICKNAMES: WHAT OTHERS SAY ABOUT US

RUSSELL AND LANGE; Humble and Proud; Truelove and Letcher. Surnames from nicknames bring us right up close to people, telling us what they are born with, how they behave, and how they appear to others. They record what those first-namers notice – redheads, the merry and the gossipy, the cunning, the brave and the pretentious. In these names we find what our ancestors value and laugh at. Today, when people get together, ten to one they will be talking about others. 'She's a terrible flirt ...'; 'He looks like a ghost ....' Our medieval ancestors gossiping in the market place are just the same – and they have the power to take the gossip and make a name. These names document observations and attitudes not found in any conventional record.

This chapter covers first those nicknames that are overtly descriptive of physical appearance. Next comes a crowd from the gossip at the market place: the names that comment about person- ality, some recording ideals and more recording failings, the good and the braggarts, the wise and the dull. The next group bypasses pious sermonizing to record a crowd like us: the lively, the clever and the lovers. Then come the names of relationships or status: the Friend, the Cousans and the Pilgrim. A tiny but vivacious group describes people by their habitual expressions – Godsiff, or 'God save me'; 'Purdey', or *par Dieu*; Drinkall for 'drink up'.

138

There is a brigade of symbolical nicknames from nature: the Ravens and the Foxes. They people a stage with mirrors and shadows. Some are impossible to interpret now; for many we know one meaning; but for others, Norse, Celtic, Christian and folk traditions tell a rich story emerging from a moral, imaginative and sometimes quite alien world that is otherwise largely forgotten. We will look at those in Chapter 6.

Peopling a Society

Nicknames are some 9 per cent of all names, and about 10 per cent by numbers of individuals holding them, largely because of the popularity of the Browns, Whites and Kings. This popularity offsets many hanging on by a thread, such as Whitehead, Borne (who is squint-eyed) and Sprackling, the man with the creaking legs. There used to be far more. In medieval Exeter the proportion of nicknames declines from 34 per cent of a sample in about 1265, to 23 per cent in 1303 and 19 per cent in 1377 as the share of occupational names rises.[1] At the very least, about half the nicknames in this sample evaporate over that period – the fourteenth-century Swetemaystre, master of the *Seinte Marie cog*, and Makeglads of Dartmouth, Devon[2] – and more have done so since. But those that survive give a unique picture of medieval culture.

According to the *Oxford English Dictionary*, a nickname adds to or substitutes for the proper name of a person. Usually, it goes on, a nickname is given in ridicule or pleasantry. In medieval times there is no substitution because surnames are being added, but the humour is still there.

Many nicknames describe physical attributes. The most popular record hair and skin colour. Red-faced or red-haired people could be lechers, for red is the colour of lust. Many names show people know each other well. Anyone can name a White or a Redd as he walks by, but only one who knows him can call him lustful. It is thought that a large medieval English village could consist of about 70 families, which suggests an individual would know some 200–450 people. The nicknames to do with personalities show people have a keen eye for pretensions and failings. They record that the rather abstract Christian and chivalric ideals of the elite are common currency, but that human frailty is far more real, interesting and entertaining. Good and Humble come straight out of the church's teachings and Curtis and Valiant from tales of chivalry. But Letcher and Proud belong to the many more nicknames that have to do with failed ideals.

Society emerges from these names. They describe changing needs. Those to do with physical strength, speed and dexterity record the skills required for labouring. Those to do with intelligence and particularly stupidity tell us that success also depends on the ability to use opportunities. An intriguing idea is that to help identification people will record the unusual in names. So the great range for the dark-skinned and the overweight, for the brave and the merry, the greedy and the stupid could all tell us that most people are the opposite and that medieval England is a place of the fair, the thin, the cowardly and the dismal, and so on. The imagery and language in these names have their own story. They tell us about the namers, direct, witty and readily turning to visual metaphors, calling the greedy Wroot, or snouts, tall men Hoyte, or long thin sticks. Picture-making is intrinsic. And across all these names you hear voices in the phrases people use – Broadhead, Goodenough.

The interpretation of the attitudes in these names is helped by folk tales and contemporary church carving as well as literature like *Piers Plowman, The Canterbury Tales* and the chivalric romances that come to England in the twelfth century with Eleanor of Aquitaine and become immensely popular. Chaucer in *The Canterbury Tales* shows how skin complexions slot into a social hierarchy, with dark at the bottom and fair at the top. Many names – Crook, Borne – record a fascination with deformity; medieval church carving shows that it is sinister, even frightening. A few names have dual meanings identified in early records, so we know that Sellman, from *saelig*, could be happy or simple-minded (today's silly) and Pratt astute or cunning. Aesop tells us that the simple are often doomed to an early death and the cunning scorned. Chaucer laughs at the lecherous and the greedy, but admires the wise and the modest.

140

Humour and Language

Behind each name, like a backlight, shines the possibility of irony. Nicknames are a wonderful vehicle for humour. For some, the humour is visual: the squat Clapps from the Old English word for a hillock, the thickset Knotts contorted like a knot, and the Wagstaffs and Waghorns, officials and musicians hopefully waving their instruments as they play. Some is comment: names that record human frailty, the greedy and the mean, the lazy and the crafty. Many use the ironic opposite to get a laugh. Just as the giant is called Littlejohn, so Angels, Wises, Lightfoots and Riches could be just the contrary. The humour depends on the link between an individual and the name, so the joke about the person dies with the first generation, but the possibility is still entertaining.

Most names are Old English; when our ancestors look for the right epithet, they almost always find an English one. As with other groups of names, almost all religious nicknames are French, from Latin; the church is treated with linguistic respect. But the many names with French derivations record that the spoken language is nevertheless an inextricable mixture of English and French words. There is a tolerance of alternatives in the significant number of French/English translations that co-exist: Wise and Sage, Good and Bone from *bon*. Meanwhile, a few Old Norse names remind us of pre-Conquest priorities and cultures. Names with Old Gaelic roots seem to focus on misshapen faces (Kennedy means ugly head).

The evolution of language emerges from these names. Many, Round, Proud, Brown, still mean the same thing. But the meanings of others have completely changed. Cruise meant fierce, Stretch violent and strong, and Moody brave. With some, the contrast between the original and modern meaning adds humour: Gamble, for example, was old; Blank meant blonde; and Butt an archery target.

Our World, their World

The world in these nicknames is one we would partly recognize. Our moral standards are more diffuse, but we might still

141

characterize people by fraud, avarice and lechery and laugh at hypocrisy and vanity in much the same way. We admire wisdom, modesty, generosity and, in the right context, courage. And we still call people by their opposites – the dismal happy – or by metaphor, such as the runner after his legs.

Yet some names record a reality that is quite different. Physical attributes like speed, strength and dexterity would probably not be the first thing we might notice. We would not worry so much about the deadly sin of greed (in those days generally greed for alcohol), notice gossiping or swearing as much, or regularly see evil or cruelty close by. Nor would we lay such emphasis on courtesy or be so suspicious of the clever. Scorn for stupidity may be within our social experience, but we would be reluctant to express it and would not condemn it. We are not afraid of deformity, nor would we make a ready link between physical appearance and inner qualities as medieval people see in Crook someone who is crook-backed and sly. And the recognition of the savage and violent potential of man shows a different moral outlook based on different experiences. Many of the last group of names are symbolic and discussed in Chapter 6, but some non-symbolic names carry the same connotations. These names also record lost realities: that pilgrims, pagans and wildmen are part of life, that legal issues can be settled by champions in the duelling ring and that those you call friend are probably kinsmen.

Why did nicknames become hereditary? This question is more relevant than for other types of surname; nicknames record physical or behavioural attributes that are more personal than occupational or locational names, and are less applicable as time goes on and, in any case, might be offensive. Bassett, or small, might not help recognition after the first generation, but is at least not objectionable. But what of Pickersgill, meaning thief, or Harmes, an evil-doer? Yet such names are inherited across England, and one can only guess that the need to carry on a surname is more important than the meaning. Perhaps once given and written down on a tax record or title deed they are difficult to change.

There are caveats. Many nicknames straddle classifications and some simply fit too many. The biggest overlaps are between nicknames and occupational names. Bowler could mean a maker of bowls or a drinker from them, so a tippler. Another overlap is between nicknames and locational names. The Woods and all their variants might be dwellers in the woods or mad, like Chaucer's carpenter who thought the flood was coming. Some names have two or more derivations that have quite different meanings. Love from the Old English *lufu* means love (it is a popular woman's name); from the Anglo-French *louve,* she-wolf, it means fierce and savage. Moor from the Old French *Maur* means as swarthy as a Moor; from the Old English *mor,* it refers to someone living near a moor, marsh or fen. Today's names could have come from either derivation. We mention many overlaps as we go along. Often, they arise from the conflation of similar-sounding words with quite different roots and meanings. But often a dominant meaning slots them into the overall classification.

Colouring it in

Going by the sheer numbers of nicknames and the numbers of people that still carry them, medieval people notice colour of skin or hair most. Of the most popular, a third relate to colour, and the top three are Brown, White and Read with its variants for red-heads. Browns and Whites are among the top ten most popular names overall.

There is a pretty even balance of names for blondes, brunettes, redheads, and white- or grey-haired people. Gold, Bright, Blanchard, Gwyn and the lovely Lillicrap are all blonde; Black, Brown, Dunns, and Moors are brunette; Reed, Russell, Rudge plus variants are redheads; and Grey, Lloyd ('grey' in Welsh), Whites and so on are the old guard.

There are many more Brounyngs and Browns, Moriels and Redes than Blanchards and Goldes in medieval documents for Devon. The 1332 Lay Subsidy lists for the rural Hay Tor Hundred in Devon alone has four synonyms for Brown. Since this is the time when names are stabilizing, the carriers are likely to have been the first generation to have them and it is a fair assumption that most of the people these Brounyngs and Redes live with are blonde.

The popularity of White and its many less popular synonyms

(including the evocative Lyllyecroppe) could be telling us that people do grow old, unless they are white before their time. In medieval Tuscany, a surprising 9.5 per cent of the population is thought to be sixty-five or over.[3] This compares with 16 per cent in Britain in 2009. The names for the white-haired also suggest a good sprinkling of Celts in the population. Even today, people with Celtic ancestry go whiter earlier than other races.

But even descriptive names can be ambiguous. The Blacks or Blakes could be bright and shining as well as swarthy from two different Old English words and some of the names for the whites and the blondes could overlap. Richard le Whyte could have been called so not because he is grey but extremely fair, and all the Blanches could either be young blondes, from the French word for white, or old greys. Fair, that good Old English name, means light hair and complexion, but also bright and beautiful.

Colour has social as well as aesthetic connotations. Chaucer's *Canterbury Tales* give us a social ranking. His shipman is swarthy 'The hoote sonne had maad his hewe al broun', and his Forester has 'a broun visage'. The more affluent Miller's beard 'as any sowe or fox, was reed', and on his nose he has a wart 'and ther-on stood a tuft of heres,/Reed as the bristles of a sowes eres'. The redheads have the social edge over the dark-skinned people. One of the best-born is William Rufus who, as William II, ruled England from 1088 to 1100. Thor, the Viking god of thunder, had a red beard and red hair. But red is also associated with debauchery, often of clerics. Cherubs are painted with red faces in the churches. Chaucer's lecherous Summoner 'hadde a fyr-reed cherubynnes face'.[4] Nicholas, the clerk in the Miller's Tale prowls after the old carpenter's pretty wife in red stockings.

Yet the real elite, whether religious or secular, are the blondes. In Chaucer's Knight's Tale, the beautiful Emily, 'fairer was to sene/Than is the the lilie upon his stalke grene' has yellow hair 'broyded in a tresse'.[5] In Scandinavian mythology the light elves are beautiful and the dark condemned to live underground, too ugly to be seen. And Finlay is a fair hero; Finn, the warrior hero of the Irish Celts, is fair-headed. White is also the colour of the Christian pure. In *Piers Plowman* 'He who walks without blemish and does the works of justice' wears the white robe of integrity.[6]

Heads, Shoulders, Knees and Toes

Size and shape are recorded in names. There is a long list for short people – are most people tall, or is height important? Petty, Pettigrew and Bassett (from the French *petit* and *bas*), Short, Little, Small, Smallbones, and Vaughan (from the Welsh) are all small. Then we have the Lilleyman or little man and the more imaginative Grigg (dwarf from a Middle English word). There is something special about dwarves. In German and Norse legend, the wonder-smiths with supernatural powers are mostly dwarves. And in the Bayeux Tapestry, a dwarf holds the horses as William's riders ask for Harold's release in his pre-Conquest visit to Normandy. It is thought he was Turold, the artist of the tapestry. More evocative are the Peppers and Pepperalls (from the Old French for peppercorn) conjuring up small, round men who are also probably dark-haired and fiery-tempered to boot, and the Moles or Moules, from an Old Norse word meaning a crumb, suggesting someone insignificant as well as tiny.

These names contrast with the tall, the Langes, the Longs and the Grants (also sometimes great), some of the Highmans and the Haymans, the Hoytes, an evocative name from the Middle English word meaning a long stick, and the Hexts, the highest of all. The Mitchells could be Michaels from the French Michel, or they could record someone big, from the Old English *mycel*.

Then comes the fat brigade: the Broads, the Rounds, the Groses (from the Old French *gros*) and the Craces or Crazes (Old French again). Imagination reappears with the Guts, pot-bellied and called after their guts; the Barrells, who look like them (but could have made them, too); the Peakes, from the Old English word for a hill (they could also live by one) who are sturdy and thickset; as are the Butts, from the Old English for a stump, which also leads to their other meanings of an archery target or an archer. Then come the Clapps, from the Old English *clop*, a hump or a hill, and the Knotts from the Old English word for knot – a vivid image of someone corded around with muscle or fat – and the heavy or thickset Kippens. As for the thin, we have the Meagers, and for tall and thin, the Hoytes, mentioned earlier. The much greater variety of names for fat suggests there are fewer fat people – not that surprising when most were living at or below subsistence level.

Names record a focus on legs, important for speed and endurance. We have Leggs, Games (or little legs), as well as Longshanks or Langbeins meaning the same from the Old Norse. Then we have Foots and Footes, Whitefoots and Blampeys and Blampieds, which mean the same thing in French. The really marvellous Spracklings or Spratlings, named after Old English and Old Norse words meaning the man with the creaking legs, tell us exactly what the first holder of the name sounds like. (Spratling could also mean a little sprat.) Literature confirms the importance of legs; describing his Reeve, Chaucer notes:

> Ful longe were his legges, and ful lene,
> Y-lyk a staf, ther was no calf y-sene.[7]

Legs mean the named could be particularly speedy, or slow, but could also have attractive legs; medieval mens' long-fitted leggings show them off, after all.

Other names record speed directly. They include the Lightfoots and Golightlys, also messengers; two nice Old Norse names meaning fleet of foot, Snarey and Skeat; and the Pettifers (Old French), who are are good walkers on their iron feet. Winch, which means 'a leaping twisted flight' from the Old English word for a lapwing, might describe someone's peculiar walking or running style. The Slacks and Slough, Slow and Slowman are slow or, perhaps, lazy.

The Hands, Maynes and Mains are the men with the hands (or they might also be strong, or come from the French province of Maine). Perhaps they are deft with them, and are skilled craftsmen. Perhaps they just have big hands, or none, or only one, or one that is deformed. Left-handedness is also recorded in names to indicate clumsiness. One of the several meanings of Keys or Kays, left-handed or left-footed from the Middle English *kei,* traditionally has sinister connotations.

Heads come in for particular comment. First, hair: the Balls, Howells and Chaffers or Chaves are bald and the Notts and Pollards close-cropped or short-haired. The Crisps, Cripps and Locks are curly haired (although, as mentioned, the Locks could also be lock-keepers (on rivers), while the Hurrens are shaggy. Absolon, the third son of David, killed when his hair was entangled in a tree, is usually a personal name, although could also describe someone with a fine head of hair. Then the Nutts have neat, round and perhaps brown heads, the Broadheads big ones, the Kennedys ugly ones from the Old Irish, while the Heads themselves probably have unusual and noticeable ones. The Beards and Bairds are bearded while the Garnhams have moustaches. The Bayeux Tapestry shows men with moustaches and the notes to one naked man say the moustache shows he is English. Then the Lears have distinctive cheeks or faces and the Giffords and variants have bloated ones (they might also come from an Old German personal name meaning gift hardy). The Hacks have hooked noses, Camerons crooked ones and the Campbells crooked mouths, while the Borns squint. Does this mean the norm or ideal was a neat head of straight long hair, good features with good skin and good eyes? Images in tapestries and manuscripts suggest it could have been.

Colour, size and shape are obvious ways to recognize someone, but names recording other physical attributes tell us more about what medieval people value. Strength is admired, as in Armstrong (perhaps an archer), Burridge (from the Old English *burgric*, fortress-powerful), Drew, meaning sturdy and perhaps a lover too, and Strong, Crewe, Stretch and Telfer, who could cleave through armour. Durrant, from the Old French, is hard and obstinate too. Some of the Maletts have the strength of hammers (but could be cursed from the Old French *maleit* or take the name from the Breton port of St Malo).

Chaucer's good squire is 'of great strengthe'. There are strong men all over medieval churches, people carved holding up columns, corbels and lintels. In the Church of St John the Baptist, Cirencester, a man protrudes balancing a column like a top hat on his head, bracing himself by gripping the two columns on either side.[8]

Any of these surnames could be ironic. Thus, Little could be a giant; Meager, fat: Lange, short: Short, tall; Golightly, slow; and Strong, a weakling.

Other nicknames explicitly record distortions: Wrey, Hack (who could have a hunched body or hooked nose), Crookshank, Cruikshank and Folljambs (a lovely name from the French for silly legs or useless or damaged ones). And all the names for body parts – Foot, Leg, Head, Hand – could mean that the part being higlighted is deformed. The insight that physical and mental or moral distortions can go together, which must have been based on observation, is recorded explicitly in Crook, crook-backed or sly, the tiny and insignificant Mole and the gingery Pepperall.

That deformity is also somehow frightening is borne out by medieval ecclesiastical art. Churches are full of carvings of mouth-pullers (competitive mouth-pulling could have been a game), figures with oversized penises, heads sticking out oversize tongues and monsters. The chapter house of York Minster has some superlative mouth-pullers. It is thought that these could be there to frighten people into piety, or to frighten away any devil thinking of coming in.[9] The Celts had an aversion to physical blemishes. Nobody with a blemish could be king in Celtic Ireland; King Cormac had to abdicate when he lost an eye.[10]

Nailing Human Frailty

A very large group of nicknames relate to personality. Medieval people know their neighbours sufficiently intimately to identify their defining traits, whether brave or cruel, clever or stupid, gentle or savage.

Many nicknames record that Christian and chivalric ideas carry over into popular culture. They give a nod in the direction of piety, modesty, wisdom and courage, but after turning some of them into their opposites through ridicule, the namers produce many more names that describe the blasphemous, the braggarts, the stupid and the savage. They give us a market crowd of people who aspire to nobility, but who constantly fall short. As in Aesop's fables, with the good mingle those who are too good to be true and the arrogant and boastful elbow the courteous and the humble. With the wise and the clever come the cunning and the fraudsters; with the generous, the misers, the spendthrifts and the greedy; and with the brave jostle the savage and the cruel. These people know their Christian duties. They value the gentle and the pious, the charitable and the courteous. It is just that the practice is hard.

Many nicknames leave the abstract far behind as they nail human frailty.

Contemporary literature can help to understand the attitudes behind these names. In *The Canterbury Tales*, people give up physical and worldly satisfaction to be faithful, trustworthy and generous in the Franklin's Tale, and the Knight in the Prologue is wise and valiant, meek-mannered and 'never uttered any vileness'. But in the Nun Priest's Tale, the hen Pertelote requires her cockerel, Chanticleer, to be 'hardy, wyse, and free' as well as trustworthy.[11] By equating cockerel and knight, is Chaucer saying such ideals are ridiculous?

The Good and the Sinful

There are many names recording the ultimate ideal, the good. We have Good and its French equivalent Bone and Bunn, Thorogood and Goodfellow and Goodman, Goodrich and Goodheart. There is a family called le Bon in thirteenth-century Dartmouth, who seem to have a seal of a tree sheltering a figure on either side.[12] Then come Bullivant, from *bon enfant*, Goodchild and Goodbairn, which mean the same thing, Dowse, from the French *douce*, who is sweet-natured and Ambler who is easy-going, like a slow-moving horse – Amblers could also be enamellers. Nice members of this group are Sweet and Sweetman and its variants. (No Sweetdame, notice.) A poetic lost nickname from Dartmouth is Swetemaystre, shipmaster of the *Seinte Marie cog*, protected by the king to carry victuals for the Duchy of Aquitaine.[13]

Medieval sermons focus mightily on the sins of indulgence and their corresponding virtues of temperance, modesty and generosity. A few names record the modest and the humble – Humble, Meek and some of the Pews or Pughs, pious from the French (others might be from the Welsh ap Hugh, son of Hugh). The Sadds are serious and discreet from the Middle English word, not sad then. Turpin, usually a personal name from the Viking god Thor, can also mean humble, a transformation of a Latin/French word for disgraceful or base that eventually becomes abasement.

The sin of greed, for money, pleasure, wine and food, is

recorded in many more names than the corresponding virtues. Gluttony, lust, and greed for money are three of the seven deadly sins. Greedy, Gulliver (from *goulafre*), both very common nicknames, Bowler and Saffer (from *saffre*) meaning glutton all record medieval disgust with excess. The Wroots, from the Old English for a snout, and the Gotts, from the Old English again for guts, meaning someone fat or greedy, are wonderfully evocative names for gluttons. Letcher, a lecher, is specifically greedy for sensuality. Many of these names are symbolic, Hogg being too good an image to miss, and discussed later in Chapter 6.

Medieval literature is uncompromising about gluttony, usually involving too much wine. Chaucer's Pardoner, the ultimate hypocrite, identifies gluttony with original sin:

> O glotonye, full of cursednesse,
> O cause first of our confusioun.[14]

William Langland associates greed with sloth and evil:

> Too much leisure and too much food
> Encouraged evil's vilest brood.[15]

Medieval art laughs at the drunk. An appealing fifteenth-century misericord in the south choir stalls in Ripon Cathedral shows a drunk woman waving a bottle being pushed along in a wheelbarrow by, so the scholars tell us, her husband.[16]

Other names could reflect the attitude in contemporary morality tales that if you have wealth, you should be generous; luxury is a deadly sin. The Riches are just wealthy; Alexander le Riche who buys wool over a fifty-mile radius from Wiltshire to Somerset in 1270 is probably the first one in his family with the name.[17] Large and Frank are generous and the names are kind. Chaucer's parson in *The Canterbury Tales*, who is poor, but 'riche ... in holy thoght and werk', is generous to poor parishioners. He consciously sets an example: 'first he wroghte, and afterward he taughte; ... if golde ruste, what shal iren do?'[18] After all, this is the time of Robin Hood, a popular theme of minstrels' songs.

While some names record the generous, many more describe

the various ways to be miserly or extravagant. Several comment on money, greed for it and what not to do with it. Thus, Penny and Winpenny and some of the Hains and Haymans could be mean and acquisitive, while Scattergood, and some of the Spendloves, are spendthrifts. Penny is thought to have come from the name of Penda of Mercia (632–54), one of the first minters of English coins.[19] Then some of the Slacks and Carless are careless with money as well as other things.

Surnames recording the avaricious and the extravagant are likely to be critical. Chaucer's Prioress despises 'vile gain', and in *Piers Plowman* Lady Meed's greed for silver destroys society through lies and lechery. The message from *The Canterbury Tales* is quite clear. The mean, cheating Miller gets cuckolded, and the Pardoner pronounces 'Avarice is the root of all evil'. By contrast, the unworldly Parson who does not hire out his benefice or run to London for a better living is admired. As for the spend-thrifts, contemporary literature is contemptuous of rich wastrels who 'greedily go through their wealth, buying fancy clothes and extravagant meals' instead of giving to beggars.[20]

Sloth and pride, other deadly sins, appear in nicknames. Langland's Waster is a sloth, wasting time rather than money, and Slough, Slowman and some of the Slacks are lazy as well as slow. These are Aesop's grasshoppers who sing all summer. On a bench-end in Holy Trinity Church at Blythborough in Suffolk a man sits comfortably under his bedclothes propped up against his pillow.[21]

We still have the arrogant and the braggarts – those deadly sinners – in the Prouds, the Boggs (bold, too) and the Braggs (who could also be lively) as well as some of our Bretons – Bretts, Brittains and Brittons known for their boastfulness (although these could also be Celts). Chaucer's admired characters in *The Canterbury Tales* are universally discreet: the Sergeant-at-Law and the Clerk, the Parson and the Knight, There is a dire warning against pride in *Piers Plowman*. Langland sees the seven sins as a manifestation of pride, with greed for material wealth being its most potent form. Thomas Proute of Dartmouth (his name a variant of Proud) might have been named after his habitual quarrels that landed him in court for assault between 1504 and 1512. He got to know the courts so well he ended up a juror.[22]

A Nod to Ideals

The Courteous and the Opposite

The meek, the gentle and the pious stand to remind us of the Christian ideals that medieval people try to live by. Other ideals are brought in by the chivalric romances. Curtis means courteous or well-educated, one of the most admired chivalric qualities, referring more to a way of life than a habit of interpersonal relations. The motto of medieval Winchester College is still 'Manners Makyth Man'. Chaucer's knight is 'a worthy man' who 'loved chivalrye,/ Trouthe and honour, fredom and curteisye',[23] and as for the prioress 'In curteisye was set ful muche' her delight. Our Gents and Gentry, which mean well-born, also, by extension, mean well-mannered and courteous, as are Nobles. Nicknames show that these ideas filter through to ordinary people. The universality of the knightly ideal of courtesy is evident across medieval documents which have Curteis and Courteys, who are townsmen and clerks, a far cry from damsels, chivalric poetry and tournaments.

The courteous do not swear. All our Bretts and Bretons might be named for obscenities as well as boastfulness, while our Turks, a name introduced at the Conquest, are just rowdy. Langland's loud-mouthed Breton challenges Piers Plowman to 'go and piss on your plough, you goddammed bastard ...'.[24] Our Purdeys and Pardews, mentioned later, are swearers from the French *pardieu*, the nicknames recording their own expletives. Chaucer's Plowman lives 'in pees and parfit charitee', while the hypocritical Pardoner says young peoples' oaths were 'so grete and so dampnable,/ That is grisly [horrible] to here hem swere'.[25] Langland's Haukin is scorned for 'boasting and bragging, backing it all up with audacious oaths'.[26] He gets his come-uppance from Hunger who smacks him, upon which the knight 'with the courtesy that was part of his calling' comes along to help. Swearing becomes such an issue for the church that early Franciscan friars in England have to give it up formally.[27]

Contemporary literature scorns gossiping as a sin because it is destructive and makes enemies. In *The Canterbury Tales* the modesty of the discreet parson, clerk, knight and reeve are

152

admired, whereas the gossips are the despised Friar and the mocked Miller – that 'loose talker and ribald joker'.[28] Most gossips have symbolic surnames, but the braggarts mentioned above and the mendacious Vauses are probably gossipers. The name Gossip itself, from the Old English, means a godfather or godmother, later coming to mean a friend.

The Wise, the Stupid and the Clever

Chaucer's knight 'was wys' and a standard of behaviour. So we can take it that the Wises and the Wisdoms, the Sages (from the French), the Frouds and the Glews (the last two are also prudent) as well as the Vizards (from the Old Norse *vizkr*) are named approvingly. An appropriately named Walter le Wise represents Tavistock in Parliament at Westminster in 1295 to review a new tax proposed by Edward I.

More names record stupidity than wisdom. The Neates can be ox-heads (heads again), and our Dumbles and Dullards, and some of the Gordons (also a place name in Berwickshire in its Old English sense) and the Folletts, from the Old French *fol* or foolish, are stupid. The Sealeys and Selleys, as noted, can be happy, fortunate souls or simpletons. Gordon is an interesting name; known as Scottish today, it appears in England in early medieval times when it means dull or stupid, from a diminutive of the Old French word for gourd. Some of these names combine physical and mental traits; the Dodds, can be rounded, lumpish or stupid – a lump for a body and a lump for a brain (Dodd from the Old English could also mean a deceiver, or be a place name).

To be stupid is mocked. The clerk who notes down a bond tenant in Berry Pomeroy in Devon in the late thirteenth century as William Dulle Sparke is surely laughing at him. 'Men should marry in accordance with their condition' intones Chaucer, with no pity for his 'sely carpenter' so hilariously cuckolded by the clerk Nicholas in the French farce of the Miller's Tale.

A pragmatic step for the wise is to become clever. The Smarts, Snells (from the Old English) and Keens are on the ball as well as bold, and the Sharps are just that. In *The Canterbury Tales*, the

Sergeant-at-Law is 'wary and wise' and Chaucer seems to admire the discretion, learning and judgement that brings him wealth, as he admires the judgement and capability of the reeve who sits on a good steed and wears a fine coat but always rides modestly at the back of the group wending its way to Canterbury.[29] Intelligence, for Chaucer, must be borne modestly.

The Cheats and the Honest

Clever is good, but you can be too clever; cheating is not on. The Pratts and the Quants (chiefly a Devon name), the Inghams (also a place name in the east), the Crooks and the Slays, Sleighs and Slys and the tricky Tranters, mainly from Devon again, are all names that mean astute, but also cunning, so reflect a suspicion of people who are too quick. A William Quantell, shipmaster from Plymouth, was astute enough to capture, with accomplices, three vessels laden with wine and many others laden with pork and other goods in 1412.[30] The Sleighs could also be weavers, from the slay, a tool used in weaving, and the idea of deftness that arises from both meanings also gives us sleight of hand. The Vauses are frankly false or mendacious (or come from Vaux).

Aesop's crafty foxes sometimes win out, but most medieval documents are full of scorn for trickery and fraud. Langland's Greed in *Piers Plowman* 'a wretched creature' goes in for falsehood, fraudulent weights, stretching cloth, clipping silver coins, and doing sharp property deals, while his wife dilutes her ale.[31] Medieval art is direct about cheats: a misericord in the Church of St Laurence in Ludlow from the early fifteenth century shows a barmaid being tossed head first into a gaping mouth of hell clasping the tankard she uses for false measuring.[32] Church art of the Middle Ages often records theft. In Wells Cathedral, on four capitals in the south transept, is carved the story of a man stealing grapes and being thumped by the farmer.[33]

Names tell us that traders can be fraudsters. Barrat means commerce or fraud, which could reflect experience with all sellers of goods, and Tranter, a carrier or a hawker, can be conflated with *trant*, a cunning or tricky person. Contemporary literature also reflects hostility to trade. Aesop, that purveyor of ancient folk opinion, has Jupiter adding a little infusion of lies into the making of tradesmen, with most going into the horse-dealers. All tradesmen lie more or less, but they none of them lie like a horse-dealer.[34] Langland's Truth will not give merchants a pardon because their way of life is synonymous with dishonesty. Even Chaucer's Miller (Chaucer has a less dogmatic morality than Langland) is a thief, 'Wel koude he stelen corn' and is farcically cuckolded by the students he is proposing to cheat. Dress declares which side of the fence you are on. Chaucer's Merchant is 'in mottelee', which we gather is looked down on from the fact that his modest knight is not finely dressed and his lean and sober clerk has a 'ful threadbar' cloak.[35] All these names suggest it is important to be on the ball, quick and smart, but to be too smart with money is scorned.

Just as dishonesty is despised, truth and honesty are valued. These are recorded in the Trows, the Truemans, the Goodhews (trusty fellows, although some were good servants), the Triggs, the Justs and the Veritys. The Holy Church in *Piers Plowman* tells of an order of knights established by King David who swear on their swords to serve truth at all times, and to support every man and woman who stands up for truth and honesty, and never to abandon them.[36] Those who do not come in for even the gentlest mockery by Chaucer are the honest, the Parson, the Clerk, the Plowman and the Knight in the Prologue. According to the *Chronicle of Battle Abbey*, an Elfin Trewe is one of the peasants picked to be allotted a house and land to commemorate the Battle of Hastings after 1066. The name probably did not survive him as a surname then, but it does reappear later.[37]

The Brave and the Savage

Courage is a chivalric quality that, as names show, carries over into everyday values. The regiment of names to do with personal bravery is as nuanced as the group to do with intelligence. Bray (a Cornish name), Hardy, Harding, Moody and Mudie, Prowse and Valiant all mean courageous. The Snells and Keens are brave as well as smart and wise. The name Sturdy means brave, but also impetuous, while the Starks are firm but inflexible and the Cruises and their variants are fierce. Do these second meanings suggest you should not take courage too far? Oliver, in the *Chanson de Roland*, says yes: when he sees the number of the enemy, he counsels Roland to call on Charlemagne's help.[38]

Courage has a long tradition as one of the supreme qualities of heroes in Celtic and Norse myth. Finn fought witches, giants and magic animals and when Fenrir is bound by Odin's son Tyr, he puts his arm into the wolf's jaws, knowing he will lose it.

Nicknames take chivalric valour beyond romance into the real world. A step beyond bravery lie savagery, violence, and cruelty. Ramage, Savage, Grimes and Stark, Hardman and Stretch all capture this trait. All the names based on Wild – Wildblood, Wildman and Wilding – also fit here, because wild men have violent potential. Medieval people take cruelty for granted and these names may not have been derogatory. In *The Canterbury Tales*, the Prioress sweetly tells a blood-curdling story about the martyrdom of a little boy – they cut his throat and threw him in a cess pit – and the knight's story is a glorification of war with no backward glance at the suffering it causes. The many symbols of cruelty in animals mentioned in the next chapter recall the dark side of medieval thinking and traditions.

But Ramage, Savage and other names referring to an untamed nature could also suggest strength and freedom and, perhaps, innocence. Underneath a miniature of Saul sending Doeg to kill the priests of Nob in the Macclesfield Psalter is a little scene of a horseman pointing towards a tall, naked man – a wild man – under some trees who is looking at the horseman and pointing in the opposite direction, telling him where to go. A gracefully inclined lady stands between them, obligingly pointing in the direction indicated by the wild man. Here we have the wild man showing the sophisticated the way. A wild man brought up by animals in the forest is a popular medieval story, echoing the Roman myth of Romulus and Remus. The north choir of Ripon Cathedral has a misericord of a wild man carrying a club walking through an oak wood.[39]

Wode can also mean mad or frenzied as well as wood, the connection arising from pagan veneration of trees, which could explain why some of our Woods and Woodings will have been wild men or even pagans. In the Miller's Tale, Chaucer has the young wife and her lover mocking her old husband: 'They tolden every man that he was wood'.[40] Here the sense is definitely mad because he believes their story that the flood is coming.

Just beyond the natural forces of savagery and cruelty lies the attribute of evil. Most of the names that connote evil are symbolic; many, Orme and Drake, meaning serpents, and Raven and Corbett have deep roots in Norse and Christian culture and are discussed in Chapter 6. We would have expected other, more explicit nicknames to have died out, but a few remain. Pickersgill, from the Middle English word *pyker*, means a very common and human evil-doer, and is a thief and a robber from the Old Norse for a footpad's ravine, implying that all ravines harbour thieves (it is also a place). Armes and Harmes are the more significant perpetrators of harm, injury or evil. The Lawless and Petchs are explicitly sinners, although the Petchs, from the Old French *péché*, could also be fishmongers. (The French word has the same twin meanings.)

Celebrating the Lively and the Sexy

A solid group of nicknames records everyday behaviour. First, the names for the merry, the epithets we think of as typical of medieval England rather than the clever or the fraudulent, the brave and the violent. Chaucer's Host 'spake of mirthe' and welcomed 'so mirie a compaignye'. And after the Prioress' rather gruesome tale in which the little chorister is martyred, the host begs the nun's priest to tell a tale to make 'our hertes glade; be blythe', which he does, with a chilling tale of vanity rewarded by death.

There is a coachful of names for the lively. We have the gentle and merry Blythe and Bragg; the light-hearted and joyful Gay, Joy and Gale; the vivacious and lively Cock, Joliffe, Jolly, Spark and Spragg; the changeable Geary and its many variants; the more temperate glad, cheerful Roote; and the playful Voisey and their variants from the Old French *envoisie*. A spark was a mystical concept too, relating to the Holy Spirit, and Meister Eckhart (1260–1327) refers to the 'Divine spark at the apex of the mind', giving depth to the nickname.[41] But Gale and Voisey can also be wanton and lascivious, Geary and Spragg could be giddy, and Waller a showoff (if not a stonemason). To be happy could also mean to be simple-minded as Sillman, Sellifant, Sealey, and Selley record. Chaucer's old carpenter who chooses the wild young wife in the Miller's Tale is 'sely'. The friendly come down to us with the Anglo-Saxon Wine and Wynne.

Then we have love. These nicknames include some of the Loves from the Old English *lufu*, now indistinguishable from names from the Anglo-French *louve*, or she-wolf, which means fierce and is discussed in Chapter 6. Loveman, Lowman, Lemon and Leaman also record a lover or sweetheart, as does Truelove. Dearlove or Darlow mean secret love. To be a lover could be a courtly role. The son of Chaucer's Knight is the Squire, who is 'a lovyere, and a lusty bachelor'.[42] Batchelor then meant a young man waiting to be made a knight. But Chaucer sets up a real-world opposite of the knightly ideal in his prowling red-stockinged Absolon of the Miller's Tale, and other names carry more explicit and earthier connotations. The Letchers are identified among the sinners, but other names give a more human view. They can suggest that people appreciate endurance in love; the Drews and Drurys, who are strong, are also lovers (or could, if the derivation is Old German, be named after Charlemagne's son Drogo). Finnemore, from *fin amour*, has the French distinction of being a fine lover. A wonderful name for heart-breaker, Crawcour and its variants from the French *crève-coeur*, has joined the ranks of the Crockers (or potters). Then we have the evocative Spindlows and Spendloves who are lavish, or foolish, with their love.

These nicknames describing personalities are all very straight-forward, one would have thought. Except, as with all medieval names, irony is never far away. The Goodenoughs and Toogoods are surely named sarcastically as people who are too easily satisfied or maybe not good at all. Similarly, there are Angels, Perfects and Darlings who cannot but be the opposite. In the same vein the generous and the meek, the Wises (remember the wise men of Gotham?), the Truemans and the brave could all be ironic. As can all the Lovemans and Leamans. In The Miller's Tale, Chaucer calls the parish clerk Absolon, doomed to be disappointed and mocked by the sly Alison and slick Nicholas, 'a joly lover'.

Relationships

Cousins

Names of relationships seem to focus on the extended rather than close family, and on important others like heirs, friends and foreigners. Kin is recorded in Child, Cousans and Ayres (or heir), important enough to be recorded separately. Both Cousans, kinsmen as well as cousins, and Ayres have many variants, the former seventeen and the latter twenty-three, suggesting the relationships are widespread and important. Names for close relatives like Fathers, Mothers and Brothers seem to stand for their qualities – Fathers for a protector like a teacher, Brothers for a kinsman or fellow guild member. Son is captured via the suffix '-son', as in Robertson, which only begins to appear in documents in the fourteenth century, as well as through a final '-s' added to another name, such as Locks or Parsons, and through the prefix 'Fitz-' (which does not mean bastard), such as Fitz-Stephen. These names ending in '-son' and '-s' show people live in close communities. So we have a William Dulle Sparkson as son of William Dulle Sparke in Berry Pomeroy over 1300–50, a joke that has become permanently enshrined.

Then we have Friend, Guest and Bellamy, from the Old French words for good friend – 'Thou bel amy, thou Pardoner' says the host in *The Canterbury Tales*. Other significant people are the strangers in the community, and Newman and Newcombe (for newly arrived strangers) and Walsh record these. Walsh and Wallis are interesting; they are from the Old English names the invading Saxons called the Celts, originally meant a foreigner or a slave, and only coming to mean Welsh later.

On why names of relationship seem to focus on the extended rather than close family, Marc Bloch suggests that the modern interpretation may be misleading. In his work on medieval kinship ties, he notes that in medieval France and Germany kinsfolk are called *amis* and *Freunde*, or friends, and quotes an eleventh-century legal document from Île de France that runs: 'his friends, that is to say, his mother, brothers, sisters and his other relatives by blood or by marriage'. He goes on to say that friend is also used as a synonym for relative in Welsh and Irish texts. So although this does not prove that the same equivalence holds in medieval England, feudalism as a social system is very similar across Europe and England and the Normans are a powerful influence here so there is a strong likelihood that the English also call their close kin by names we would use for more distant relatives. This would explain why we have so few stand-alone siblings and so many variants for Cousans and Ayres as well as Friend and Bellamy.[43]

Pilgrims

The pilgrims are the Palmers, Pilgrims and probably the Barefoots too (although these might just be mendicant monks or friars). Chaucer, at the start of *The Canterbury Tales*, identifies the difference between Palmers and Pilgrims: in spring 'than longen folk to goon on pilgrimages/(And palmers for to seken straunge strondes)'.[44] The difference seems to be that pilgrims are ordinary people with professions and homes and set out for somewhere specific. Palmers, who typically carry a palm or some English substitute, make pilgrimages to the Holy Land and spend their lives travelling to holy places at home and abroad, living in poverty. In fact, they do not always reach the Holy Land, going usually to Rome, where the Pope often allows them the palm as if they had gone to Jerusalem.[45]

Pilgrims and pilgrimages reflect a very medieval coping strategy. From all sides people are bombarded with the dogma that life is only a preparation for death, purgatory and Judgement Day. But experience teaches people that the dice are loaded; devils, temptation and sins are too powerful for them to live the sort of life that will get them quickly to Heaven. So through pilgrimage to a holy place, the sinner can use the prayers of the pious and the intervention of ascetics and saints to reach a paradise that they would never otherwise attain.

Pilgrimages are important among all ranks of society. Kings, nobles, clerics and ploughmen go on them. The most important destinations in England are the tomb of St Thomas à Becket in Canterbury (the destination of the group in *The Canterbury*

Tales) and Our Lady of Walsingham in Norfolk. But people also visit shrines at Durham, St Albans, Glastonbury, Lincoln, York, Peterborough and Winchester among many other places. Palmers travel to Santiago de Compostela in Spain, to Lourdes, or sites in what is now northern France. Langland's pilgrim, who comes from Sinai, attests to the distances quite ordinary people travel in those days. Margery Kempe, a mayor's daughter from King's Lynn with pretensions to saintliness, born in about 1373, dictates at the end of her life an account of her visit to Jerusalem.[46]

But Chaucer's merry group, whose thoughts turn to pilgrimage in spring, suggest they might not always have been only holy ventures. In *Piers Plowman*, the pilgrims:

> set out on their journey full of sage speeches, and thereby earned the right to lie about it for the rest of their lives.... A gaggle of hermits with crooked staves set out for Walsingham, with their whores behind them ... dressed up in copes to look different from the rest, and, hey presto! They've become hermits – gentlemen of leisure.[47]

Langland's pilgrim is a fraud; the ordinary man gives his labour according to truth and honesty and the ploughman knows Truth when he sees it, but the pilgrim does not.[48] Pilgrims generally have a reputation for telling fisherman-type stories about the marvels they have seen in their travels. As for Chaucer's band, pilgrimages are also an excuse for a holiday.

Not surprisingly, the church has ambiguous views on pilgrimages. Although individual shrines enjoy the revenues from them, the church itself worries about the effect of worldly travel on its priests and makes strong and ineffectual efforts to stop monks and nuns and particularly their superiors from making them.

Pagan and its variant Payne mean pagan, not a derogatory name in medieval times but simply meaning a non-Christian. This group could include the Woods, Wodings and Wilds mentioned earlier. It is illegal not to be baptized, so pagans are outside the church. Master can mean a schoolmaster, the master of a house or a ship, or, as we saw in Chapter 3, the Master of a building project. And Noble could be a noble, one of the few non-ironic names for the upper classes, or somebody who is well known. A Noble is also a gold coin, worth about a third of a pound in the late fourteenth century.

Then we have Neal and Campion or Champion, all meaning a champion. The *Oxford English Dictionary* definition of a champion is one who is a man of valour or a stout combatant. Champions represent parties involved in land disputes. The many variants, at least twenty-three, of the ancient Gaelic Neal record how important the function is.[49] One use was in dispute settlement. Reaney and Wilson quote the case of the Dean and Chapter of Southwell owing some £750 in modern money to a champion hired to fight a duel to settle a case about the advowson or patronage of a church.[50] Early references to champions are as winners at games, an important part of medieval life and played in churchyards and on village greens, at fairs and on feast days. Periodically, either the church or the king ban games. The church bans them from churchyards during the Black Death, for instance,[51] and disapproves of them elsewhere, while during the Hundred Years' War games are stopped in favour of practising archery. Champions will have emerged from all these games, as well as forms of physical contest such as wrestling and rough ball games like mass football.[52] Apart from the Neals and Campions, our Games and Gammons are also nicknames for people good at games, and all the names discussed earlier in this chapter that mean legs or speed could have arisen from prowess at sport.

Phrases and Oaths

You can hear the immediacy and vivacity of speech in the many phrase names that enliven all the groups discussed. As well as being descriptive, humour lurks within these names.

The first group identifies people with their habitual expressions, so we hear their voices. Purdy and its variants, including Pardew, come from *par Dieu* and means for God's sake. We have Godsname, who exclaims 'in God's name', and Godber, Godbear or Godbehere (or God be in this house). It sounds as if it could also mean good beer, a nice choice to make about your name, but this is unlikely because beer did not become a common drink until after the fourteenth century. Then we have Godsiff and Dugard, from *dieu vous garde*, both of which mean God save you. Other expressions include Farrell, meaning farewell and its French equivalent Bonally, from *bon aller*, to go well. Then we have Gover, to go fairly, or gently and Drinkall to drink up. Goodyear is a nice one, for someone who exclaims it all the time. Clearly, in 1297 a William Godyer from Shrewsbury is having such a good year, being assessed at the relatively high tax rate of three shillings and owning a good riding horse, meat and some brassware.[53]

Occupational joke names describe people who have fine jobs and do them badly, so they have all sorts of connotations linked with the pretentiousness, hypocrisy and perhaps pathos of the named and the jealousy and humour of the namers. Think of Wagstaff, a minor official, which gives a marvellous visual image of him being officious with his staff of office; and Waghorn, inept with his trumpet. Similarly, the constable Catchpole who inspires laughter rather than fear. Then Benbow is an archer, having trouble bending his bow, Copestake is a very basic woodcutter, and Warboys a lowly forester.

Derivations

Nicknames are dominated by those with Old English roots, which, except in the few religious names that are based on the Latin, are more colourful, inventive and nuanced than the French. There are still many with Old French derivations, and, perhaps surprisingly, many that co-exist with an English translation, suggesting that the ordinary people creating these names are happy in either language, people saying 'Bonaller' as readily as 'Farewell', and 'Pardieu' as easily as 'Godsave'. Derivations of names are evidence that the language people speak is a thoroughly kneaded dough. In medieval records for Dartmouth, for example, French Blondes live alongside English Whites and English Loves and Lovecocks with French Finnemores, all translations of each other.

Like French/English dictionaries, for most of these groupings there are far more names in English than in French. For the colour group, for instance, we have Moor meaning swarthy from its Old French base, and Black, Blake, Brown, Cole, Dunn, Earp and Dimes based on Old English roots. For strength, we have the Old French Drew, and Armstrong, Burridge, Steel and Stretch from the English. The English names generally have many more nuances that add depth to a name – Sturdy who is not only brave like Hardy, but impetuous, Stark who is not only determined, but unyielding, and the Sillmans and Sillifants (fortunate, or silly, souls). But there are always exceptions. Telfer, from the French *taille fer,* iron cleaver, is someone able to cut right through iron armour, a wonderfully direct image. Then our Garnham with the moustache comes from the Old French *grenon,* or moustache.

In almost all groups of nicknames there are Old or Middle English names and Old French names that mean the same. For the group to do with hair and skin colour and size, Rowse means red-haired in both derivations, White exists alongside its translation, Blanche, Fair with Beal (from Belle), Whitefoot with Blampied, Short with Basset, Hoyt with Grant and Broad with Grose. For the group that relate to other physical attributes, Ball means bald in both English and French derivations, and Strong exists with the French Drew, which means the same. For the names recording personality traits, Barrat and Prowse, Beal, Fettes and Quant come from both sources, while Gale exists with the French Gay, Wise with Sage (for wise), and Good with Bone, or *bon.* For the names of relationships, Cousen is based on both derivations, and we have Friend co-existing with Bellamy, *bel ami.*

The religious names, Palmer, Payne, and Pilgrim, are the only group for which all names have Old French roots. This is similar to the derivations of religious occupational names.

Like ancient stones left out of respect in a new graveyard, the Old Norse and Gaelic names are rare, showing how easily names can disappear. Yet still they survive. Grice, or grey, Crook, and by derivation, Cruikshank or Crookshank, and Mole (a crumb), all have Old Norse roots, as do Guest, Legg, Slack, Spark and Spragg. Vizard, meaning wise, has an Old Norse prefix with an Old French ending. And the incomparable Spratling or Sprackling, the man with the creaking legs, comes from an anglicization of the Old Norse word *sprakaleggr* (unless it comes from the word for sprat and means a little one). A very few names, like Meek, Slay, or sly, and Bond come from both Old Norse and Old English.

There are a few Gaelic names: Finlay, meaning fair hero; Muir, meaning big; Cameron and Campbell, meaning crooked nose and crooked mouth; and Kennedy, ugly head. The latter three suggest that others, probably English, are the namers. The fact that most Celts are called Scott, Wallis or Ireland suggests the same. But there is still the possibility that these groups take English names.

Wit and Change in Language

Surnames record the way people see the world around them and the language in many of these nicknames tell us about the imagination of the namers. Our medieval ancestors are into direct and visual metaphors – for example, the Winch who has a walk twisted like the flight of a lapwing. There is a directness and lightness of touch in the complex names – the Spendloves and Golightlys so much more evocative than the Letchers and Quicks.

The wit often comes from a name that stands for its opposite. We know from Littlejohn and the wise men of Gotham that medieval people use the device, and it could apply to all the Speedy, who could be slow, the Shorts tall, the Megors fat, the Strongs feeble, the Humbles arrogant and the Richs poor. The wit explicit in the Toogoods and Goodenoughs lurks as irony behind all the Angels, Perfects, Wises and the lovers. Although much of this humour would come from the connection between the name and its first owner, you can still picture how it arose. There is humour in calling people after their customary phrases – *par Dieu* and drink up – and in the names that still tell you about musicians and officials being pretentious and pathetic with their symbols of office.

Time has added another interest to these surnames. Differences between the original and modern meanings show where language and ideas have changed. A surprising number of nicknames still mean what they did. The appealing simplicity we see now in all the Shorts and the Rounds, the Strongs and the Prouds, the Humbles, the Meeks and the Justs tells us that the underlying words and meanings are the same as they were. Others have changed a bit. Some changes add comment. Pollard has gone from a shaven head to a heavily pruned tree and Rust from red hair to the red etching on corroded metal, the words dehumanized in both cases. Crook, then either physically or morally bent, now usually just means a criminal, the medieval meaning simplified, as it is for Sadd, originally serious or discreet. Large was generous, and is now physically big – broadly the same idea but behaviour has morphed into appearance. Petty has gone the other way, from small to small-minded. Moody meant brave and impetuous; was the experience over 600 years that the brave were emotionally unreliable?

But the original meaning of many nicknames has changed completely. For some, the change is bewildering: Cruise meant fierce, Dowse sweet, Drew sturdy and Stretch strong and violent. The old and new meanings seem to have no connection. Then take Grant, big, Bowler, a tippler, Gamble, old and Drew, sturdy. We still make grants, bowl our balls, gamble and draw, so we might think we know what the original names meant, but we don't. For others, the contrast is funny. Blank was blonde and Belcher fair-faced – so all blondes are air-heads or have windy digestions? And Pain was a pagan. Some contrasts evoke nice images; Crisp meant curly-haired and evolved into curly potato chips; Gale was joyful and became a whirlwind; Butt was an archery target – ouch!

But however much these nicknames have changed, we can all relate to the images behind the Barrels and the Golds, the ideas in the Scattergoods and Trueloves, and the grin behind the Toogoods and the Thorogoods.

CHAPTER 6

SYMBOLIC NICKNAMES AND MEDIEVAL BELIEFS

THE NICKNAMES IN the last chapter are simplifications; people called after curly hair, happy dispositions or habitual expressions. But symbolic nicknames are quite different, because a symbol carries immense possibilities of associated meanings. So, while one meaning may be the same as that discussed in Chapter 5, the rest could mirror and extend this. This chapter explores symbolic nicknames, including ironical surnames of status, such as Bishop and Pope, Abbot and Prior, Lord and Earl. Symbols add colour and contour, depth and comment and, often, humour. They have kept alive for us medieval imagination and inheritance of pre-Conquest attitudes and beliefs.

Why call a neighbour Winter instead of White? Winter brings an image of someone whose colour has faded, but is also in the winter of his days, when life is slow, and light and energy have been replaced with the almost-sleep of nature and the sap of life with the brittleness of approaching death. The symbol carries the colour, but also the story of old age reflected in nature; winter in contrast with summer, the symbol matching and extending the full complexity of age. Then take Raven, Lilly, Peacock and Pye. At one level, these names could mean a person with black (Raven) or white (Lilly) hair, or who is rich and probably vain too (Peacock) or who is as noisy as a magpie (Pye). But lift just a little the corner of the curtain that separates our world from the world that created these names. Norse, Celtic and Christian traditions associate the raven with war, bloodshed and sin, the lily with purity and peace, the peacock with resurrection and the magpie with vanity, dissipation and evil.

A Heftier Punch

Symbolic nicknames tell a great deal about medieval life and culture. They show, as do so many other surnames, that ordinary medieval people regularly use metaphors to understand, explain and comment on the everyday world in a sense that is quite foreign to us today. Leaving aside the ironic Popes and Kings, most symbolic surnames reflect an acute observation of wild creatures, especially birds. People know their habits well, giving us the vigilant crane and the stupid coot, the warlike wren and the unlucky or chattering jay. Colour is important; black and white are fundamentally symbolic. Observation of nature is matched by a keenness of eye for the habits of people.

Many symbols stand in for the very human attributes and Christian thinking picked up in the non-symbolic names, such as strength, speed and moral failings but pack a heftier punch: Lamb versus Meek, Hogg versus Greed, Pope rather than Proud. But some of these nicknames catch the echo of cultures from quite another and more ancient world. Rather than the intimate, gossipy village of the ordinary nickname, it can be a frightening, ruthless place inhabited by the all-powerful and evil symbols that can be the only explanation of an amoral and terrifying reality. It is not surprising that these nicknames speak to people in the fourteenth century, who experience disastrous natural crises, such as famine and plague, and know a world where victim and hunter live in uneasy balance and where survival for one must mean death for the other. So when the name of Hawke, Kite, Keat or Wolf is applied to a neighbour, the threatening force of the symbol for its victim could carry over, and may mean not that the person named is strong and brave, which are human attributes, but that he is potentially as savage and ruthless as the symbol in the world of the symbol. And in the same way as in Norse and Celtic tradition heroes often changed into the animals they pursued, Hawkes and so on could be named to tap into their powers or to propitiate the threat they pose. Medieval carvings of demons in churches are thought to be there to frighten or to propitiate, to prevent other demons entering, or to prevent their doing evil. These are not the straightforward Strongs or Hardmans of the previous chapter; they warn of a different world of long association with supernatural forces and incorporate the immediate threat of an unrelenting nature.

Yet dominating much of this symbolism are strong visual images that we can still respond to; irrespective of other meanings Bull might have, pent force would be one. Almost all of these symbols, ravens, cranes, eagles, work as physical models, and the surname could simply record what people look or even sound like.

Symbolic names can also be jokes. Some are obvious even today. Research and medieval art record that fourteenth-century people regularly use opposites to get a laugh and just as the non-symbolic Little can mean big, Hart could be slow. Symbols can also stand in for social satire. A serf called Pope and a ploughman called Lord are jokes about pretentiousness and vanity. Fox is cunning; medieval church art uses the animal as a symbol of clerics. For foxes preaching to somnolent geese read cunning priest addressing his trusting congregation unaware of the threat he poses. The humour also helps people come to terms with those richer and more powerful than themselves. But some is dark. In contemporary folk tales stupidity is often rewarded with death, so calling a neighbour Coot could be a warning of a nasty end.

Some of these names may also carry the seeds of later events, presaging the early demise of the feudal system. Bishop or King carry scorn for their institutions as well as comment on the person named. The popularity of these ironic names document the scorn is widespread. After mid-century French raids on the undefended south coast and French and Spanish attacks on merchant shipping make people distrust the government and encourage scorn for its incompetence and corruption, exacerbated by its increasing demand for taxes. The Peasants' Revolt is ignited by a poll tax.

During the revolt, Essex men demand of the young Richard II

the heads of Archbishop Simon Sudbury, chancellor, as well as the treasurer, Sir Robert Hales; both are murdered. People hate the church as much as the secular elite. *Piers Plowman* with its scorching criticism of ecclesiastics is the most popular poem of its day. The church holds about a third of all land in England in the fourteenth century and its prelates consort with nobles, but it is more than envy. These are the days when its worldliness is breeding the opposition of Wyclif's anti-clericalism and that of his followers, the Lollards, that are to lead to the 1401 Act on the burning of heretics and other repressive and extreme reactions. In 1378, as surnames are becoming established, the church is in ferment with two rival popes, England supporting the one in Rome versus the Pope at Avignon.

The derivations of these names confirm findings for other groups, that the English turn almost exclusively to English words when it comes to creating names recording nature. And the roots of the ironic names of status show, interestingly enough, that the names reflecting the basic hierarchies of church and state are also Old English, so existed in England before the Conquest and survived it. The Normans expanded the rungs below the king with Duke and Baron. But the top and middle levels of the church system are already there, the Anglo-Saxon church well integrated with the continental church. This is surprising, given the French roots of other names to do with religion.

Interpretation

Interpreting these names from a distance of some 600 years is hard. We are so far from the natural world that was the source of much of the symbolism and so far from the culture and traditions that supplied the rest, that we sometimes cannot even guess at the meanings beyond the visual – Bunting, Starling, Veale and most of the names for fish, for example. But with other names, contemporary literary, artistic and folk records can help. These include, notably, the Bible, the Anglo-Saxon epic poem *Beowulf*, *Piers Plowman* by William Langland, writing by Geoffrey Chaucer, as well as Norse, Celtic and Christian oral traditions. Some of these traditions, as we know, are recorded and current in the twelfth and thirteenth centuries.

Medieval church art is a good test for what is generally known about Christian and folk symbolism because it is aimed at the illiterate. Religious themes in stained glass and on walls of churches and chapels are numerous and widespread, regularly using symbols to comment and instruct. Folk carving in less prominent places shows that most people know about the meaning of the symbols used in folk history: apes and hogs representing lust and the fox cunning. Aesop's fables are another source of information; these are sufficiently well known to appear at the base of the eleventh-century Bayeux tapestry.[1]

One cannot know whether those choosing names of symbols from pre-Conquest myth grasp their full connotations. From the derivations of our surnames we know that Old Norse and Celtic words are part of the spoken language in the fourteenth century. And the old cultures must, at least to some extent, have persisted with the language. The Viking invasions took place in the ninth and tenth centuries so medieval memories of Norse culture would be equivalent to us remembering through oral history what Henry III and Shakespeare were all about. Ordinary people in the Middle Ages would have better memories over that length of time because oral history is intrinsic to society and traditional ways are more valued.

Before getting into the detail, a word about classification. Many of these symbolic nicknames could be classified differently. The bird or animal names could mean a keeper or seller of them. Hawk could mean a powerful, ruthless person, or a hawker. Pie could mean someone as vain as a magpie, or a seller of pies. Robin could be a bird here or a diminutive of Robert (see Chapter 8). And many of these names have several meanings: Drake could be a dragon, a standard-bearer or a male duck; Brock a badger or someone living near a brook; Chubb, someone lazy or foolish, the fish or a fisherman.

These symbolic nicknames provide an insight into the culture of ordinary medieval people. They record a love of ambiguity. Not only do many names have several meanings but the symbols they use can be contradictory. Strong visual images often hide unexpected dramas and fear of ferocious animals and raptors that roam an unpredictable and terrifying world. Simultaneously, names can invoke protection; Doves and Lambs, Swans and Harts inhabit a white and essentially Christian world of ideal peace and purity. These names also describe a morality that can be quite foreign where the stupid may not survive, gossipers are in league with the devil and gluttony and vanity are serious sins. Cheek by jowl are direct and perceptive names that comment on those around – obstinate Cardons, or thistles, and smelly Brocks, or badgers, chattering Jays, lecherous Sparrows and stupidly pompous Popes and Bishops. Medieval people have a keen eye for friends and neighbours who pretend to live good lives, but descend into pettiness, excess and delusions of grandeur.

Pride in Physical Prowess

Vigilance, speed and strength are all important in medieval life, as the non-symbolic nicknames show. But symbolic names add colour, image and dimension. The starting point is the visual impact, the watchful Cock and soaring Eagle, that leads into a world of abstract qualities – the spirit with the flight of birds – tied into legends from a deep inherited culture.

A cockerel today behaves as he did 600 years ago, so the vigilance and liveliness represented in our Cocks and related surnames are immediately accessible to us. The behaviour can be readily used as a metaphor. In Christian tradition cocks greet the dawn, chasing away the darkness of evil and the Irish believe a crowing cock can stop the devil coming into a house. In Norse legends, the cocks are the watchmen. At the battle of Ragnarok when the world ends, three cocks crow to presage doom, one in the gallows' wood, one at Valholl (Valhalla), where the dead warriors wait, and one in the underworld of the dead.[2] But there is a darker side. In Celtic/Irish tradition, Cock belongs to the underworld. For Christians, Cranes and Herons are also vigilant. Hawkey is keen-eyed, a useful trait when food often has to be hunted down.

Like vigilance, speed is important; footslogging a fact of life. Hawk, Swift, Buck, Hare and Hart are speedy and the names are complimentary. The Bible has the lame man leaping as an hart (Isaiah 35.6). In Graeco-Roman tradition, the hawk is the messenger of Apollo, the epitome of speed and Bird is the messenger of the gods for the Irish Celts. Hare has nicely complex connections; it is thought timid as well as speedy. Perhaps it records those who are always running away.

Bull, Bullock, Turnbull, Steer, Lyon and all the raptors, Eagle, Hawk, Keat with its variant Kite and synonym Puttock record a solid interest in power. All start from impressive visuals.

Both Celts and Christians see the bull as powerful, but the Celts see the power as divine, while the Christians see brute force. For the Druids, the bull is the life-giving sun (the cow is the earth). Lions are a traditional symbol of power or its human interpretation courage, carried on many heraldic shields and endowed with a magnificent appearance; the carver of a glorious maned lion stretched along the end of the Dean's bench in Ripon Cathedral has made the most of it. Lyon and Lyons are popular nicknames. Christian tradition typically uses the power of the lion for good – Christ as the lion of Judah, majestic and royal. But Lyons are feared as the kings of the beasts in Aesop, who has many stories of them terrifying and often devouring weaker animals. Yet they carry nobility too, sparing the slave that took the thorn from the paw and the mouse that later freed a lion from a trap.

Eagle, Hawk with all its variants, Kites and Puttocks are powerful and rapacious. Hawks are widespread; most medieval nobles have hawkers, a status symbol, when they go hunting and the behaviour of hawks is well known. The winged eagle, the symbol of St John, is a useful image, used on lecterns to carry the Bible, outspread wings symbolizing the strength of the missionary reach of Christianity.

Good and Evil

Symbols create a world of often battling contrasts. Their sources, Christian tradition and pagan mythology, use as a vehicle animals and birds from an unpredictable and amoral nature. Some matches with observed nature apply in all traditions: the spirit with the flight of birds, solitariness with stags and crows and resurrection with the annual renewal of the peacock's feathers. Traditions also agree on colour; ideals white and evil black, the purity of the white lily in contrast to the evil of the raven or the crow. But many symbols of power, such as predators like the Lion and the Eagle can be a force for the victory of good, or the opposite.

The Christian Tradition

The Christian Dove, Doe, Lamb, Lilly and its variants, and Calf and the Celtic Hart and Swan stand for purity, peace and innocence. Nunn can mean meekness in a man, and May or Mey young innocence.

Doves are core to Christian traditions; they represent the Holy Spirit, a dove with an olive branch means peace and one with a palm is victory over death. Lambs – 'Behold the lamb of God, which taketh away the sins of the world,' according to John the Baptist (John 1.29) – are gentleness, as are Does; Langland's Soul intones in *Piers Plowman* that a generous gentleness of spirit should prevail among Christian people.[3] Lambs also represent the crucifixion, suffering and triumph. The lily is sacred to the Virgin: its stalk, her holy mind; its drooping leaves, her humility; its scent, her divinity; and the whiteness, her purity. In *The Canterbury Tales*, the Prioress refers to the Virgin Mary as 'The white lilye-flour/which that thee bar...'. The Hart, for Christians, is religious aspiration, trampling the servant of evil, and Langland, in *Piers Plowman*, says the calf stands for purity of life in those who administer God's laws.[4] In Celtic/Irish tradition, Hart is purity and Wren sacred.

Most of these names may have other meanings. Dove is sometimes a pet-form of David; Lamb could be from a personal name Lambert; Lilly could be a diminutive of Elizabeth; and Swan could also be a herdsman or a peasant or swain. Hart, instead of meaning religious aspiration, could signify speed.

Quietness and solitude are prized in the Christian tradition, and the names Lion, Crowe and Corbett, Stag and Hart all symbolize this. Ravens can also symbolize solitude and hermits. These symbols match observed nature.

The prizes of the pious, immortality and resurrection, are embodied in Peacock, Eagle, Lamb, even Lion and Swallow. Life after death is essential to Christian tradition, but is also part of pre-Christian culture. Norse gods are fated eventually to be destroyed by their enemies, the demons and the giants, but out of the wreckage of Ragnarok, when fire destroys the universe, a new cosmos emerges. Lions can also stand for resurrection, since their cubs were said to be born dead and be brought alive by their sire. Peacock and its variants mean, in addition to its other more human qualities, resurrection because the peacock renews its feathers and the hundred eyes on its tail mean the all-seeing church. The symbol only works for Swallows in the west where they resurrect the new year by bringing in the spring.

Many birds symbolize ascending spirits in a direct extrapolation of the image of flight. The group includes Bird itself, Eagle and Eagles, Hawk and Wren. In Christian tradition, Birds are winged souls and spiritual. In Celtic myth, they are the souls of the just,[5] and flights of birds are used by the Druids in prophesies. A flight of birds is said to have guided the Gauls invading Illyrium.[6]

Christians and the Norse can take the power of the Eagle and make a warrior for good. For Christians, the Eagle represents victory over sin; when it dives and then climbs it is Christ rescuing souls from the sea of sin and taking them up to heaven. For the Norse, it can fight the evil serpent in Yggdrasil, the Tree of Life.

Evil

Surnames with Norse connotations have none of the Christian attitudes towards gentleness and suffering. In their sagas, gods and giants battle over the control of the world, the emphasis on strife, heroic feats and cunning. Names carry echoes of the culture in the symbols of cruelty and evil rather than piety and humility. Several common symbolic names describe malevolence and evil. These include all the wolves – Wolf and the Anglo-French Love, Lovell and Lowell and Old French Lovett and Lowe and their variants (from *loup*, or *louve*) – Raven with its French translations Corbett and Corbin and Hawke. But there is ambiguity. In Norse tradition, gods are as unpredictable as nature. Odin, the king of the gods, could be kind and generous or violent and brutal, hunting down and killing his favourites. For the Norse, Eagle can be good or malevolent. And Bird, Wren, Drake and Orme (or serpent) are malevolent in one tradition and not in another.

Transposed onto this view is the Christian interpretation of evil. Medieval people see evil and devils everywhere in nature. Many surnames carry the connotation, from the dragons, Drake, Griffin and Orme and the black Raven, Crow and Pye to Wolf, Fox and even Hogg. For Christians, even the noble Lion can be evil; when Christians are delivered from the lion's mouth, the animal symbolizes the Devil.

There are memorable records of evil. St Edmund Rich as a young man sees at sunset a flight of black crows, which he recognizes as devils come to fetch the soul of a local usurer at Abingdon (did St Edmund owe him money?), while St Dominic recognizes the Devil in a sparrow.[7] Physical representations of demons, often with people's legs sticking out of their mouths, are liberally applied to carvings, monuments, stained glass and frescoed walls in churches. The church ensures that people have demonic images around them all the time.

Wolves and Ravens

Wolves symbolize evil and menace in all traditions. In early myths, the wolf roams at dark and is a familiar of primitive gods of the night, the time of chaos, death and madness. For Celts, the wolf swallows the sun – the father of the sky – at night, calling up the image of the baying wolf outlined against the rising moon. In Norse legend, wolves are the epitome of death and destruction. The most vicious wolf, Fenrir, swallows the sun and precipitates the final battle between the gods and the giants that destroys the universe. In other legends, two wolves, Skoll (repulsion) and Hati (hatred), chase the sun, the symbol of good, day in and day out; when they catch it, eternal darkness signals the end of the world.

Wolves have deep roots in Christian tradition, where they denote cruelty as well as evil, the Devil, craftiness and even, as the killer of the Christian flock, heresy. Even in Aesop's tales, the wolf threatens life and is rarely bested.

Celts, the Norse and Christians agree over Raven and its French translations Corbett and Corbin. Christians see the raven as the Devil and a symbol of sin, its colour making it a natural opposite to the dove. Celts see all-black ravens as a bird of ill omen (although a white feather makes it into one of good luck). The Raven of War symbolizes panic, evil and malevolence. Celts also associate ravens with prophecy; they are 'talking birds'. A similar idea underlies their roles in Norse myth, where they are associated with Odin. Two ravens, Huginn and Muninn, sit on his shoulders and fly over the world every day, representing his intellect, thought, and memory and reporting back to him on what they have seen.[8] Our saying 'A little bird told me' could revive this legend. But as the birds of death, they feed on the corpses of his battlefields. Evil and intellect are twins. For both Celts and the Norse, colour is an important attribute of ravens. Black is evil. The crows that come after that usurer of Abingdon are black.

Both the power and magic of birds can be evil as well as good. In Norse legend, the eagle is both to be propitiated and feared. It can be wisdom. Odin, the king of the gods, changes into an eagle to get the mead of poetry. But at Ragnarok, the end of the world, the rusty yellow eagle shrieking at the prospect of feasting on the dead is evil. Celts believe that birds as well as the sacred wren also represent magic powers and malevolence. Other traditions see the wren either as a little king, or as a witch. It was thought unlucky to kill one, but in England and France the tiny bird is hunted at Christmas time and taken in procession to the churchyard where it is buried to symbolize the death of the old year.

Dragons

Drake, from *draca*, in Old English meaning winged serpent or dragon, and Griffin (otherwise short for the Welsh Griffith), a mythical beast with the head and talons of an eagle and the body of a lion, are evil for the Norse and Christians. But for the Celts, the dragon is a symbol of royalty, a royal propitiation of the king of the underworld. In a similar contrast, Orme, the serpent abhorred by the Norse and Christians, is associated with healing and the god of fertility for the Celts.

The dragon, our Drakes and Griffins, is, in the Christian tradition, among the most evil. *Beowulf's* Grendel is the icon:

In off the moors, down through the mist bands
God-cursed Grendel came greedily loping.
The bane of the race of men roamed forth
Hunting for a prey ...[9]

The connotation is widely understood in medieval times when the cult of St Mark is widespread and he is frequently shown overcoming Satan in the form of a dragon. 'The great dragon was cast out, that old serpent, called the Devil, and Satan, which deceiveth the whole world' (Revelations 12.9). And the Prioress in *The Canterbury Tales* refers to 'Our firste foo, the serpent Sathanas'. But he is clever: 'Now the serpent was more subtile than any beast of the field' (Genesis 3:1). The Norse also see the serpent as evil. The serpent Jormungand coiled around the earth is the most formidable of the enemies of the god Thor, and a serpent, Niohogg, gnaws at the base of the tree of life before the final battle in which the universe is destroyed.[10]

Medieval church art is festooned with dragons and griffins. In a misericord in the south stalls of Ripon Cathedral choir, there is a beautifully carved griffin gnawing away at a detached human leg.

The Sinners

The Greedy, Angry and Gossipy

There is a clutch of names that match observed nature with the sinners.

The greedy and the lustful appear in Hogg, Hare, Gudgeon (a freshwater fish used for bait), Bevin (from the Old French *boi vin*, or drink wine), Kite again, Sparrow, Pinnock (a hedge sparrow) and Pye. Most of these have other meanings.

Gluttony in the Middle Ages usually means excessive drinking rather than overeating. 'Boozing gluttons ...' Langland calls them 'whose god is in their belly'. Greed devours the man; Langland's Greed has thick lips, inflamed eyes, cheeks that flap like a leather purse, a grease-covered beard and a hat crawling with lice. Langland is quite clear about where he stands on lust. In a wonderful metaphor he sees the flesh as a fierce wind blowing 'such violent gusts of sensual desire as to rouse men to look at sights that lead to folly'.[11] His target is usually the church; *Piers Plowman* is spattered with over-eating and bibulous priests who dread dying in mortal sin, but cannot help themselves.

Hawks also stand for rapacity and greed for material things, a popular target for scorn; *Piers Plowman* humanizes and pastes the symbol into a morality tale. Langland's protagonist, Haukin, symbolizes man, a clothes-horse for all the sins that man could pursue. He wears a coat of Christian faith, but 'Here it was stained with pride and there with angry, violent words – scolding, mocking and unreasonable behaviour' and his prime focus is on ways of getting rich.[12]

Anger is a deadly sin. One example identifies the wolf with anger. Robert, Earl of Yvery, is nicknamed Lupus in the eleventh century, because of his violent temper.[13] By extension, many of the names meaning savage or fierce might also refer to people with nasty tempers – Love, Lovell, Lowe, Grime, Cruise and Hawk.

Hoggs are a wonderful image of gluttony; large, pink, tight-skinned, snouts enormous, tiny eyes, both snouts and trotters in the trough. In a medieval record, the aptly named John Hogyn shocks some Hampshire magistrates by refusing to work and by sleeping all day, spending his nights at the tavern.[14] Pigs are also frequent symbols of lust in medieval church art, often playing music, another symbol of lechery. On a misericord in Henry VII's chapel in Westminster Abbey, a pig playing the flute watches an old man, his arm around a woman in a low dress, reaching into his purse to pay her as she holds out her hand.[15] Chaucer uses a surprising symbol for lechery, a sparrow; his Summoner 'was lecherous, as a sparwe'.[16]

Gossiping is a sin. Gossipers are strongly identified with raucous birds; the wonderful Old Norse Screech, Pies and Pyes from the magpie, the Cornells from the French *corneille*, crow, and the Jays. One of the several meanings of the Keys and Kays is chatterer, from the Old Norse *kei*, or jackdaw. The Daws, from the Old English for jackdaw, also belong here (although the name can also be a pet form of David).

These are not 'a-nice-cup-of-tea-and-a-chat' names. Gossiping leads to bitterness and conflict. Haukin, in *Piers Plowman*, engages in insults and lies that turn friends into enemies. Gossip is mischief and the sound unattractive. Of the rich man calling out to Christ in *Piers Plowman*, Langland says 'I believe that his voice will sound in our Saviour's ear as raucous as the chattering of a magpie.'[17] A misericord in Ely Cathedral shows two gossiping women, one with a book and the second a rosary, both being embraced by the Devil.[18]

The Vain

Pies, Peacocks and Daws (also thieves) are vain. Christians dislike magpies as representing vanity, dissipation and the Devil, probably because vanity leads to the other two. A painting of Phillip II of Spain in a manuscript now in Cambridge University Library shows him as a gorgeous peacock, the lands he claimed listed on the tips of his outspread tail feathers, standing atop his family's emblem, the pomegranate, a big bite taken out of it.[19] People will have readily understood this metaphor for his vanity, greed and destructiveness.

Vanity, connected with pride, is one of the main targets of medieval morality tales. Langland fears for nobles who have spent their lives listening to flatterers when the moment of their death approaches.[20] The symbols of status discussed below have a lot to do with vanity. In *Beowulf* a king:

> ... entrusted with ancient treasures ...
> His vanity swelled him so vile and rank
> That he could hear no voices but his own. He deserved
> To suffer and die.[21]

But Aesop has fun with vanity – the crane who can soar to the clouds while the fine peacock has to sit on the ground, and the jackdaw who dons everyone else's feathers only to have them stripped off again. While the moralists fulminated, everyone else laughed.

People Like Us

Metaphors connecting observed nature and peoples' behaviour create infinite possibilities. The clever and cunning or stupid can be Smart or Dullard. But how much more evocative are the cunning Fox or Tod, its mostly northern equivalent, and the more unexpected stupid Woodcocks, lusty Sparrows and fertile Hares. Finches are silly, perhaps because the bird is overcurious and has a short sharp squeak.

The Clever and the Simple

Foxes in folk tales are clever. Christians liken them to the Devil; clever for evil purposes, cunning, deceptive, fraudulent. Then they also imply sleek speed, nimbleness and agility. Like wolves, they travel by night, and the Scandinavians call the *aurora borealis* the light of the fox.

Popular culture seems to like the cleverness. In Aesop's fables, the fox gets the better of the lion and the bear, the crow and the goat. In The Nun's Priest's Tale in *The Canterbury Tales*, the fox neatly bests the pretentious, vain and stupid Cock by well-judged flattery and determination to get him in the end. In much church art, Foxes stand in for rapacious priests. The Partridge is cunning too, but is deceitful and a thief to the bargain in Christian tradition (although, oddly, it could also represent the truth of Christ). In Aesop's tale about the fowler, the partridge and the cock, the partridge's wit saves its life. For once, the symbol does not match visual reality. The calculated intelligence of the partridge seems inconsistent with its clumsy lopsided flight and dumpy appearance.

Arm-in-arm with the cunning go the simpletons – Finch, Chubb, Gordon, Coot, and Woodcock. (The French translation of Finch, Pinsent, means gay, but not foolish; perhaps that's just what the surviving records show.) Finch calls up the picture of a small curious bird, with a stupid call and a habit of staying too close to danger. But ambiguity comes in again; finches are also admired; they are supposed to eat thorns, including the thorns on Christ's crown. There are many medieval carvings of Jesus holding a finch and a crown of thorns. Aesop, whose bread-and-butter is the idiot animal, from donkeys and crows to lambs, allows a lion to flatter even a bull into removing his horns so the lion can devour him more easily. But in another fable the bull sensibly walks away from the lion's trap; Aesop is more interested in the morals of his stories than the characters. Parrots and Jays are mimics – the jay, says the Summoner in *The Canterbury Tales*, can shout 'Walter' as well as the pope – and stupid too.

The price of stupidity can be high. In Aesop the bull gets eaten by the lion, and the frogs by their king, the stork. In the Nun's Priest's Tale in *The Canterbury Tales*, the stupid and vain cock who believes the fox when he says he comes 'only for to herkne how that ye singe' and is 'ravisshed with his flaterye' meets a grisly end.[22] There is humour in these episodes where the fox's victims may die because of their stupidity, but it is black. Yet the camel who tries to dance like the monkey only gets chased away with ridicule. Laughter is punishment enough for just being pretentious, but death is nature's way of rewarding the truly dim. All the surnames meaning stupid could have been given with humour, or as a warning of a bad end.

Everyday Habits

Then comes a quiverful of little traits based on intimate observation that we can all relate to. The Nightingale sings sweetly. The Jays and the Pinsents are gay, while the Wildgoose, a lovely poetic image, is shy and retiring. (The name is concentrated in Derbyshire, particularly Bakewell.)[23] The obstinate are captured in Brock, or badger, and the difficult in Bramble and Cardon or

Carden, a thistle, from the French *chardon*. We still call people prickly.

All these have wonderfully appropriate matches in nature. Brambles in Aesop's fables are impudent, prickly, catch at what they've lost instead of what they lack, but because they are insignificant, they survive the logger's axe. In European traditions, the badger is clumsy but is also a weather prophet, so he has his uses as well. Then the Brock and Hogg are smelly; people notice when you have not washed. The Bees are probably busy, but in Celtic tradition they are popular because they come from Paradise and have secret wisdom. Aesop echoes this connection with the gods when his queen bee from Hymmetus takes honey to Olympus. But their stings are evil.

Several names symbolize fertility, the Hare again in the Christian tradition and the Hogg and Raven in the Celtic. These symbols must have been based on observation. Fertility inside marriage is approved of by the medieval church, as a constraint on lust outside it, but even so the parsons try to stop married couples having intercourse too much, banning it on holy days and especially in the run-up to Easter.

The Visual Image

All the nicknames that could draw on medieval traditions might also simply record straightforward visual images. Cocks, rather than vigilant, might be strutting young lads. The Foxes of the *aurora borealis* could just mean people with red hair. As well as stupid, the Chubbs and Spratts are short and the Chubbs dumpy, too, giving us our 'chubby'. Crane and Heron and Pyne could be tall or long-legged and the Sparrows could just be small and insignificant rather than evil or lecherous. Although St Dominic sees the devil in one, for Bede the insignificance of the sparrow becomes a haunting metaphor for human life, when he quotes a Northumbrian noble comparing life to the flight of a sparrow through the king's hall 'coming in from the darkness and returning to it'.[24] Ralph Pynnock is a small tenant farmer in early thirteenth-century Devon; his name, meaning a hedge sparrow, might be telling us he is physically small, or that his land is small beer next to that of his neighbours, or might say his little plot is known for its sparrows.[25] Similarly the Ravens and the Crows, malevolent or not, could just be black-haired and Snow, Winter, Hoare and Frost white-haired.

As for the immortal Peacock and its variants, in at least one contemporary document the extravagant bird simply means rich. In *Piers Plowman*, Langland refers to the peacock and the peahen as symbols of 'rich men in their pride' who cannot rise up in the air because of their trailing tails.[26] Fine feathers impede the good life.

For some symbolical nicknames we only know the visual image. Oliphants, based on the Middle English word, are nicknames for someone who is large and ungainly. They could also be dealers in ivory or ivory horns, and in the *Chanson de Roland*, the horn that Roland blows to call Charlemagne back to save the day against the Saracens is called his Olifant. Scarfe is a cormorant, from the Old Norse, so is long-necked. Then we have the little people: the Flays, or fleas, who leap about; the Lobbs, or spiders, who are all arms and legs (but who might also come from a place); and the Wiggs, or beetles (or makers of fashionable beads or wigs), who have long bodies, short legs, and are dark and unattractive. Although Aesop has a nice story in which the beetle, too small to be noticed, gets the better of the eagle.

There are two wonderful metaphorical names describing the skin: Greeley, which means pockmarked, comes from the Old French word meaning hail, and gives us the vivid picture of a pitted complexion. Then some Mackerells and variants, also French, describe legs with skin scorched red by fire (other meanings include fishermen and bawd). These images could not be given in a single unsymbolic word.

So the physical image may predominate in the naming process, particularly for the names recording creatures with striking looks or habits. When all is said and done, whatever their spiritual qualities, the 'smale fowles maken melodye'.[27] Irrespective of how aware people are of their inherited cultural traditions, they know the bull out there on the meadow is something to be reckoned with, and when someone close to them is called Bull, the name evokes the massive shape, the small eye, the brooding presence and the potential for colossal impact.

The Jokes

Jokes are a leitmotiv running through all these names. Even where the symbol is relevant for understanding the name, irony could creep in. Some images are just funny, like calling someone Bramble or Cardon (thistle). Then humour could arise from a surname meaning the opposite to what the named person is like, Crane describing someone short, for example, or Hart and Hare slow. In Wells Cathedral, three unnecessary ribs in the processional way are being eaten away by a dragon carved at where they stop. So Dragon and Griffin might not be symbols of evil but of whatever needs doing – dragons as servants.[28] Then Nunn cries out for being a joke name for some prissy or womanizing man. Humour could come from bringing high-sounding names down to earth; Marlowe, in the *Jew of Malta* in the sixteenth century says: 'Now I will show myself to have more of the serpent than the dove; that is, more knave than fool.' Down at the village pump, Sunday sermons are given a spin. A visual cameo of medieval irony toward grand symbols is a carving of a group of lions clinging for dear life to a ledge high up on the chapter house roof of York Minster.[29] Lyon, after all, might just be a coward.

Mockery

The possibility of joke names leads directly to the names of many clergymen and aristocrats that are given in mockery. Priests come in for a lot of vilification in medieval literature. Many will have lived exemplary lives but enough will not for Langland to cry that greed has a stranglehold on clerics and priests; 'The dove they feed is called Greed' and 'They gobble up their "charity", then fight and squabble for more'.[30] Our churches are full of satirical carvings of monkeys as monks, foxes in priests' robes preaching to geese and apes as bishops. The satire here uses symbolism as a joke to give a serious message: monks are hypocrites, the priests are after your soul, you are a fool and the bishop's an ape, a frequent symbol of lust in medieval art. If symbols are used as a vehicle for irony and comment in art, it is reasonable to suppose they are used in the same way in naming, drawing on the same rich sources of observation of nature and the foibles of man, wit and contemporary fables.

Medieval England is a secular and an ecclesiastical nation, ruled by a king in London and a pope in Rome. Both have courts and laws and both raise taxes. These names say as much about how the elite are viewed as those named. Most people will have known about their kings from the songs of minstrels and reports of battles. More tellingly, they blame both the aristocracy and the church for the failing war that exposes undefended coasts and merchant shipping and for the increasing demands for taxation and for men to go to war from what they see as an inept, corrupt and extravagant government. Both the secular and the church elite are targeted during the Peasants' Revolt of 1381.

Peoples' derision for church and state are in the names they take. Etymologists have found the following nicknames are often used in scorn. These include names like Pope, Bishop, Archdeacon and Deacon, Dean and Parson (or Persoun as he was called in some records), Vicar and Priest. Then for the monastic orders we have Abbot, Prior, Monk, Nunn and Frear and its variants. Churchmen, particularly the local ones, are a favourite target for mockery. Secular targets include King, Prince, Duke (then usually a royal), Earl, Baron and Knight, plus the generic Lord.[31] Noble, brought by the French, seems not to have been a title then, but a nickname for the well-known or noble, although it can be ironic. There are many of these names around today. While we struggle to find a few Pies, Cranes and Peacocks, King is in the top five most popular nicknames, while Knight, Earl, Bishop, Abbot and Pope are not far behind.

There are other possibilities. These names might refer instead to a servant of the relevant person. Less likely, a few could be genuinely inherited from clerics careless of their reputations. Churchmen have vowed to be celibate, but many records of clergy at all levels as well as contemporary literature prove they are not.

Countless cases in the diocesan courts deal with concubines and the fines convicted clergy have to pay for having them. Their children might either have their father's title as a name, a name like Parsons, recording that they live at their father's house, or the name of the mother. The latter is the case with Robert Busse (also called Robert Bonus), the controversial Abbot of Tavistock in the early fourteenth century. He is the son of a priest, Master Robert de Yoldelond, but takes the name of his mother, Joan Busse.[32]

A few of these could be 'pageant' names, names for roles in pageants acted on holy days and feast days. King could come from the King of the May for example (no Queen of the May in those days). The earliest reference to May Day customs is 1240 in Lincoln.[33] Pope, Bishop and Knight are names from other pageants or burlesques. Bishop could also be given to the boy Bishop in the rather charming custom of role reversal in which a boy, usually a chorister at the cathedral, can be elected each year to act as bishop between St Nicholas's Day and Holy Innocent's Day (6 and 28 December).[34] Some of these actors and boy bishops will be the ancestors of our Bishops, Kings, Knights and Popes.

And for the rest, there is a standard: a stereotype that is monstrously exaggerated is meant to be laughed at. Calling a ploughman or a small trader a Bishop or a Baron meets the standard.

The humour is two-edged, saying something about the person named as well as what ordinary people think about the institution. The named are being mocked for pretending to be less worldly than they are. The same inspiration underlies Aesop's stories about little vain people who pretend to more importance – the ass who eats the grasshopper's food to sing like him, the bullfrog who puffs himself up to be as big as the bull and bursts, and the jackdaw who paints himself white because he envies the pigeons and ends up an outcast.

As for the symbols of church and state, there seems to have been a fairly common recognition of what these clerics and lords stand for. Contemporary literature and art tell us that the names of the clerics are likely to stand for hypocrisy, pretence of piety, greed for money and drink and lust. Those of the aristocracy are thought to stand for overweening arrogance, pride and vanity.

The Church

The church owns some 33 per cent of English land. Baptism and church attendance are compulsory; refusing to pay tithes to the priest warrants excommunication. However, the substance of religion is obscure to most people. Texts are in Latin, few can read them and the word of God is anyway read silently in church. Just when surnames are stabilizing, John Wyclif, and his followers, the Lollards, are to lead a popular movement demanding forms of worship that bypass much of the clergy. Wyclif's translations of the Bible into English are pronounced heresies by the Archbishop of Canterbury (in 1382). The ideas divide the secular elite, but are enough of a threat to lead England, up until then free from the worse forms of religious extremism prevalent in continental Europe, to pass the Act of *Haeretico Comburendo*, or the burning of heretics, in 1401. The first victim is burnt that year.

In medieval church art, often in out-of-the-way places, carvers record the views of ordinary people. A misericord in Wells Cathedral carved around the 1330s has a fox preaching to four geese, the nearest already asleep and en route to being gobbled up. One in Ripon Cathedral takes the story one step further and shows the fox bearing away two geese for his dinner.[35] Our Foxes and Tods could be stand-ins for a crafty church, lulling its gullible parishioners doomed to have their souls devoured. Or they could be the Devil (perhaps Lollards), wresting the pious away from God. Either way, the congregation are the stupid geese and the fox the cunning and threatening church.

Ecclesiastical surnames go to the heart of one of the great hypocrisies of medieval times: the piety and asceticism of the church. Hypocrisy can be laughed at, but to a deeply religious people the hypocrisy of a church that is meant to lead and protect them from purgatory is also to be feared. The church is the butt of widespread criticism from the educated for its worldliness, hypocrisy and greed. Langland's *Piers Plowman* is bitterly anti-clerical and is immensely influential and popular. Symbolic surnames show that ordinary people hold the same views about the church as Langland.

Junior Clergy

The clergy closest to villagers are the local parson and unbeneficed priests who help in the parish, hold masses or are chaplains to important people. There are about 9,000 parishes in England in the Middle Ages and some 20,000 priests.[36] Clerics are meant to live according to the principles of celibacy, poverty and obedience. They collect tithes from their flock; in principle, divided equally among the rector, the church for its maintenance and the poor. They charge fees for indulgences, burials, and so on.

Priest or Prest, Parson, or, more usually, Parsons and Vikkers, the lowest rung of the church and closest to the ordinary man probably stand for the intimate failings you see in neighbours – someone who pretends to high principles and acts all too humanly. Most parishes are administered by peasant-born vicars standing in for rectors who are often gentry, unordained, appointed for life by patrons and usually absent.[37] Vicars are ill-educated, poor and too dependent on fees to be respected. People will know what their local clergy are like and how they live. Unsurprisingly, they watch what their parsons do with their tithes, and there are records that they know. By law, parish priests had to give a quarter or a third of their income to the poor, and the people of Bishop's Cleeve at the end of the fourteenth century, for instance, are aware that their rector only gives wheat worth 4–5 shillings a year out of an income of £100.[38]

In *Piers Plowman,* Langland shows a priest called Sloth, who prefers ballads to prayers, gossip and girls to visiting the sick and fasting, and hunting hares to chanting psalms. In the Prologue, worldly and greedy rectors and vicars complain to their bishops that their parishes are destitute, and ask permission to live in London and 'sing mass there to a more profitable tune – the sweet sound of silver'.[39] By contrast, of all the cheerful group setting off for Canterbury, Chaucer is most generous to the Parson. He is poor:

> But riche he was of holy thoght and werk,
> He was also a lerned man ...
> Benigne he was, and wonder diligent,
> And in adversitee ful pacient[40]

It is hard to know which of these views is the standard. A primary source of information on the medieval church is the record of bishops visiting their dioceses, but these only focus on failings. An episcopal visitation in 1397 in Hereford finds priests who are married, neglect their buildings as well as their services, and whose parishioners accuse them of usury, forgery, sorcery, visiting taverns, trading and embezzling. Marriage or concubinage of priests, incontinence, is a major issue in the archdeacons' courts. But it rarely seems to lead to removal, which will have irritated parishioners even further.

Given the poverty inherent in the position, the rise of a Thomas Vicars, who must have been only a few generations removed from the vicar's house, is impressive and tells a great deal about opportunities for social advancement. Either he or his recent ancestor has become a considerable farmer and horse breeder. On his two demesnes in 1451, he grazes almost 800 sheep, nearly 200 cattle and 92 horses.[41]

Most grand houses have their own chapels and Chappells and Chaplains, clergy without a parish, often peasant-born, who work for a fee. The Redvers documents record a chaplain, Osmund, in the early twelfth century.[42] These might also have been named in irony. Others will not.

Other names related to the church include the Bells, who could be the bell-ringers (as well as living near the church, or having Bell as a nickname for beautiful or indeed as a pet form of Isabella), and the Chantrells could be the ringers of the treble bell (or treble singers). And finally we have our Porteous, the writer of breviaries, or portable prayer books; not a common name, given for a function much less common than that of a clerk, but the surname ensures he is still with us.

Senior Clerics

Deacons, Cannons and Deans are all in a position to take bribes just as archdeacons are, and the first with the surname could have been a corrupt local official, perhaps a reeve or a beadle ready to forget about a minor infraction in return for a penny or two.

The archdeacon is powerful, well-positioned to be dishonest, and comes in for mighty criticism. Archdeacons are the bishop's deputies in the diocese. Generally well-born or able, they are often lawyers who have risen through the courts. They preside over the diocesan courts and handle the more difficult matrimonial and testamentary work and breaches of canon law, such as usury. They earn money via benefices, legal fees and fines. A contemporary writer, Giraldus Cambrensis writes:

> this office is so wholly given over to rapacity nowadays ... that the name of archdeacon rings in some men's ears with a sound as horrible as that of arch-devil; for the devil steals men's souls, but the archdeacon steals their money.[43]

Rural deans are elected by the clergy, and one is appointed per Hundred. They are unsalaried, but collect fines from dealing with matrimonial, testamentary and moral issues. Canons do parochial work where the church has been endowed to the monastery.

Bishops, responsible for exercising spiritual leadership, are often enormously wealthy and powerful; distant but easy and popular targets for the ordinary bloke's wit. Most are foreign and distinguished with either secular or clerical backgrounds. They could be of high birth or have risen through service to the king. There are fourteen in England under William I, sixteen under Henry II, and twenty-plus shortly before the Reformation. Most are able and energetic, good administrators, supporters of education and enthusiastic builders. In the fourteenth century, William of Wykeham, a civil servant made Bishop of Winchester, builds what becomes Winchester College and, in Oxford, New College. But many often live at court, when vicars general or archdeacons act for them in spiritual and administrative matters. If the archdeacon is away, the rural dean steps in.

Many stories focus on the ignorance, pride, greed, lust and ostentatious ways of bishops. The fact that many are foreign and most absent from their dioceses, allowing spiritual standards to lapse, cannot have helped. In 1318, the Benedictine chronicler Greystones writes of Louis, Bishop of Durham that he 'was illiterate ... not understanding Latin' and was unable to read his public profession at his consecration. 'When ... ordained and came to the words *"in aenigmate"* [through a glass darkly] he said "... by St Louis, that was no courteous man who wrote this word!"'[44] Today, you feel for him; then you would have thought that at least a bishop should know his Latin. Their life styles are criticized. Reason, in *Piers Plowman,* looks forward to the time when:

> Bishops, instead of buying fancy horses, will spend their cash on housing the homeless beggar, and sell off their hawks and hounds to provide for [the] religious who are vowed to poverty.[45]

Even medieval church art satirizes Bishops. Critical images are not in prominent places, often on misericords, high up on ceiling bosses or in the stained glass windows of side chapels, but that they are there at all is surprising – and intriguing. Apart from the carvings of foxes as bishops preaching to sleepy geese, the lust of bishops is a target. An early fourteenth-century book of hours in Trinity College, Cambridge, shows an ape, symbol of sensuality and unbridled passion, dressed as a bishop. And early fourteenth-century stained glass in the Lucy Chapel of Christ Church Cathedral in Oxford has a monster in a bishop's mitre, his dragon's tail ending in a women's fashionably done head turning to look at him.[46]

Despite the jokes, some bishops are energetic, competent, conscientious – and around. The reformer John de Grandisson of Exeter is one. Finberg writes of him:

> Throughout the forty-two years of his episcopate John de Grandisson devoted himself wholeheartedly to the care of his flock, preaching, writing, constantly visiting every corner of the diocese....[47]

The More or Less Reclusive Orders

Monks and Friars, Freres and their other variants are a frequent target of scorn, often for their failure to abide by their vows. Villagers would know their monks and friars. Monasteries are important sources of charity and other support and if the local monastery owns the church, parishioners will have even closer contact with them. Some orders, such as the Carthusians, are reclusive, but others go out into the world. Four main orders of friars, Franciscans, Dominicans, Carmelites and Austins, appear in England during the thirteenth century and almost every considerable town has at least one friary. Friars are committed to poverty, so have no property and cannot receive endowments, and live by begging, often competing with the parson for confession and burial fees.

Monks and friars in medieval literature are worldly hypocrites. Chaucer's monk, despite his vow of poverty, wears 'of gold y-wroght, a curious pin', and fur-trimmed sleeves, and 'was a lord ful fat ... His botes souple, his hors in greet estaat.'[48] A monk in *Piers Plowman* hunts like a noble with a pack of hounds.[49] But Chaucer's friar is worse: licentious, irresponsible in absolution, a drinker – 'he knew the tavernes wel in every toun' – and was a brilliant beggar.[50] Langland's friars, without a secure position in the ecclesiastical structure, adapt religion to demand – no fasting for his congregations.[51] These people vowed to chastity, poverty and obedience are licentious, wealthy and cunning enough to fashion the rules to their own ends. People will see that and predict their downfall. On a misericord in St George's Chapel at Windsor Castle, a demon pushes three monks along in a wheelbarrow steered by a fox into the mouth of hell.[52]

Abbots and Priors are often no better than the Bishops. John de Grandisson's registers of his 1328 visitations record that the Abbot of Tavistock, Robert Bonus, 'hath since his first arrival held himself aloof from all religion and all worship of God.'[53] (Tavistock had large and wealthy estates, covering eighteen square miles at Domesday.) Once elected, Bonus begins to remove the Abbey's treasure, in one episode taking away £1,200 in cash at night. He is later accused of embezzlement, assault, battery, manslaughter and sexual misconduct.[54] Among faults recorded by Grandisson in Abbot John de Courtenay in about 1348 are overspending, foolishness of dress and secular finery; allowing monks to break their rules; wasting money on a pack of hounds; and embezzlement. Priors could be the same. The prior of St James' Priory near

Exeter, William de Bittendene, in 1334, is 'oftentimes convicted of embezzlement and fornication.'[55]

Chaucer's serious social irony is directed at the hypocrisy of ecclesiastics. *The Canterbury Tales* includes a great deal of gentle humour about the failings of ordinary people – the cheating Miller and the Wife of Bath with her many husbands. But failing church-men come in for uncompromising satire. Whereas students who cuckold the Miller and the old Carpenter make for entertaining stories, the Pardoner, the Summoner, who travels the country summoning people to the ecclesiastical courts, and the Friar come in for bitter comment for *their* lechery. The difference is that *they* are churchmen who have taken holy vows.

In the Peasants' Revolt of 1381, abbeys at Lesnes in Kent, Bury in Suffolk, Waltham in Essex, and St Albans in Hertfordshire are attacked, as well as the archbishop's palace at Canterbury. At the same time, Archbishop Sudbury, the Prior of Cambridge, is exe-cuted by rebels. The church is seen as the enemy as much as the king and the nobles. When so many people begin to be called Pope and Bishop, Monk and Frere because of their ostentation, hypoc-risy and greed, it is a sign that, at the very least, criticism of the medieval church is widespread.

The Secular Elite

The surnames King, Prince, Duke, Earl, Baron, Knight and Lord would not be taken by people with these as titles who tend to have locational surnames after their properties. So these surnames are usually nicknames, recording qualities of the aristocracy seen from below. Medieval records have many Kings and Dukes assessed at the lowest tax rates who could not possibly be even fallen aristo-crats. The John Baronn assessed at 7d tax in Shrewsbury in 1306 on the basis of his movable property being one cow and three pigs,[56] and William le Duke assessed at the lowest rate in Lowton-with-Kenyon in Lancashire must have had the names as a joke about their behaviour and aspirations. (1d is a penny.)

The aristocracy would have been known as the local landown-ers, the charterers of the ships and the commissioners of the courts sitting on cases of national interest. Barons and Lords make no vows to be chaste, poor and obedient, but they can be mocked for pride, arrogance and ostentation, as well as incompetence, fraud and corruption, one of the principal causes of the Peasants' Revolt.

As for those named, the titles seem to have been given as jokes to the lowly but pretentious dressed in fine leggings, jackets and gowns which seem to have been seen increasingly after the Black Death. Some of these will have been our first Kings and Barons. The name of Robert le Kyng, who holds more than twice the land of most of his neighbours at the end of the thirteenth century in Bishop's Cleeve, Gloucestershire, tells you what he is like.[57] But the hapless Peter Kyng, servant to a London merchant and sent to Dartmouth to recover his master's stolen wine and oil, set upon by local shipmasters and robbed of everything he possessed, is hardly treated like a king.[58]

Knights might not always be named in irony. The dictionary defines the word as knight or footsoldier. Knights had to own land worth at least £40 in the fourteenth century, when Chaucer's pension in 1367 was worth a bit over £13. They tend to be the more wealthy minor landowners, and there are some 1,000 of them in England by the end of the thirteenth century.[59] They are the lowest rank of the aristocracy, the wealthiest overlapping with the lowest barons and the poorest with the squires and the gentry, so they may not have had the funds to be ostentatious. They serve on grand juries and go to war, providing their own armour and horse. This function of Knights makes them the heroes of contemporary literature and ballads in which they embody courtly love and prowess in battle, differentiating themselves from the richer merchants joining them as gentry. Chaucer's Knight is a fine man who:

> ... loved chivalrye,
> Trouthe and honour, fredom and curteisye,
> Ful worthy was he....[60]

Devon records have a bunch of pseudo-knights who must have joke names. Roger Knight, an unfree tenant in Werrington in about 1366 and the Knyghts who pay 12d tax in Paignton or

8d in Buckland Barton and Kingskerswell in 1332 when others are paying 10 shillings and more must have been named for their behaviour.[61] Langland calls two of his knights Sir Do-Well and Prince of this World, surrounded by lions and flatterers, so haughty and self-regarding.

Derivations

Two-thirds of these symbolic names are English. Only 15 per cent are Old French and the same share is either English/Old French.

With the symbolic nicknames from nature, when our ancestors want to find an equivalent to say something about their neighbours, they very rarely turn to French; the words they use are from their native tongue. This is consistent with other groups of names from the natural world that are almost all from English words. This must reflect their everyday language, but might also be a matter of choice where English/French translations exist.

The derivations of the ironic names of status show a chronology in the development of the hierarchies of church and state. Most of the ecclesiastical names, surprisingly, given the French roots of other names to do with the church, are either Old English or Old English/Old French. This goes for Pope, Bishop, Deacon, Abbott, Prior, Priest and Monk. The French bring Dean and the clergymen close to the people, Frere, Vicars (from Latin) and Parson. Dean and Parson seem to pass into Middle English after the Conquest. Similarly, King, Earl, Knight and Lord are only Old English, in England before the Normans, while the French bring Prince, Duke and Baron.

These results suggest that the basic hierarchy of church and state under Pope and Bishop, King and Earl were established in England before the Conquest and survived it. The Normans, by adding Duke and Baron to the secular elite essentially expand the rungs below the king. But the top and middle levels of the church system were already there, the English church already well integrated with the continental church.

There are still some Old Norse names: Duffin, a fish; Scarfe, a cormorant. Raven, so important in Norse legend, and Swann could be either Norse or English. Pike of the many meanings could be Norse, English or French.

The symbols used in these surnames are, apart from the Lions and mythical dragons, predominantly from the English country-side. When they come to describe those around them, medieval people turn to birds, animals and fish and sometimes to plants and seasons. More than three-quarters of the symbols are birds. This is the world they know.

* * * *

They march past, a parade of little people, passing through a violent world that largely ignores them. The surnames they give each other record their fear of a terrifying reality and invoke the protection of natural predators as well as the symbols of a Christian world. At the same time, they add their own commentary about themselves and their society in the names that record the sinners, the good, the silly and the cunning. And in the ironic nicknames they laugh at the farm workers in bright jerkins and tight, fashionable hose, the misguided and the envious who try to ape the rich and the powerful. These ironic surnames are also a way of bringing down the people at the apex of the feudal system, humour helping ordinary people come to terms with the rich and the powerful. But they carry a warning.

CHAPTER 7

PERSONAL SURNAMES AND
MULTICULTURAL TRADITIONS

THIS CHAPTER IS about continental surnames. (In this context
'continental' is used to describe multicultural names, although,
strictly speaking, these include names with a Scandinavian root as
well as a European root.) It will look first at the many indigenous
personal surnames that have two or more roots (for example,
Willard that could be German or English, or Oswald that could
be English or Norse), and the common concepts they carry. It will
then look at the classical/biblical names of the saints that similarly
arise from European traditions.

The drumbeat of English resounds through personal names.
By the ninth century, Old German single names had been taken
by almost everyone in what is now northern France and we know
that these names, often in French forms, largely pushed out the
pre-Conquest single English names when the Normans came to
England. But as they choose personal surnames, the English
resuscitate many early names and heavily anglicize those of the
Norman invaders.

In medieval times, personal surnames, based on surviving
records, are at least as popular as nicknames and occupational
names.[1] But records are highly likely to understate their prevalence.
Their revival seems to have been the choice of the least privileged

who fall below the nets of records. Of 640 jurors and suitors in Devon in 1238, 15 have these indigenous names, single then, while 120 offenders have them. A century later, they are even less fashionable among the privileged. Only ten of 950 burgesses admitted to the freedom of Exeter have them in 1348.[2] Because these surnames are associated with the poor, others might have avoided them. Despite an important effort made in the Middle Ages to record Welsh and Icelandic oral folk poetry and epics, Chaucer and Langland hardly mention indigenous names or culture; virtually all names in *The Canterbury Tales* or *Piers Plowman* are Norman or classical/biblical.[3]

These names show more clearly than others how the attitudes of the poor majority of the population towards the Normans had adjusted over the three centuries after the Conquest. As people return to indigenous names they may want a change from Latin sounds, or to record their own roots in an England that was Saxon and multicultural rather than the introverted state the Normans had made. Their choices show a preference for English as a language and for an English culture. But they also show that this English outlook is rooted in an Anglo-Saxon world view that is still accessible to and valued by medieval people. Some names cannot be otherwise explained, demonstrating that continental mythology is well known to the medieval people who choose them. These medieval surnames recalling heroes, gods and saints still tie us to a common pagan and Christian culture that existed across northern Europe and Scandinavia well before the eleventh century.

The medieval English seem to treat saints' names differently. Saints are important in the Middle Ages. Local churches are dedicated to them, ships are called after them, and occupations and groups have patron saints. So it is not surprising that people are named after them. Yet while many indigenous Old English and some Celtic saints' names have survived as surnames, often in much changed forms, most come down to us as Norman versions of original classical or biblical names, such as Dennis from Dionysius or Giles from Aegidius. The English seem to accept the Norman dominance of the church. The English church had always looked outwards.

Language Links

During the first decade of the 1500s, a John Gerard of Dartmouth is in and out of the mayors' courts. Despite being called variously Gerard, Gerrard, Jelard and Jerard, he is probably the same person. He lives in le Ford lane, where he thoroughly annoys his neighbours by dumping 'Robell' and 'various things'. He is involved in several assaults, using a 'fletcher', a knife and a poignard, usually drawing blood. He goes through bad times. He is sued for a debt of £32, a large amount, and his creditor 'enjoyed' all his lands and tenements in Dartmouth and the outlying parish of Wodelegh. His apprentice connives with a Robert Breton, carver, to steal his possessions. His character emerges from these tribulations: quick to anger, a bad judge of character and careless of the future.[4]

John Gerard is not so interesting for his rubble-throwing and poignarding as for his Norman name. This small-time Dartmouth felon is a rung in the ladder by which descends to the present day Gerrard, the haughty Earl of Roussillon in the *Chanson de Roland*. This English Gerard shows us the place we used to occupy in a continental world.

More than any other group of names, personal surnames, particularly those with multiple roots, open a window onto an overarching pre-Conquest culture that encompassed England, northern Europe and Scandinavia. Other records, both physical and linguistic, contain the same evidence. But that of surnames is more comprehensive and compelling. They record invaders who had family links with the invaded and show that the English, the Norse and the Germanic tribes drew on the same traditions and subscribed to the same world outlook.

The connections arise out of the links among the relevant languages. Celt, Norse, German, Frisian and English are all Sanskrit languages. The last four are Germanic: Norse is north Germanic and German, Frisian and English are west Germanic. By the eighth century, the Celts had largely been pushed out to Brittany, Cornwall and Gaelic-speaking Wales, Ireland and Scotland, where the same words were current. Old Norse, introduced in the second half of the ninth century, was spoken by all Scandinavians. At the Treaty of St Clair-sur-Epte in 911, the Norse raiders of the northern European coast had been granted territory called after their name – Normandy, the land of the Northmen. But at the Conquest, barely 150 years assimilated in their new land, the Normans already spoke a sort of French with Latin roots. They found a Saxon England speaking Old English. There was an English alphabet in the seventh century and Alfred, in the ninth century, had begun to establish an English literature. Yet connections survived; the Normans brought some Old Norse from their origins and some Celt from Brittany and in England they were to find a strong element of Norse from earlier Norwegian and Danish invasions and Celt still surviving on its peripheries. At the same time, their own 'Norman' names had elements common to English and Norse.

Scholars believe that over the 300 years after the Conquest, about 10,000 French words were introduced into English and a large amount of Old English was lost, some say as much as 85 per cent.[5] Chaucer's language in the fourteenth century *Canterbury Tales* is fairly close to modern English whereas the English of the late tenth-century Anglo-Saxon scholar Aelfric is incomprehensible today. Middle English began to appear in the eleventh century and modern English after William Caxton first started using a press in 1476, although features of older versions continued to be spoken for generations after the newer had emerged, and strong regional dialects confused the differences among them.

Fragments of Celt and Norse are still current in the Middle Ages. A tympanum over the door of Pennington church in Lancashire from about 1100 has a Scandinavian runic inscription, so a Scandinavian language was still used there after the Conquest.[6] Chaucer's Reeve of Norfolk, as late as about 1386, says 'ik am old' instead of 'I am old', the Norse *ik* a sign the reeve is from the Danelaw and its use evidence that English readers would immediately recognize that.[7] Norse culture had an enormous influence on pre-Conquest England. While tenth-century England was a monarchy under one king, it meant co-existence with mutual respect for tribal differences. Laws for the Danelaw differed from those of Wessex and Mercia, and Scandinavian areas were administered through wapentakes according to Scandinavian custom while other parts were administered through Saxon Hundreds.

Names with multiple roots

Baldry, Harding and Willard could have German and English roots.

Hammond, Harold, Howard, Randolph, Reynolds, Ralph, Roger and Simmonds are German and Norse, and Goodman English, Norse or German.

Ayliffe, Brothers, Oswald, Otter, Raven, Sewell and Wyman are English and Norse.

Griffiths and Howell could be Welsh or Breton; Brian Irish, Norse or Breton; Duncan Irish or German.

When many of the words used across these cultures are similar, to find that that many of their names are the same and mean the same is hardly surprising. You cannot miss the matches between Hamon (German), Hammundr (Norse) and the English Hammond, for example; Sigmund (German), Sigmundr (Norse) and Simmonds; Haraldr (mostly Norse) and Hairold (German) for Harold; and Osweald (English) and Asvaldr (Norse), and so on.

These multicultural names tell about the times and values of the medieval people who take them. Our Simmonds, Wymans and Griffiths are evidence not only that people in the Middle Ages like these names, but by picking up names with pre-Conquest roots, they show they like memories. At the same time, the appearance of surnames from Norse and continental legends and epics like *Beowulf* and the *Chanson de Roland* – Finn, Simmonds, Turpin, Rowland, Oliver – shows that seventh- and eighth-century continental myth still speaks to the English of the Middle Ages. When people call a neighbour Turpin, it tells us that Thor and the panoply of Viking gods and the sagas are still at least nominally in peoples' cultural memory in the fourteenth century. It might also mean that after famines and four devastating attacks by the Black Death that coincide with the naming period some might be harking back to pagan beliefs. The range and persistence of these names show the vitality of the Norse and Saxon cultures.

These names also illuminate the Anglo-Saxon world. Combining their meanings and connections gives rich material about the social and political background as well as the oral history, beliefs and priorities of the Anglo-Saxons. Names with multiple roots show intricate linkages among the northern tribes. They can also reflect, despite patchy records, migration and settlement patterns that can be quite specific. The meanings of the names echo preoccupations among all races with conflict and the courage and judgement associated with success, the importance of protection, magic and gods as well as fame that outlives death. The same or similar names appear in the same guises across Norse, Teutonic and even Celtic legends and reflect a common world view – of elves, boars and warriors with 'sig-' and 'thor-' names.

Names Unique among Records

Other records of early culture are sparse. Stories and records were oral, mostly sung, vulnerable to loss and change from social upheaval. Christianity must also have inhibited repeating and recording them. Many records were lost. Viking and Danish invasions destroyed monasteries and monastic life throughout eastern England and Northumbria, so the early history of East Anglia and the eastern Midlands is virtually unknown. That of Northumbria, where the cream of monastic scholarship was concentrated, is only partly available because Bede's *Ecclesiastical History of the English People*, which ended in 731, was distributed outside Northumbria and abroad and was later recovered.[8]

Fortunately, a renaissance of interest in folk culture in the Middle Ages rescued the records we have. Between about 1150 and 1350, early Welsh poetry was collected in four manuscripts. In the twelfth and especially thirteenth centuries, three centuries after paganism had faded as a religious force, scholars painstakingly collected and wrote down the oral poetry and epics of the Vikings then available in Iceland and Scandinavia. These 'Icelandic' texts are the bedrock of our knowledge of Anglo-Saxon, Norse and Teutonic culture. The *Chanson de Roland*, the most famous of the *chansons de geste*, was recorded as it is now in the late eleventh century. Little remains of German myths. The *Niebelungenlied* is thought to have been combined from disparate myths in the late twelfth century in the Austrian Tyrol.

Beowulf, written in the seventh to eighth centuries, is the only surviving English epic. Dunstan, one of the most important church reformers of the tenth century and an Archbishop of Canterbury, is known to have enjoyed heathen poetry – he was criticized by his peers for preferring it to studying his books – but if he made a collection, it has not survived.[9] There is one early poem in English that uses the verse form of oral epics for a Christian theme: Caedmon's poem about the creation that he, a cattle herder at the Abbey of Whitby, was told to write in a vision.

Physical evidence and place names record the same links among northern cultures. Excavations of Anglo-Saxons sites show some of these continental linkages in widely sourced objects. A sword from about the seventh century in the Sutton Hoo vessel has a Rhenish blade, jewels worked by East Anglians and a Swedish pommel.[10]

Common words based on the early similarity of the relevant languages appear in place names spanning northern Europe. Thor, the Norse god of thunder, was the favourite god of the Icelandic Vikings who came to north-west England. The Old English and Germans had the same god, Thunor and Donar. Germany, Iceland and England still have place names commemorating Thor, some twenty in Iceland, some thirty in Norway and a number in England, including the Essex Thurstables and southern Thursleys.[11] All the '-wik' towns record early trading patterns, from Schleswig and Brunswick on the continent to Norwich, Ipswich and Droitwich, a large producer of salt in the Middle Ages, in England. Hamwic and Lundenwic were early names for Southampton and London. *Tre-* (farm) names – in Wales Trefasser and Trefecca, in Cornwall Trewithin and Tregony, and Trebenden and Tregastel in Brittany – echo the footfall of Celtic saints. The Breton name for Finisterre is still Penn ar and Cornwall's holy headland is Penzance.

But the many personal names that could have arisen anywhere in England, Scandinavia or northern Europe are a far more comprehensive and dynamic proof than archaeological relics or place names of the cross-cultural integration of Anglo-Saxons.

Names – the Sticky Sandals of Migration

Etymologists have been able to show how a few Old Norse personal names with at least one other root (for example, Neal, Brian and Murdoch) record where the Viking and Danish invaders into England came from and where they went. It is worth describing these invasions briefly because they are so important to understanding the surnames that record them and where surnames with different roots emerged and settled.

From the mid-seventh century, Norwegians from the western fjords sailed to the western islands of Scotland and Orkney, the Isle of Man and Iceland and were in Ireland by the first decade of the ninth century. From there, they went to north and north-west England, especially in 890–93 and then 919–52. They established themselves in north-western England to the west of the Pennines from the Wirral, south of Liverpool, north along the coasts of Lancashire, Westmoreland and Cumbria to the Solway Firth beyond Carlisle from the end of the ninth century. They left unambiguously Scandinavian place names there: Hanaby, Upperby and Lazonby around Carlisle, Kirkby, Greasby and Frankby along the Wirral and Formby, Soulby and Appleby in between. (The suffix -by is Norse for farm or town.) From there, they crossed the Pennines. These early Norse settlers were joined periodically by invasions from the Norse kingdom of Dublin.

The Danes and other Norwegians came from south Jutland along the Frisian coast to harass the shores of both south and east England and what is now northern France. In 793, 794 and 795 they sacked Lindisfarne, Jarrow and Iona, the great monasteries of Northumberland and centres of Christendom in Britain. Around 850, some of these Danes went on to Ireland too, and could have joined the Norwegian invasions of the English north-west. From 835 a series of major attacks against south-east England culminated in the great Danish invasion of East Anglia in 865. In 867 both Northumbrian rulers were killed and English Northumbria's political pre-eminence was destroyed. The Danes attacked East Anglia from York the following year and from 874 began to settle East Anglia, Yorkshire and the East Midlands, establishing a dynasty of semi-pagan kings at York. The last of these, Eric Bloodaxe, was only expelled in 954, after the combined forces of the Norse in Dublin under King Olaf Guthfrithson, the Scots and Strathclyde were defeated by Aethelstan and Edmund at Brunanburh. By 955, after Guthfrithson's death in 941, England had become a single kingdom under Edmund. He was succeeded by the weaker Aethelred the Unready who was unable to stop further raids by professional Danish armies under Thorkell the Tall and Svein Forkbeard, among others. Of the five kings ruling England in the eleventh century before the Conquest, three were Danes. The last, Harthacnut or Cnut, was replaced by the English Edward the Confessor as late as 1042.

Migrations of the Norse

A few surnames record the trajectory of the Norse who came via Iceland and Ireland. Oman, from the Old Norse Hamundr, from Orkney and the Shetlands, documents the first stop of the Norse on their way west. Norse/Gaelic names that appear on either side of the Pennines from the end of the ninth century tell us the Norse had intermarried with the Irish Celts before they arrived. The Old Norse Njall, our Neal, was taken to Iceland and then Ireland by the Vikings and, acculturated as the Old Irish/Gaelic Neal, went from there to north-west England and Yorkshire. Gille is another Old Irish and Norse name that must have had a similar trajectory. Brian, Norse and Old Irish/Gaelic or Breton, and probably Duncan, Old Irish/Gaelic, were taken from Ireland to Cumberland, and thence over the Pennines to Yorkshire. Murdoch, Old Irish/Old Welsh, was also probably brought to Yorkshire before the Conquest by the Norse migrations from Ireland. Coleman, from the Old Irish names Colman and Columban, the name of a sixth-century Irish saint, and the Old Norse Kalman, travelled with the Norse from Ireland to Cumberland, Westmorland and Yorkshire. Duncan and Murdoch, also arose separately in other Gaelic-speaking countries, particularly Scotland.[12]

Some of these names have been identified as also coming to southern England later with the Normans, and others probably did too. Njall, for example, seems to have gone with Scandinavians to Iceland, back to Norway, then to northern Europe and ultimately England with the Normans. Brian was also brought later by Bretons at the Conquest. The Old German version of Coleman might also have been introduced to the south from the continent.

In general, Norse/Norman names occurring in the north-west, Midlands or East Anglia will probably have come directly from Scandinavia or via Ireland and in the south via Normandy. They include rarer names with mixed roots like Askell with its Norman equivalent Ankell, Osborn, Osmund and Rolf as well as the common names highlighted in the box on page 202. Norse names (which could also be Danish and/or Swedish) like Brand, Swaine, Grime, Gunn, Knott and Orme will have had the same distribution.

It is less easy to identify where names with Norse/English roots come from because many English with English names live in Norse areas as well as outside them. But first records can help. First records for Otter, for instance, are all in the Danelaw. Algar (noble or elf spear, Old English/Old Norse/Old Danish) recorded by Reaney and Wilson in a number of Danelaw counties as well as Sussex and Kent in the eleventh and twelfth centuries and by Hey in Berkshire and Essex in 1377–81, is likely to be Norse in East Anglia and Anglo-Saxon in the south.[13] So the Aelfgar who lived in Bishopsworth and had invested in ten houses in Bristol in the tenth century is probably English.[14] Algar is only recorded in East Anglia and London in the nineteenth century and Hey thinks it likely that just one or two Algars produced the surname.[15] Wyman is likely to be from the Norse Vigmundr or Vimund, battle protector, in records found in Lincolnshire, Leicestershire and Norfolk, and from the Old English Wigmund, war protection, in other places and so on.

But over time, many personal names have acquired other meanings, often as similar-sounding names combined, and deducing their origins from first records can be hazardous. To take just one example, first records show Goodmans in Hertfordshire, Hampshire and Suffolk. A Goodman in the Danelaw could have a Norse root from the Old Norse Guthmundr, battle protection.

Elsewhere Goodman could be from the Old English first name Guthmund or German Godemann. And either in the Danelaw or outside it could be from Old English or Old German words meaning a good man or a householder. An English monk called Godemann, who went on to become abbot of Thorney on the Isle of Ely, wrote in about 980 a *Benedictional of St Athelwold*, a beautiful illuminated manuscript in rich colours in the Carolingian style.[16]

Early records can help to narrow the origins of a personal name with other meanings if it is relatively rare. Earp, from its English root *earp*, means swarthy. But records show it is a northern name, occurring in Staffordshire from the sixteenth century[17] and here it is likely to be from the Erp of Teutonic mythology. Erp was one of the many warrior sons of Etzel, or Attila, King of the Huns in the fifth century, killed in a battle by Witege, his head cut off by the sword Mimung. In one legend he was killed by his brothers for refusing to avenge the death of Swanhild, daughter of Sigurd. Jarvis is usually from the Old German/French personal name – a popular variant was Gervase – but in Yorkshire it could be from Jervaulx in the North Riding, where the first Cistercian abbey in England was founded in 1132.

Battling Overwhelming Odds

Combine the multi-rooted personal surnames with their meanings and a common world view emerges from across Scandinavia, northern Europe and England. Medieval people are keeping alive the beliefs and traditions of Anglo-Saxon times.

Names with derivations from English, German and Norse show widely held perceptions of a violent and threatening world. (For derivations of names with multiple roots see page 202). Otter means terrible army (among other meanings) and Harold army power. An Otter, an early hunk, was the human lover of the Scandinavian and German fertility goddess Freya who transformed him into a boar to be able to keep him in Asgard, the home of the gods. People record magical weapons: Roger is fame spear and Algar elf spear. The heroic 'Sig-' names in Sewell and Simmonds mean victory ruler and victory protector. Many multi-rooted names invoke protection, including Wyman, and Hammond. Randolph, shield-wolf and Osborn, god-bear, invoke the protection of powerful and feared animals. Courage is celebrated: Harding, brave warrior, and Willard, resolute and bold. Rulers must be powerful: Oswald is god-ruler, Baldry bold ruler. Good judgement is important: Reynolds is counsel might and Ralph advice wolf. Gods protect. Thor names tying the migrant tribes together include Thurban, Thorold, Thurgar, Thurgood, Thurkettle, Thirkill, and Thurstan. Turpin, from Thorfinnr, the race of Thor, is first recorded in England in 1066, although, since Thor was so popular in Iceland, versions of the name are likely to have been in north-west England much earlier.

The outlook and attitudes that appear in these names show experiences of mortal threats so great that the only protection can be from superhuman countervailing forces. There is a strong focus on elves, gods and magical nature, from the elf-counsels of the English Alfred to the god-bear in the Norse/English Osborn, the eagle power of German Arnold and the power of the wolf in the English Woolrich. Magic and gods cross cultures. All the surnames from feared predators could be a way of absorbing their powers, as the Norse Halfdan mentioned later ate the heart of a great wolf. Heroes have a code of loyalty and honour: Aylward is noble protector, and Aldred noble counsel. The concept of fame outliving death occurs across the legends that have survived from the Norse to the Teutonic, and names from all etymologies record it, from Robert, German for fame bright to Aylmer, English, noble famous.

Names combine rule with warrior and superhuman attributes. The gods of Teutonic myth invoked by Oswald are picked up by kings. English and Celt dynasties traced their lineage back to the gods. Seven of the eight surviving Anglo-Saxon genealogies go back to Woden, the English Odin, the Norse king of the gods and father of Thor.[18] Woden still appears in English place names, such as Wednesfield, earlier Wodnesfield, in Staffordshire and Wensley in Derby.

Wolves and elf spears are called on for protection in Randolph and Algar. Elf is virtually the same word across the languages:

aelf in Anglo-Saxon; *alfi* in Icelandic; *alp* and *elfe* in German. In Norse mythology light elves were beautiful and dark the opposite, living underground. In some legends the two are different from dwarfs, but in others they were also associated with the wonder-smiths like the dwarf Weland, who had magical powers and made weapons and jewels of unbelievable strength and beauty essential to the prowess of heroes and gods. The elves and dwarves of German folk tales belong to the same tradition. Ellwood and our Aubreys, from the Old German Alberic, are elf-rulers; an Alberic guarded the hoard of the Niebelungs in Teutonic legend and in Norse myth and in the *Nibelungenlied* a dwarf Alberich with a cloak of invisibility fought Siegfried.

Gods and Heroes

Thor is one of the few Norse names that generated several variants and almost the only one to invoke a god. The names came from all sides of the Channel. A Thurbrand from Yorkshire caused the murder of Earl Uhtred of Northumbria in 1016 as he entered Cnut's court, beginning a family feud that lasted generations, in which many on both sides met premature and violent deaths.[19] Thorkell the Tall, a Dane, was a persistent harrier of the English in the early eleventh century, burning Oxford in 1010. Meanwhile, in 943, a Norman Thormod was trying to convert the young Duke Richard of Normandy to paganism. First records of Thurkells occur across England, from the north, where they are probably Norse, East Anglia, where they might be Danish, and Worcestershire, where they might be English.

Svein Forkbeard, or Tjuguskegg, Thorkell's contemporary and co-raider, gave rise to a warming story about a Thurkill from East Anglia. Svein had sworn to invade England, kill King Aethelred, and drive him from the land, and was, indeed, briefly recognized as king in East Anglia, long enough to send one Thurcetel to collect tribute from the Flegg Hundred in Norfolk in 1013–14. Thurcetel heard Svein had died as he was riding back with the money, whereupon he turned around and returned it to the contributors.[20]

Thor legends throw a net across the turbulent tribes of northern Europe, Scandinavia, Iceland and Anglo-Saxon England. From France, there is Archbishop Turpin, a name that means the race of Thor, the eighth-century bishop of Rheims fighting with Roland against the Saracens in the Pyrenees in the *Chanson de Roland*. A militant churchman, he stays with the hero throughout the fateful battle. At one point, riding against a King Corsablis:

> He breaks the buckler, he's split the hauberk's steel,
> Into his breast driven the lance-head deep,
> He splits him through, on high his body heaves,
> And hurls him dead a spear's length o'er the lea.[21]

A Thurkillus was a Danish hero, Christian in some Norse legends and fighting giants and monsters in others. He consorts with gods; in one legend he describes seeing Thor drive red-hot pokers through the giant Geruthus and smash the backs of his women with thunderbolts. An early Icelandic Thirkell shows sacrifices were often made for personal reasons such as vengeance. A Thorkell the Tall (in Víga-Glúm's saga) who went to Freyja's temple with an old ox, wanted revenge for being expelled from his land by a certain Glum, saying 'now I give you this ox, so that Glum may leave the land of Thvera [in North Iceland] no less compelled than I leave it now. Let some sign be seen whether you accept or reject it.' It was recorded that the ox was so moved that it bellowed and dropped dead.[22] It is a good example of man making a deal with his god.

Heroes and demigods have the same names across races. Goodman, the name of a giant in late sagas, could be English, Norse or German. The name means battle protection, and sagas talk about the Norse Gudmund of Glaesisvellir (the Shining Fields) who ruled with his brother, Geiroo, their land divided by a river spanned by a bridge of gold. Harding from the English Hearding or the German Hardwin, was the name of a son of a Norse hero, Halfdan, our Haldanes, who was given magic powers by Odin. Called 'the hairy' because he vowed to cut neither hair nor beard until he had avenged his father's death, he killed and ate a great wolf, eating its heart to take on its might and ferocity, and killed

Svipdag, his father's murderer, who had changed into a dragon.[23] The name would be German or English, but the legend is Norse.

All the Simmonds and Sewells belong to the group of 'sig-' or hero names that appear across Norse and Teutonic legend, Siguro in Norse and Siegfried, hero of the *Niebelungenlied*, on the continent, killing dragons, fighting giants and gods. Simmonds, in England before the Conquest, comes from the greatest Norse warrior, Sigmund, who draws the sword of victory from a tree. He reappears in *Beowulf* as the Teutonic Siegemund who wiped giants from the earth and destroyed a 'treasure-rich' dragon, swinging 'his sword so savagely that it slit the creature/ Through, pierced its flesh and pinned it/ To a wall'. Brought down by vanity, he 'deserved to suffer and die.'[24] A Norse Sigmund lived in the forest like a wolf, fighting giants. Siward, the Danish warrior appointed by Cnut to tame the Northumbrians in the eleventh century held one of these 'Sig-' names that could have come from the English Sigeweard or Danish Sigwarth, victory ward. The Celt heros Drystan and Finn have similar weapons and life stories to these Teutonic 'Sig-' heroes. Finn, from the Norse, Danish, Swedish and Celtic Irish, was a Scottish giant, appeared in the eighth century *Beowulf*, and had links with the Teutonic Sigurd.

Memories of Epics

Beowulf is a good example of a shared continental epic tradition and view of history in Anglo-Saxon England. It is a story in English about a Danish king and sixth-century tribe from southern Sweden, the Geats. Beowulf, the strongest Geat, chooses the bravest and the best to sail to Denmark with him to vanquish the monster Grendel who is tormenting the Danes. An eventful story, written in wonderfully powerful and visual English by an Anglian poet, it assumes the island people knew about and were interested in the doings of sixth-century Danes, Swedes and Frisians and understood the many allusions in the poem to characters and events in Norse and Teutonic legends.[25]

Six centuries after it was written, the medieval English take names recording the Geats who strode out to slaughter Grendel.

Woolvett is wolf Geat; Sait is sea Geat; some Elliots and Ayletts come from Aedelgeat, noble Geat; Marryatt and Merrett come from the Old English Maergeat, famous Geat; and Levett is from Leofgeat, beloved Geat. There are Levetts in East Anglia and the south-east, Levitts further north, particularly in Yorkshire, and Levicks that could originally be Levitts. According to the Domesday Book, in Wiltshire one Leofgeat held land held by his man in King Edward's day: 'This Leofgeat made and makes orphreys for the king and queen'.[26] A Lovet in Dartmouth in 1507 'caused much annoyance at le conduit near le Thorn'.[27] So the memory of the continental tribe of heroes lives on.

The *Chanson de Roland* was a classic medieval *chanson de geste*. Roland, the most famous of Charlemagne's knights, leads a group of heroes into a trap at Roncesvalles in the Pyrenees, where they are vastly outnumbered by the enemy. But 'The French all say: "Foul shame were it to flee" and they fight to the death.[28] These names have stayed with us down the centuries in our Rolands or Rowlands and Olivers (Roland fierce and his friend Oliver wise), Gerards (Roussillon's haughty earl revived by John Gerard of Dartmouth), Odgers, from Ogier the Dane (never meek of mood) and Turpins – recalling the warlike Archbishop. Rowland, Oliver, Gerard and Turpin or Thor names are still strong today. Even Ogier, although scarce, survives, often as its variant, Odger.

Paganism?

Thor names raise the question of whether medieval people are consciously harking back to paganism when they choose these surnames. Thirkell, Thurkettle and even just Kettle mean sacrificial cauldrons and keep the memory of pagan ritual alive.[29]

Much of England was christianized by the tenth century. King Edwin of Northumbria had been baptized in 627 at York with many of his retinue. And Alfred had converted the East Anglian king, the Dane Guthrum, in 878. By the Norman Conquest, only the Scandinavians and Finns in Scandinavia and Finland were formally pagan. In about 1030, an English missionary, Wilfred, was drowned in marshland by heathens in Sweden after he had

publicly smashed an idol of Thor with a very symbolic double-headed axe – Thor's weapon.[30]

At the same time, Viking paganism ripped but did not destroy
the English tangle of religious cultures. While in the north-west,
English pagans worshipped Woden and Turold, Christianity
was actively practised in Wales and Cumbria, Strathclyde and
the south-west. But the sacking of the monasteries shattered
Christianity's intellectual and spiritual culture and by 900
monastic life had disappeared from the north and the Danelaw.
And although most of the Norse invaders from Ireland had been
pagan, early churches dedicated to St Patrick along the north-west
English seaboard suggest some brought Christianity with them.
Some Norse were even atheist. Our Kettles have an antecedent in
the self-reliant hero Ketill Hoengr who, in what must have been
an ironic comment on his own name, claimed: 'I never gave sacrifices to Odin, and yet I have lived long.'[31] Nor were all Normans
Christian, as is evident from the pagan Thormod who tried to
convert the Duke of Normandy. But paganism in England must
have been significant enough to lead Cnut to renew anti-pagan-
ism legislation in the eleventh century. The story seems to be that
paganism and Christianity co-existed among the Norse invaders,
the Anglo-Saxons and even the Normans right up to the Conquest.

Surnames emerge some three to four centuries after paganism
ceased to be an active cultural force in England. Although this
sounds a long time, it is less than that between ourselves and
Shakespeare. At the same time, the conditions that spawned the
Norse and Teutonic legends and made them relevant apply to
the fourteenth century. Norse legends of heroes, gods and magic
evolved out of a period of intense social and physical upheaval in
Scandinavia and brought the same dislocations and uncertainty to
England in the ninth and tenth centuries. These conditions were
to persist in England, first with local rebellions and repression
and then the foreign wars of the new Norman kings that imposed
an enormous burden of tax and manpower on ordinary people.
In addition, medieval England is to see cataclysmic disasters
– famines between 1315 and 1322, in which a quarter of the population is thought to have died and several episodes of the Black
Death, in which a further half is believed to have perished.

It is entirely possible that the Norse surnames that tell us people remember their Norse roots may also be saying that they continue to need Norse beliefs. Surnames like Pagan and Paine and all the Wild names indicate a few had always been outside the church. But for most, the church dominates medieval life and many surnames, particularly nicknames, are evidence that its precepts are fundamental to peoples' thinking, even though some names suggest a healthy scorn for the practices of churchmen. Yet these Norse personal names might suggest an openness to paganism among some in difficult times.

An image common to pagan and Christian England could be telling. Grey horses and death were popularly associated in Norse myth and in the Christian Middle Ages the Black Death is shown as a man and a woman riding greys. At the very least, whether people knew the details of what these names mean, they may also reflect a perception of a violent and unpredictable world and a real need for the support of legends and myths that served at an earlier, similar time.

And Wade was Miles away

Two names that cross cultures tell everything about the international world of the Anglo-Saxons. Our Waylands can be from the Old German Weland, the wonder-smith of Teutonic and Norse myth, whose work became the stuff of legend. Beowulf, anticipating death, bestows his armour, made by Weland, as a great treasure:

> And if death does take me, send the hammered
> Mail of my armour to Higlac, return
> The inheritance I had from Hrethel, and he
> From Wayland.[32]

In early myths, Weland forged a magic sword of victory, serpent rings and a chain that could capture the wind. He is pursued for his skills by gods and kings, and in one legend fashions wings to soar away from the island of the tyrant Nithud.

In about 700, in Northumbria, a whalebone casket – the Franks casket – was made that still survives. On its front panel is a carving of this Norse/Teutonic Weland, who has just killed the tyrant's sons before escaping. He is offering a cup made from one of the skulls to the king's daughter, Beaduhild.

Weland has a son by Beaduhild, called Wado, our Wades, who became a legendary hero himself and had a magic boat, Wingelock, which could cover hundreds of miles in a moment. Wade is mentioned in several medieval texts and later Arthurian legends. In the Merchant's Tale in *The Canterbury Tales*, Chaucer's old widows, when blamed for something, swear that, like Wade's boat, they were miles away when it happened. The memory of Wingelock is said to have persisted in northern England until the Reformation, an echo of a story that originated far beyond this island's shores.[33]

The Saints

Medieval people are very conversant with the saints. Virtually everyone belongs to the church and saints' days and homilies on their lives are a large part of the church. The first Life is thought to have been of Samson, written within fifty years of his death at Dol in about 560. It was followed by many more, some more reliable than others, some entirely fictitious. Trades, crafts and other groups have patron saints. Nowhere is the popularity of these names more vivid than in the names of their ships. Vessels plying the Exeter port in the eleventh and twelfth centuries bear a high proportion of saints' names, including names of apostles – particularly Thomas, John, Michel, James, Paul, Nicholas. All are preceded by Seint or Seynte. Out of a sample of sixteen names, more than half are of apostles and evangelists and the Holy Family like Marie and Anne. Other names are generally religious, like *la Trinite, la Grace* or *Sancti Spirit*.[34] These names must have been chosen to invoke protection and inspire confidence in the face of risk. Some have particular connections to travel. Christopher, James and Thomas were travelling apostles, the latter reputed to have been to India and other places, and the fourth century

Nicholas, bishop of Myra in Asia Minor, was the patron saint of sailors and merchants (as well as children, pawnbrokers and others).

Many saints' names take the Norman form of the classical/biblical root, recording the profound influence of the continental church evident in other ecclesiastical names. But a sprinkling of Anglo-Saxon and Celtic saints' names are still around, witness to the tenacity of some local heroes. The earliest saints whose names influenced medieval naming patterns were martyrs or holy men, who might have been scholars, teachers, missionaries, bishops or even kings. Many never existed, or, if they did, the details of their lives cannot be proved. The boy Hugh of Lincoln was one of these (see page 220). There are literally thousands of saints today; one compendium, the *Roman Martyrology*, lists 4,500, and is still not exhaustive. But here, we are interested only in the shorter list of those who had been recognized or canonized by the Middle Ages – canonization began to be taken over by Rome from the tenth century – and whose names influenced surnames.[35] Many saints have been canonized since then and many early saints do not seem to have been recorded in surnames, or at least names that have survived.

Saxon, Norse and Norman surnames came to England with invasions of people looking to raid and to settle. Saints' names came and went with another type of invasion, with people who looked to convert. In our surnames, you can trace the incoming wave of evangelists from Rome who converted the early Anglo-Saxons and the returning tide of particularly Celtic missionaries who came to convert the British and especially the continental heathens. Although few have Celtic names, language links seem to have forged the chain that led these Celts on, from Ireland and Wales to Brittany, often via south-west England. Christianity had been established in Britain as early as the fourth century, when three British bishops are recorded attending the Councils of Arles in 314 and Rimini in 359. But the barbarian invasions of Gaul had led to the British church evolving independently from Rome until the eighth century. Many travelled for consultations, education and appointments between English and continental institutions. There are many records of English saints in France today.

Names from a Continental Church

Very popular saints' names include Norman names like William, Richard, Robert, Hugh and Henry and classical/biblical names like Bartholomew, David, John, Lawrence, Matthew, Nicholas, Paul, Philip, Simon and Thomas. The latter are quintessentially saints' names. All have many variants, Thomas and Nicholas almost as many as the Norman Richard. Looking just at common medieval saints' names, and excluding the very popular Norman names, out of a sample of thirty names, almost three-quarters are Hebrew or Aramaic, Latin or Greek. Only one, Cuthbert, is purely indigenous.

Since most of the popular names belong to kings, statesmen and legendary heroes as well as saints, while an early saint, such as an apostle, may once have been the origin of the name, by the Middle Ages one might assume it must have lost a clear link. Simon, for example, has fine credentials as a saint in Simon Peter, but the surname today is Simmonds with its many variants, which could also be from the popular Old Norse or German Sigmundr or Sigmund. Simund was a common form of Simon after the Conquest, and Wyclif used it in his translation of the Bible. So it is hard today to tell which Simmonds belong to the saint and which to the similar Sigmundr.

Yet British saints might have influenced the choice even of some of these most popular names. Simmonds could have been called after the English saint Simon Stock who died in Bordeaux in 1265 and was prior general of the strict Carmelite order for almost twenty years. Paul, a very early surname, could record the sixth-century Paul Aurelian, or Paul of Leon, a British Celt. His life was written towards the end of the ninth century and is well known in medieval England, describing his missionary work in Brittany, where he died. Richard could be from Richard of Chichester and Gilbert from Gilbert of Sempringham, the twelfth-century founder of the only truly English religious order. There is even an English saint called William, that most popular Norman name of all. Margery Kempe, a controversial holy woman from Bishop's Lynn (now King's Lynn) who dictates her memoirs in the early fifteenth century and is punctilious in ticking off all the best holy sites from Jerusalem to Walsingham, visits the shrine of St William of York, who died in 1154 and was famous for miracles of healing.[36]

John must be one of the most common saints' names; there are sixty-four entries for Saint Johns in the *Roman Martyrology*. They include two English Johns: the eighth-century John of Beverley and the fourteenth-century John of Bridlington. Variants of the name hold the same ironic connotations you find in nicknames for ecclesiastics. Jankin, from Jan and then John, means a fool, and Chaucer's reference to a Jankin in The Shipman's Prologue in *The Canterbury Tales* is a mocking reference to a priest. Clergymen are often laughingly called Sir John.[37] Jack has the same connotation, and a book of jokes published in 1604 is called *A Jack of Dover*.

Three particular saints are most likely to have influenced the choice of three of the very popular names in medieval England. The first is Thomas à Becket. Killed in Canterbury Cathedral by knights loyal to Henry II in 1170, his shrine becomes one of Europe's most popular, and wealthiest, pilgrim destinations. William Langland criticizes its opulence in the popular *Piers Plowman*, his hero Piers swearing by all the wealth in St Thomas' shrine that he will not accept pilgrims' fees. Thomas, in his years of estrangement from Henry II, spent time at Sens in northern France, and an early thirteenth-century window at Sens Cathedral tells the story of his last days at Canterbury, the detail being as important to the French congregation as his chapel in Canterbury is to the English.

The second saint who is ever-present in medieval lives is James of Compostela. His shrine then ranks with Rome as the second most important holy site after the Holy Land. It was first recorded in the ninth century when the story of the disciple's missionary work in northern Spain was revived, visions seen and the pilgrim tradition established. In May 1394 in Dartmouth a licence is given for a ship, *la Charite*, to take 100 pilgrims to Santiago de Compostela 'to pay their vows and bring them back', a nice record of the professional responsibilities of the captain.[38] Margery Kempe visits the shrines at both Canterbury and Compostela.

Finally, we have Hugh, a French form of the German Hugo,

vastly popular. It was the name of several continental saints, but, for the English, the twelfth-century Hugh of Lincoln is very important. He seems to have been very appealing: protective of ordinary people and firm with his superiors (even Henry II and Richard I), facing down mobs rioting against Jews, playing with children. A contemporary poem mentioned in Chapter 3 describes him helping to build his cathedral, carrying 'the hewn stones in a kind of hod, and lime mortar also'.[39] Margery Kempe, our indicator of the popularity of medieval saints, visits his shrine. But she also visits the shrine of Little St Hugh of Lincoln, a child said to have been murdered by Jews in 1225, whose story, recounted in medieval ballads, seems to have been fictional, or at least sufficiently without substance to exclude him from modern lists of saints. The Prioress in *The Canterbury Tales*, recounts the story of a very similar child murder but sets it in an Asian city.[40] Both Hughs might have been invoked by medieval namers in all the variants they make out of Hugh.

Norman Saints Take Over

Saints popular among the Normans become so among the English. Alexander, Austen, Bernard, Brice, Dennis, Giles, Gervase, Gregory, Harvey, Hilary, Lambert, Magnus (rare today), Maurice, Martin, and the womens' names Ellen, Brigid and Luce, have all been linked by etymologists to saints liked by the Normans. Some Breton/Celtic saints were also popular with them – Allen, Coleman, Mallet, Petherick and Sampson; these are discussed later.

Lambert was a seventh-century missionary-bishop from Maastricht, introduced by the Flemish, with many dedications in the Low Countries. Martin, said to be from Martin of Tours, a fourth-century missionary saint, was the founder of French monasticism, revered on the continent and with many church dedications in England. Chaucer's Knight in The Tale of Gamelyn refers to the original St Martin, from Hungary, a knight serving under Constantius and Julian who opposed the Arians and helped the poor, dying at Tours where his relics were preserved.

It seems to have been straightforward for the English to

adapt and use popular Norman versions of these classical saints' names rather than anglicizing them. Quite a number of these are unchanged and have few variants and many are Norman, mostly French, forms of names with classical roots. Some popular abbreviations emerge early on – Austen instead of Augustine, Bennet for Benedict, Ellis for Elias, Luke for Lucas. Chaucer, in *The Canterbury Tales*, already talks of 'seint Beneit' or Bennet, from Benedict, and his Host swears by 'seint Austin' rather than Augustine.[41] Others include Giles from Aegedius, Gregory from Gregorius, Maurus from Maurice, and Piers, like Langland's protagonist, or Pierce for Peter, as well as Hilary and Dennis. Giles was a revered seventh-century hermit from Arles; Hilary was popular in France particularly because of the fourth-century Hilarius of Poitiers; and Dennis came from the third-century martyr Dionysius, popularly known as the patron saint of France.

Some of these continental saints might have been chosen for their English connections. Bernard is thought to have come from the twelfth-century Bernard of Clairvaux, a founder of the Cistercians who established Rievaulx, Jervaulx and Fountains Abbeys in Yorkshire, but the same name also existed in England before the Conquest. Ellen is from St Helena, the mother of the Emperor Constantine, thought, incorrectly, to have been a British princess. But there are only continental connections for many others, including Lambert, Hilary, Dennis and the very popular Martin.

Some English Names

The examples quoted earlier of Thomas à Becket and John of Beverley show that some English saints also take classical or biblical names. Many names like Benedict, Piers for Peter, Stephen, Thomas and John were known as monks' names in pre-Conquest England. When, in 718, at the age of about forty, Wynfrith of Crediton left England to convert the German heathens, never to return, he took the name Boniface and it is as Saint Boniface the martyr that the Anglo-Saxon Wynfrith comes down to us. There are still Bonifases in Devon. After the Northumbrian Biscop

Baducing went to Rome in the seventh century he took the name of Benedict in France before returning to found the great monasteries of Wearmouth and Jarrow in Northumbria that, under his influence, became famous for their libraries, paintings and relics. Bede was taught by Benedict Biscop at Monkswearmouth.

But some monks, friars and priests seem to have kept indigenous names. Etienne Harding, an Englishman with a very English surname (although he did take a local first name), was the third Abbot of Citeaux from 1108–33. He sent Bernard to found the abbey of Clairvaux in 1115 and establish the Cistercian Order and his own effective organization at Citeaux may have influenced the Cistercian rules.[42] Harding is also remembered for commissioning a magnificently illuminated Bible that still exists. English saints with Old English names included Cuthbert, from Cudbeohrt, a seventh-century Northumbrian bishop of Lindisfarne, almost the only English saint invoked by the pilgrims in *The Canterbury Tales*. The Lindisfarne Gospels, written in his honour, are one of the finest surviving examples of Hiberno-Saxon art. Edward was either from the tenth-century English martyr or the later Edward the Confessor.

Saint Edmund was the King of East Anglia who died leading the East Anglian army against the Danes in 868. According to legend he was bound to a tree, pierced with arrows and beheaded, to be honoured as a saint within fifty years. A magnificent retable in the church at Thornham Parva in Suffolk, painted around 1330, probably for a local Dominican priory, includes St Edmund with a line-up of seven other saints and a crucifixion, all miraculously still intact. The other saints are two Dominicans, St Dominic and St Peter, three important preachers – St Catherine of Alexandria, St John the Baptist and St Margaret of Antioch recording the mission of the medieval Dominicans – and St Peter and St Paul, the principal founders of the church. To have included Edmund with this group shows his continued prominence some five centuries after his death and after the huge cultural change introduced by the Normans in the eleventh century. It is another signal of the long memories of the medieval English.

Three important English saints, Dunstan, Aethelwold and Oswald – two Englishmen and a Dane – kept their indigenous names and come down to us as Dunstan, Ellwood and Oswald. They were the tenth-century churchmen who spearheaded a revival of monasticism in England under first Edmund and then Edgar after it had disappeared in England in the second half of the ninth century. Dunstan rebuilt Glastonbury Abbey where he had studied and then became Archbishop of Canterbury, concerned with education, teaching Latin, reading and psalms. Aethelwold, Bishop of Winchester from 963, wrote the *Regularis Concordia*, which established common rules for monastic life in England and set the foundation for a nationwide monastic tradition. Oswald, from Asvaldr, god-ruler, bishop of Worcester, is remembered for establishing a monastery at Ramsey, on the edge of the fens and in the heart of Scandinavian East Anglia. The fenland monasteries he established with Aethelwold survived the next onslaught of the Danes and the monks they trained established the Benedictine tradition in England and secured its links with the continent, even sending missionaries there.[43]

Alphege, the Norman form of the Anglo-Saxon Alfheah that is Elphick today, was the English archbishop of Canterbury martyred by the Danes in 1012 for refusing to allow himself to be ransomed on the grounds that his people had already paid the Danes enough tribute. Some Danes were so shocked they crossed over to Aethelred the Unready, bringing with them forty-five ships.[44] Wulfstan, our Woolstones, was a long-serving bishop of Worcester in the eleventh century, who supported William I and kept his diocese after the Conquest.

There are a handful of British saints with Norse names. Their stories reflect the eclectic mix of names and races in the early Middle Ages. Eskil, a Norse name common in England both before and after the Conquest and still with us as Askell, was an Englishman martyred in Sweden in 1080 after protesting at a heathen festival. Although he was English, his name suggests why he went to the country where he was martyred. Osmund was an eleventh-century Norman who came with the Conquest. His name was Norse, a legacy of the Norse invaders to what is now northern France. He became bishop of Salisbury, chancellor to William I and connected with the Domesday Book. He died in 1099 and was only canonized in 1457, the last English saint until

1935. Magnus was the name of many Scandinavian kings, having been taken by Magnus I of Norway and Denmark who died in 1047 after Charlemagne, who was called Carolus Magnus. The name was very popular in Shetland, reflecting the close linkages between the islands and Norway, and Saint Magnus of Orkney, who died in 1116, was the son of a local ruler. In Scotland, the name became McManus.

Most Celts Choose Continental Names

The Celtic saints were enormously important for the early church after the Gauls had been conquered by pagans. It is thought that Wales was Christian from Roman times. The conversion of the northern half of Ireland is associated with St Patrick in the fifth century when the south was already Christian. From then until the mid-eighth century, when the Celtic church was finally absorbed into the Roman, Celt missionaries from Wales and Ireland travelled, following tracks of language.

The fact that the Celtic church was active so early seems, understandably, to have affected the take-up of the names of its saints in surnames. Celtic saints had both continental and indigenous names and surnames suggest the former survived better – Patrick, David, Samson and Mallet from Malo. Out of a sample of thirty-four Celtic saints in one compilation, twenty-one (or 62 per cent), most with indigenous names, do not seem to have produced surviving surnames, although many were important enough to have churches dedicated to them and places called after them. Yet the Cornish Petherick from Petroc, although only first recorded in the sixteenth century, shows that indigenous names can be revived as surnames. So all the Budocs and Cadocs, Dyfrigs and Illtyds who did outstanding missionary and monastic work in evangelizing Wales, south-west England and what is now northern France may not be lost but may survive in surnames that have changed out of all recognition, rather like Malo thought to be hiding in Mallet. Alternatively, and looking at the proportion of Celtic saints who took classical/biblical names, Celtic names were simply unfashionable.

Well-known Celtic saints have continental names. The pre-eminent Welsh saint Samson could have a classical name, although it is likely to have been Celtic in Wales and the south-west; Sampsons are recorded in Dorset and Devon in the thirteenth century. Samson took the popular trajectory, particularly for the Welsh, to Armorica, the core of present Brittany, in the early sixth century after travelling with his family to Cornwall and became abbot of Dol. He had studied at the great monastic centre of learning of St Illtyd in Llantwit Major, Glamorgan. There is an evocative record of a Sansom Cornuwala at the Cistercian abbey at Riveaulx in Yorkshire in about 1170. Five centuries after the saint's death, a namesake from Cornwall was reaching out to abbeys in the north.

The Celtic Dewi, the sixth-century abbot/bishop of Cardigan who became the patron saint of Wales, canonized by Henry I as part of his campaign to win over the Welsh, was popular among the medieval English as the Hebrew David or its Scottish/French form Davy. He worked in Wales, a strict ascetic, founding twelve monasteries, and went on pilgrimage to Jerusalem. Patrick, a Romano-Briton, the best known Celtic evangelist, was a missionary bishop. Born somewhere between the Clyde and the Severn, he established an organized church in northern Ireland, where he had been enslaved as a youth, beginning in 432. He set up his see at Armagh. Malo, the popular form of Maclovius, was a sixth-century Celt, who also probably originated in south-west Wales and went on to Armorica, where he gave his name to St Malo in Brittany. Today's Mallets are thought to include early Malos.

Paul Aurelian is another British Celt who took a Latin name. He was a sixth-century Bishop of Léon, popular in France, and a powerful missionary in Finisterre. There are traces of him in Wales and he is also said to have been educated at St Illtyd in south Wales. The twelfth-century Irish bishop Lorcan ua Tuathail became Lawrence O'Toole. Archbishop of Dublin in 1161, he is known as a simple monk and abbot who became involved in the politics surrounding an Anglo-Norman invasion.

A Few Choose Celtic Names

The names of a few saints who kept indigenous names have survived as surnames. Petherick from Petroc was an active sixth-century missionary from Wales, popular in Devon, Cornwall and Brittany. Little is known about him except his Welsh origin – Petroc is from Pedrawg. He settled in Padstow, where he landed from southern Wales, from where he is said to have gone on pilgrimages to Rome and Jerusalem and even established a hermitage on an island in the Indian Ocean. The ancient Cornish church was very close to the Welsh.

The Irish Colman was among the seventh-century Irish who established Iona off the coast of Mull and the great Northumbrian monastery at Lindisfarne under Oswald, Oswy and Oswin, all to be destroyed by the Vikings in the late eighth century. He was Bishop of Lindisfarne in about 661, carrying a name that had morphed from the Irish Columban into Colman and the Norse Kalman. It was an early and common name and a Richard Coleman recorded in Yorkshire in 1177 might commemorate the saint, but the name has many other meanings.

Saint Blaan was a late sixth-century Scottish missionary to the Picts, giving his name to a foundation at Dunblane, churches in Bute and elsewhere in Scotland and to the clan MacBlain, who are still with us. Finbarr was a seventh-century Irish saint associated with David in south Wales and left his name to Barra in the Outer Hebrides. There are places called Barr in Ayrshire and Renfrewshire and people with the name in Lothian in the early thirteenth century. Today's Barrs might originate in the name of the saint. There are several Finns – saints recalling the Celtic hero, from the sixth-century Finnian of Clonard in what is now Brittany, who made that monastic centre famous for its principles of religious life and learning, to Finan, a seventh-century missionary monk from Iona who became bishop of Lindisfarne.

Allen, an Old French/Breton name, came with the Bretons at the Conquest, particularly to Lincolnshire, linked to a Welsh and Breton saint. It was very popular in the Middle Ages. Some of our Furseys could come from the seventh-century Irishman who died in France in 648. He worked first in East Anglia where he established monasteries and then went on to Gaul. His tomb at Peronne became a place of pilgrimage and Bede describes him as a man of outstanding goodness.

As they travelled, these saints' names scattered with them, leaving place names and ancient dedications in churches, although many of these have since been changed. Early dedications to Celtic saints from these islands are enduring evidence of the linkages among the Celts on either side of the Channel and include those at Dol Cathedral and other churches in Brittany to Sansom, Allen, Fursey, Malo, Paul of Leon and Petroc.

So Saints Live On

Most of these saints' names became popular in England among lay people only after the Conquest. This seems to have been particularly true for the 'monks' names' Stephen, Thomas and John, but also for names like Cuthbert (later popular in the north), Lawrence, David, Dennis, Lambert, Matthew, George (which came with the Crusaders) and Nicholas. David was widespread in Wales (often as Dewi) before the Conquest, and Martin, Maurice, Patrick and Bernard occurred in England, but not, it seems, the names of early martyrs like Stephen or Lawrence, apostles or evangelists. There is a view that the ordinary secular Anglo-Saxons avoided saints' names out of respect.

But, if this were so, by the Middle Ages, the English have adopted the Norman familiarity with saints' names, as is evident from the ships' names quoted earlier. Marjery Kempe, in her early visions, is sufficiently easy with the Holy Family to see herself as maid to the pregnant St Anne and the Virgin. The pilgrims in *The Canterbury Tales* carry many saints' names – Simkin from Simon, Nicholas, Absolon, John, Piers for Peter, Hubert, Robin, Gervase and Geoffrey. The list includes some women, Helen, Molly from Mary, and a few Old English names like Cuthbert and Edward. They make many references to saints like Paul, James and Thomas. Several invoke saints that have very personal associations: the Host calls on the charismatic St Augustine; the Yeoman wears a St Christopher medallion on his travels; the extroverted Franklin invokes the patron saint of hospitality, St Julian; the highly civilized Prioress calls on St Helen, the gentlest of invocations; the corrupt Pardoner refers to the overstrict rules of St Benet and St Maurus, important Benedictines. Their saints are important element in their lives.

Medieval records feature many names of saints. While all might not be inspired by the saint, some certainly are. Dartmouth, the third largest town in Devon in the fourteenth century, is a cosmopolitan port with numerous inhabitants called after quite distant English and foreign places. Its medieval records refer to many people with saints' names, particularly those brought by the Normans. Several are held by chaplains, chantry priests and churchwardens – Martin, Dennis, Thomas, John, Alexander, Piers – and are likely to be after the saint, while others, like Lambert, carry names that are otherwise unusual. There are substantial numbers of Davys, Pauls and Sampsons, all Celtic saints and even more people called James, possibly after the James of Compostela whose shrine Dartmouth vessels plied with their cargo of pilgrims.

Some of these names have other meanings that will have helped them to survive. Over the years, names that sounded the same, often in different languages, seem to have been combined. We have mentioned Sigmund. Simpson is usually a personal name from Simon, but in Devon it could be from one of three places originally called Siweneston, which might help to track it to an original family. Dennis could be from the Greek Dionysius or mean a Dane from the Old French. Maclovius became Malo and Malo became Mallet, which might be nicknames for somebody cursed or steely (from two French words) or be from a diminutive of Mary (from the English). Lambert, the name of the saint from Maastricht, could also mean lamb-herd from the Old English, so the present surname might be from a Flemish saint or an English shepherd. Maurice could be the saint who assisted Benedict, or could be a nickname for someone swarthy both from the Latin derivation Mauritius or a Moor.

Put together the surnames from these saints' names and they tell the story of Christianity in Anglo-Saxon England. Our Gregories, common in the Middle Ages, recall Gregory the Great, who died in 604 and sent forty missionaries from Rome to pagan

England in 596, led by Augustine, our Austens, who became the first Archbishop of Canterbury. Chaucer's Host in *The Canterbury Tales* invokes 'seint Austin'. Bishop Lawrence of Canterbury went with Augustine, and Justus and Paulinus followed in 601. The story of the early Celtic church begins with the Romano-Briton, Patrick, born 385, who went to Ireland and this missionary work continues over the next three centuries with Samson and Malo, our Mallet, who went to Brittany and Paul who went to Léon. They are just examples of the many others who left from Wales, Cornwall and Ireland to evangelize on the continent of Europe.

Three eminent Northumbrians represent the flowering there of the church and scholarship before the Viking destruction: Oswald, the Christian king who brought Aidan and other missionaries to convert his kingdom, Cuthbert, the missionary bishop and Benedict Biscop, our Bennet, who founded the monasteries of Wearmouth and Jarrow and established the great libraries used by Bede. All three are surnames today. Edmund and Alphege stand for all the others martyred by the Danes. Oswald of Worcester, Aethelwold, or Ellwood, and Dunstan were the three tenth century church reformers who re-established monasticism in Anglo-Saxon England before the arrival of the Normans.

The next chapter will focus on what the personal names with only or mainly Norman and Old English, Norse and Celtic roots have to tell about medieval society and the Anglo-Saxon world.

CHAPTER 8

THE SURVIVAL OF NATIVE PERSONAL NAMES

MANY PERSONAL SURNAMES have single or dominant roots. William is Norman, Edward English, Harald primarily Norse, and Morgan Celt. These have much to say about both medieval and Anglo-Saxon society and are the focus of this chapter. Through the namesakes of these surnames in myth and legend, medieval people revive pre-Conquest culture and ensure it comes down to us. Chapter 7 talked about the shared cultural inheritance and world view in multi-rooted personal names. Here, we show how the continental inheritance is grounded within the English context.

How Do English Personal Names Survive?

The odds are against the revival of indigenous names in the four-teenth century. The great majority of freemen in southern England had exchanged their single indigenous names for unchanged Norman ones by 1200.[1] By the surname period the Old English, Old Scandinavian and Celtic first names have largely disappeared from the records. In Devon, only about 2 per cent of taxpayers have these names in 1332. Cole, Alfred or Alured, Edmund and Edward are among the few survivors in Devon and Dorset.[2] As noted in Chapter 7, indigenous personal names seem to have been kept alive by the very poorest.

The speech of the medieval English is in these surnames: English, Norman French, based on Latin, together with some Norse and Celt. More like a wide-brimmed hat than a pyramid, the power structure of medieval society has very few Normans and normanized English making a small crown, with the vast majority of the population forming the brim below. Languages invert this hat, with the English brim on top, Norse and Celt at the tips, and Norman French and Latin underneath. The language of personal surnames shadows this upturned hat. While single Norman names are the basis for the most popular names in this group, most are heavily anglicized. The majority of unchanged Norman names – Williams and Richards, Hughes and Roberts – are here because they are massively adopted by the Welsh some two to three centuries after the English and so do not reflect medieval English culture. As they change the Norman names, medieval people also go back to ancient indigenous names that are Anglo-Saxon, Norse and Celt.

It is the culmination of the development of a pride in English and its Anglo-Saxon roots. Listen to the Franklin in *The Canterbury Tales* when he asks the other pilgrims to excuse him for his 'rude speche' and firmly says 'I sleep never on the mount of Pernaso,/Ne lerned Marcus Tullius Cithero'. He goes on to say he only knows such 'colours as growen in the mede'.[3] His English is the language of the countryside, of the ordinary people, not the literate elite. One of Chaucer's good pilgrims, with the parson and the knight, the Frankleyn distances himself from the classical French tradition and sets his tale of knights and ladies squarely in ancient Britain and Armorica in present-day Brittany. *The Canterbury Tales* is written in English in about 1384, when surnames are stabilizing, and both assert the new strength of the English voice.

English Rooted in Anglo-Saxon Culture

These surnames reveal a great deal about the namers. The anglicization of Norman names reflects nostalgia for the form and beat of ancient single names. Rick, Will and Hodge take you directly back to the sound and the style of the Bottas, Hoccas, Dodas and Ulfs, the Old English names of the Domesday Book, and Dawkins and Hancock to twin-structured Anglo-Saxon names like Godwin and Aelfheah. These anglicizations show attitudes. In changing Norman names so dramatically, people clearly do not believe the patronage of anyone with the original name will do them any good. Then the sound and rhythm of these names, the transposed consonants and vowels, rhymes and alliterative suffixes echo a pure joyfulness in playing with language. And Alldridge from Aelfric shows the name of a great Anglo-Saxon scholar is at least nominally still in peoples' memories in the fourteenth century, while the many names from Norse and Celtic legend recall the pre-Conquest culture that people in the Middle Ages are famil-iar with. To an extent, the recording of folk history during the naming period may have strengthened these choices, perhaps by validating their importance, perhaps by making more information available.

These Old English, Norse and Celtic names recall and extend our knowledge of ancient cultures. They document times of conflict as kingdoms were consolidated and invaders repulsed and absorbed and the need for protection, toughness and good judgement. They echo the heroic morality of Norse, Teutonic and Norman legends, heroism in the face of unpredictable and enormous odds, the search for fame and the importance of friendship.

Understanding these surnames adds to what records tell of social history and the integration of cultures. From Alfred to Edward the Confessor, English kings gave their sons English names and Scandinavian kings gave theirs Scandinavian names. Royal names reflected tribal origins. But the great English earl Godwine under the Danish Cnut gave two of his younger sons English names, Tostig and Leofwine, and two of the older ones Scandinavian names, Harold and Svein. Ambitious nobles balanced their loyalties.

Whether you were an English or Scandinavian king, it was important in unifying and ruling England to engage both tribes. Thus the English king Edgar, who ruled between 959–75, busy reclaiming English land from the Danes and crowned at York as the English king, appointed three bishops to drive forward the Benedictine revival – the Englishmen Aethelwold and Dunstan, he who enjoyed heathen poetry, and Oswald, a Dane. The Danish King Cnut appointed three great earls, Godwine earl of Essex, Leofric of Mercia, and Siward, a Dane, to rule in tumultuous Northumbria; again, two Englishmen and a Dane. This Siward was to marry into the ruling Northumbrian family, but he called his son Waltheof, an Anglo-Scandinavian name, and Waltheof was to pursue a famously violent intergenerational feud with an English neighbour, as discussed on page 262.[4]

The roots of the personal surnames chosen by medieval people largely record where the different races settled in Anglo-Saxon England, although many English must have taken Norse names, and vice versa. Norse surnames tend to concentrate in the north-west and the east, while Old English and names brought by the Normans are further south and west and the Celtic/Breton names in the Welsh borders and the areas of Breton settlement.

Characteristically local names are still a common phenomenon. This is remarkable, given the political and social confusion of the ninth and tenth centuries and the reconquest of the Danish counties east of Watling Street up to the Tees by the son and grandsons of Alfred the Great in the tenth century, followed by 300 years of Norman rule. Medieval records particularly of Norse names still in their original areas show the profound effects of the Viking Age on Anglo-Saxon society. This concentration of tribal names in tribal areas will have helped ancient cultures to persist; traditional societies have long memories. Surnames ensure the cultures survive.

It is impossible to know whether people choosing these indigenous names just know them or whether and how much they know the legends and the culture they sprang from. Scandinavian traditions were strong in England before the Conquest. Scandinavian areas kept their own laws and customs and although the last Danish King of York, Eric Bloodaxe, left in 954, there were Danish kings of England almost up to the Conquest. More importantly, language is the vehicle for history and legends and records show Norse continued to be spoken in some areas at least until the twelfth century, suggesting the oral tradition of Norse legends, just as personal and place names, continued to survive the Conquest.

The need these personal surnames fill could be for variety, or for a change from Latin sounds to the sound of the English that most people speak. Perhaps, as they alter the Norman and return to indigenous names, people want to record their own roots, or are nostalgic for Saxon England. Based on their own experiences of famine and plague, people may identify with names describing a violent and unpredictable world and need its magic and heroes.

But, at the very least, the choices show, first, that English is the preferred medium of expression and, second, that an English voice and an English culture exist, rooted in an Anglo-Saxon world view that is still accessible to and valued by ordinary medieval people. When the English had earlier exchanged complex and evocative single Old English names for those of the invaders, English had also appeared to have lost the battle of the languages. As the English go back to English versions of these new names and their pre-Norman culture for others, it is a tide that raises all ships. Shortly thereafter English emerges as the dominant language.

The caveats that apply to the etymological information in all surnames are particularly relevant to indigenous personal surnames. Because they seem to belong largely to those who fall below the recording net of tax and court, it is hard to establish a chronology for them; pre-Conquest records are rare, and even those between the Conquest and the fourteenth century, when a surge in written documents occurs, scarce. Then, too, many of these names are difficult to track because they change form, combine with others, or simply disappear.

The Norman Names and the Welsh

Personal surnames based on Norman single names are vastly more popular than others. Typically brought with the Conquest as single names, many were nevertheless in England earlier. They are Old German or Old French. Their modern success comes from two facts: within very few decades of 1066, most people had dropped Anglo-Saxon single names in favour of Norman ones; and the Welsh, taking surnames some two centuries after the English, liked them.

The most popular single names from fourteenth-century records are: John, William, Thomas, Richard, Robert, Henry, Roger and Geoffrey, in order of importance.[5] John, William, Thomas and Henry are in almost the same order in modern lists of the most popular Norman surnames.[6] When employers, guardians and potential benefactors almost all have the single Norman names the English had adopted after the Conquest, one would expect the first personal surnames, particularly, to record beneficiaries called after them.

But what happens next reverses the post-Conquest switch. When they become surnames, many of these popular single names fracture into a multitude of very English variants – abbreviations, pet names, rhyming alternatives, and diminutives. Hodge and Dodge from Robert, Rick and Ricketts from Richard, Wilson and Willcock from William ... the variations are enormous. Hugh alone has more than ninety. While single Norman names sound different to English or Norse names, the new versions the English make of them are closer – Hudd from Hugh or Richard reminds one of the Anglo-Saxon Hudda and Watte from Walter of Wuffa. The transformation shows a newly confident people detaching Norman French from its origins.

The Welsh dominate those forms of the most popular Norman personal names today that are closest to the original single names. The top five most popular Norman surnames are there now mainly because the Welsh take them around the Act of Union of 1536. Most of the Jones, Davies and Williams, from John, David and William, are Welsh, and half or more of the Hughes, Richards and Roberts. Jones and Evans come from John; Evans is the Welsh form of Ieuan, and Jones from Ioan, the translation adopted for the Welsh authorized version of the Bible. The Welsh pick predominantly popular personal names; they have few nicknames, occupational or place names. In a sample from Cardiff in the 1960s, nineteen of twenty-one names are personal surnames. Nor do they like variants or pet forms, usually preferring the forms quoted above that end in '-s', although there are exceptions, such as Parry instead of Henry, Pritchard for Richard and Probert for Robert. The names starting with 'P' are usually contractions of the original Welsh prefix '*ap*', which means son of.

These names start in medieval England and many English still hold the unexpurgated versions. Jones and Davys are Old French names and Williams, Henry and Robert, Richard and Hugh are Old German, Robert coming to England with Edward the Confessor.

Many Welsh are of course in England during the naming period. They are usually called Welsh or its variants, such as Wallace or Wallis, after their origins. *Wealas* was the name the invading Angles, Saxons and Jutes called a foreigner or a slave. There were over a hundred Waleis or Walensis in the Domesday Book (see Chapter 4). A few Welsh personal names – Bowen, Maddock – emerge in the English/Welsh border counties in the twelfth and thirteenth centuries. These become surnames at the same time as the English and are hereditary long before surnames are known in Wales. Most families with these names today have lived in England since the time English surnames were established.

The Fracturing of the Norman Names

Few other surnames have as many variants, pet forms and diminutives as those from the very popular Norman single names. Hugh has the most, but there are not many fewer for Richard, Robert or William. Many of these variants are more popular than their originals – there are vastly more Watts than Walters, for example, and Hutchings than Hugh (excluding the Welsh Hughes). Some of these variants are obvious – Ugo belongs to Hugh – but some are not so – Hotchkiss belongs to Roger via Hodge. Many are confusing: Gillot, with its French diminutive, could belong to Giles, Julian or Guillaume, for William; Hancock and Hann to Randolph, Henry or John; and Hawkin could come from Harry or, via a rhyming form of Raw, from Ralph. Wyatt could be a diminutive of Guy or William.

It is hard to identify patterns in the proliferating variants of these Norman surnames. But there are some. They show a strong urge to abbreviate. A list of rioting peasants is given by John Gower in his poem about the Peasants' Revolt, *Vox Clamantis*: Watte, Thomme, Symme, Bette, Gibbe, Hykke, Colle, Geffe, Wille, Grigge, Dawe, Hobbe, Lorkyn, Hudde, Judde, Tebbe, Jakke and Hogge.[7] All are abbreviations or pet forms of Norman first names that are the source of surnames. Watte is obviously from Walter, Thomme from Thomas, Wille from William, and so on. But Hudde, for instance, could have been a form of Hugh or Richard, both Norman names, or could have come from the earlier Old English name Hudda, Colle from Nicholas or the English/Norse Cola. All these names echo Anglo-Saxon personal names like Botha, Drabba, Mugga, or Hocca that gave us Hockin. The names of the invaders are anglicized, sometimes into oblivion, by the imagination of the invaded.

But abbreviation is often only the first stage. Suffixes are frequently added, making the new name quite different from but often just as long as the original if not longer. You cannot help thinking that people are consciously following the Anglo-Saxon practice of integrating two ideas in the same name as they do this, as Godwine came from two words, meaning good and friend. These suffixes reflect the linguistic influences on medieval culture. The '-kin' in Wilkin, Simkin and Hotchkin (from Roger), which is affectionate, is thought to come from Flanders. The '-cock' in Jeffcock (and Jeffcot and Jeffcoat as well) and Wilcox is Old English, and adds the thought of youth and liveliness. Other suffixes make diminutives and are French; Howett from Hugh, Dixon and Ricket from Richard, Wilmot from William and Rabbit and Robin from Robert. Robin Hood is a popular folk hero and the first written reference to him is believed to be in *Piers Plowman*, written in the 1370s, when Sloth refers to ballads about him.

Making Music

Collect these names, and you hear gusto in the sounds and rhythms of the English language. John is from the Old French Johan, Jehan and Jean and gives us the popular Welsh Jones and Evans, as well as Joan, Johnes and Joynes. After that, our ancestors seem to play ball with the name. Johan and Jehan turn into Jan and Jon, then come the diminutives Janin, Jenin and Jonin; then up goes the ball and comes down as pet forms Jankin, Jonkin and Jenkin; then over it goes to someone else and comes back as Hancock and Hankin. Priests are mockingly called John and Jankin means a fool. There seems to have been no end to what you could do, with some imagination, to a one-syllable name.

A lovely group is there just because it rhymes. So Richard becomes Rick, Dick, Hick and Hitch; Roger becomes Dodge and Hodge; Robert becomes Robb, Dobb, Nobb and Hobb. From Gower's list Hykke is clearly a rhyming form of Richard, Hobbe of Robert and Dawe could be more indirectly from Ralph which first became Raw. All of these variants have their own suffixes – Dickson from Dick, Dodson and Dudgeon from Dodge, Dawkins from Dawe, and so on. Even the pious William Langland, in *Piers Plowman*, shows the same gusto for rhythmical alliteration with his Jack the Juggler, Friar Fix-it and Friar Flatterer, Randy Robin, Robert the Robber and old Muggin the Miller.[8]

Consonants and vowels are readily transposed. You can see this in the rhyming forms. Raw to Daw, Dick to Hick and so on. Roger attracts different consonants but the 'o' doesn't vary until you come to Dudgeon. Robert seems to attract 'a', viz. Dabb (and Dabinett), Nabb and Rabson. Richard sticks with its 'i' until Hedgecock appears. William keeps the 'i', then produces a 'y' instead with Wyatt. Walter becomes Wat. The Old English names hiding in these variants include Hudd in Hugh from the Old English Hudda and the Old English Dodda in the Dodd from Roger. Hopcyn, a Welsh name used in Wales from the thirteenth century, could be in our Hopkins from the diminutive Hobb from Robert.

Regional Versions

The anglicization of these Norman names brings regional variations. Jeffcock, a pet form of Geoffrey, is recorded east of Sheffield in the fourteenth century and is still pre-eminently a variant from the Sheffield area. Rumball, from the Old German Rumbald, is in Essex in 1191 and the fourteenth century and is still from East Anglia, the south east and East Midlands.[9] Other variants have broader distribution: Hitchins, Hitchcock, Hiscock and Richings are all southern variants of Richard. Hudd appears chiefly in the south west, especially Gloucestershire. That these names are still in the areas where they first emerge is consistent with most research, despite the evidence that many disappeared as male heirs failed or families migrated.

The adaptations denoting sons are regional too. The suffix '-son', a Norse characteristic and almost always a feature of northern surnames in medieval times, gives us our Robinsons and Thompsons, Wilsons and Jacksons, Watsons and Simpsons, who are all in the list of most popular names in the modern sample. It is generally the most popular names that have these adaptations; you do not find them added to names like Baldwin or Gerard, Randall or Osmond. Most Norman single names survive best in these '-son' forms. They were often transcribed in Latin in early records rather than as the English name – as *filius Robertii*, for instance, instead of Robertson. But by the fourteenth century the Robertson form is being used.

Later than the '-sons', and in the south, an '-s' is added instead, to make Williams or Gibbs. It is also added to a few indigenous names like Howell and Powell in the English counties bordering Wales. But the added '-s' could also mean anyone living at the relevant house, so a son or servant, and the earliest examples almost always mean a wife or daughter. The upper classes use 'Fitz-' as a prefix to mean a son, so you get Fitzherbert for example. Adding '-man', as in Harriman, identifies a servant.

Contemporary Examples

As well as William and Richard, the medieval English take Norman names that are common then but seem more unusual today. These tend not to be abbreviated and to have fewer variants. Baldwin, Walter and Giles, Jeffery, Guy, Wyatt, Herbert, Lambert, Ralph, Jack and Oliver are all popular after the Conquest. A John Baldewyn is among the wealthiest assessed for tax in Shrewsbury in 1309, with an inventory that includes a very expensive riding horse, quite a bit of cash and expensive clothes, jewellery and silver plus armour, so he may have been a soldier.[10] Baldwin could have been popular because it was the name of five kings of Jerusalem spanning the twelfth century when the Crusaders held power there after the first crusade took the city in 1099. Baldwin de Redvers, created First Earl of Devon in 1141 and born in the early 1100s, might have been called after these crusader kings.[11]

Norman names are common in medieval literature. The wanton merry Friar in the Prologue in *The Canterbury Tales* is Hubert, there is Robin the Miller, and Gervase, from Jarvis, the smith in the Miller's Tale, Alisoun, from Alice, the 'wilde and yong' wife of the Carpenter in the same story, Geoffrey for Geoffrey de Vinsauf, the thirteenth-century poet and Sir Russel, the fox in the Nun's Priest's Tale. Similarly, a 1377 tax list from Dartmouth in Devon includes, as well as Henry, Rogger, William and its pet form Wilcock, Davy and Michel, both common French names, Gerard and Piers from Pierre which has given us our Pierces and Perrins. Piers is the name Chaucer gives to the Monk accompanying the Nun who tells the story of the chanticleer and the fox. In his study of Devon names, Postles finds names like Martin, Ellis, Jordan and Davy more frequent second names than William, Richard or Robert in the fourteenth century.

Not all Norman names came with the Conquest. Although our knowledge depends on haphazardly surviving records, scholars believe many did – notably William, Hugh, Roger and Richard. But Baldwin, Robert, Ralf, Simmonds, Walter and many others were popular in England before then. A Viking Walter founded the Norman dynasty, and fragments of a poem called *Waldere* are thought to record an epic similar to *Beowulf* about Walter of Aquitaine that would have been known to the Anglo-Saxons. Many more Old German names must have circulated in England before the Normans came. Although Herbert is thought to have arrived with the Normans, a seventh-century memorial stone to Herebert, an unknown priest, at Monkwearmouth in Northumbria shows a Herbert in England centuries before 1066.[12] England was part of continental culture well before the Conquest.

Old English Names

The striking feature of the popular Norman names is how much they are changed. And the way they are changed, by contraction and then re-expansion, has meant their original meanings can be hard to identify. Although Anglo-Saxon names seem on the face of it more likely targets for alteration, Aelfsige seems less easy on the modern tongue than Roger or Hugh, in fact many Old English surnames stay fairly close to the original twin structure and meanings characteristic of most Anglo-Saxon names. Elsey, for instance, is closer to Aelfsige than Hodge is to Robert. Most Anglo-Saxon personal names consisted of two concepts – Edgar, prosperity spear, or Godwine, good friend. The structure of these revived Anglo-Saxon names reflects a nostalgia for Saxon rhythms.

Compared with the popular Norman names, Old English names have few variants, suffixes and abbreviations, although names ending in '-ing' are entirely English and denote a dependent. Wilding, Gooding, Harding come from these names.[13] Many carry information on Anglo-Saxon times. Their meanings mirror those of the names discussed in Chapter 7, but it is illuminating to show how connected they are to their English context, suggesting these meanings are important to the namers. They echo warrior kings who traced dynasties back to gods, the wars and invasions that united England and the Anglo-Saxon world view and ethics of nobility and courage. They revive stories and heroic principles that were centuries old and arose far beyond the shores of the island that was their home. They show the strength of this culture where many surnames stay local to the areas where the first migrants had brought them, suggesting they have not moved far from their Anglo-Saxon roots. Understanding the background to and etymology of names illuminates ancient records in a unique way.

Edward is probably the most popular English name, with solid ecclesiastical and secular precedents in the tenth-century Edward the Martyr and the eleventh-century King Edward the Confessor, who preceded St George as the patron saint of England. In a tax record from Shrewsbury in 1313, of the 179 listed, only one Old English personal name occurs: Edward. Other relatively popular

English names include Cole, the royal names, Alfred, Edmund and Eddy from Eadwig, Goodwin, Woolrich from Wulfric, Mitchell and Cuthbert.

There is a group of appealing single-syllable English names that have survived into modern surnames in their own right. These include names like Botta (now Bott), Hocca (Hockin), Hudda (Hudd), Wuffa (Wade), Cutha (Cade) and Frow from Freowine. (The final '-a' was masculine.) In the eighth century an English merchant called Botta was recorded living and working in Marseilles – giving a glimpse of Anglo-Saxon trading networks and how they operated.[14] The relatively rare Drabble from Drabba has survived in the Sheffield area. Cola and Eddy are perhaps the most popular of this type of name, and records are full of them. The Devon Domesday Book has many others, including Hecca, Doda, Ulf, and Wado. Gower's list of the participants in the Peasant's Revolt show how medieval namers revive this single-syllable tradition in the way they treat Norman names. The predilections of the medieval English for simple names have not changed since Anglo-Saxon times.

The Warrior Kings

The world view in Old English names has to do with battles, war, the qualities of heroes and the importance of protection, magic and the gods, themes echoing those in the names of the Normans and the Norse. Conflict was ever-present in Anglo-Saxon England. In about 600, England had twelve kingdoms. Over the next 250 years these consolidated into three or four, with Northumberland pre-eminent in the seventh century under Edwin, Oswald and Osiu, Mercia in the following century under Aethelbert and Offa and then Wessex under Egbert and Alfred. The Norse and Danish invasions of the eighth to tenth centuries virtually destroyed all save Wessex. But they motivated unification. As Alfred's son and grandsons – Edward, Aethelstan, Edmund and Edred – reclaimed the land lost to the Scandinavians, the last Scandinavian King of York was expelled in 954 and England was united as a Christian kingdom under Edgar, crowned King of England in 957. But continued Danish raids meant no relief from the threat of war and the need to wage it successfully.

So the English monarchy in Anglo-Saxon times depended on the success of its warrior kings. Their names recall the attributes they needed – noble counsel, prosperity protection, hardness, prosperity war and prosperity spear – names that record the need for protection of a land under attack.

Ironically, Alfred, who began the consolidation of England, and Aethelred, who lost it to the Danes, share the quality of good counsel – Alfred means elf-counsel, and Aethelred (our Aldreds), noble counsel. Alfred was the classical combination of warrior and scholar and Aethelred, feeble and hesitant, was known as Aethelraed Unraed, literally noble counsel no counsel. 'When the enemy were in the east, our army was kept to the west, and when the enemy were in the south, then was our army kept in the north,' recalls the contemporary Abingdon chronicler of Aethelred's campaigns.[15] Alfred's ambitions for his kingdom are strikingly clear from the names of his son and grandsons: Edward prosperity guard; Aethelstan noble stone; Edmund prosperity protection; and Eadred prosperity counsel. With his consolidation of the kingdom of Wessex Alfred had stemmed the tide of invasion. His descendants had to preserve his success with boldness and judgement.

Not only did they conserve it, they expanded his kingdom into a nation. Three Edwards ruled England in these difficult times, but Edward the Elder, son of Alfred, seems to have deserved the name the most. He ruled from 899 to 924 and with his sister Aethelflaed conquered the bulk of the Danelaw, driving the English frontier north to Bakewell in Derbyshire. His son Aethelstan (our Alstones and Astons), extended it into Northumbria, invading Scotland. He and his half-brother Edmund won the decisive battle at Brunanburh (a place that has never been identified precisely) in 937 against a coalition of the Norse kingdom of Dublin, Strathclyde and the Scots, a battle that historians recognize as creating England as a single kingdom.

Edwy from Eadwig (prosperity war) ruled only from 955–9, and his name – a common one – is echoed in its diminutive, Eddy. Edgar, prosperity spear, succeeded him. These two kings, predominantly the latter, presided over a revival of Benedictine monasticism, all but destroyed by the Danes and the Norse by 900, and Edgar is remembered as the first king of England to have been crowned. The ceremony took place in Bath in 973 and the church played a large part in it.

The Saxon word for kingdom is *rice* – recorded in names like Godric, Woolrich, Aldrich and Loveridge. A sheriff called Godric, good or god ruler and Goodrich today, at the time of Edward the Confessor, is remembered for giving his maid quite a bit of land in Buckinghamshire as long as she taught his daughter to make orphreys, or gold embroidery – a nice example of the value of the skill of doing gold embroidery. The freeing of a slave called Wulfric (Woolrich) describes the orderly way in which the Anglo-Saxons liked to manage things. Wulfric was liberated at a crossroads, a symbol of his new freedom to choose where to go. His liberation had three witnesses, including the priest and the clerk who recorded it.[16] And so he is one of the very few slaves to have a voice through his name today.

King is *cyning* or *cyng*, which became a nickname rather than a personal name, although it did exist as a personal name because Kingson is derived from it. But there are several names based on *cyne*, or royal: Kinman, Kenward and Kenway are examples, meaning, respectively, royal man, royal guard and royal war. Kinsey is *cynesige*, or royal victory.

War, Magic and Heroism

Saxon kings traced their ancestry back to the gods in royal genealogies that were important subjects of poems and epics. Seven out of eight surviving Anglo-Saxon dynasties go back to Woden, the English version of Odin, the Norse king of the gods.[17] Oswald means god ruler. Usually English, the best-known Oswalds today are associated not with pagan myth and magic, but Christianity. An Anglo-Saxon Oswald was one of the three strong seventh-century rulers of Northumberland who made his kingdom so powerful it dominated the south for the only time in Anglo-Saxon history. A Christian, he was responsible for establishing the religion in Northumberland, bringing in monks from Iona and elsewhere in

Scotland to establish and strengthen his monasteries. One of these was Lindisfarne, already created by Aidan from Ireland in 635, which became an important centre of teaching and scholarship until abandoned in 835 under the onslaught of the Danes. Oswald the Dane is among the saints mentioned in Chapter 7 as pushing forward a revival of monasticism in England in the tenth century.

Components of Anglo-Saxon Names

All could be prefixes or suffixes

– *aelf, elf**	– *raed, counsel*
– *aedel, noble**	– *ric, rule*
– *beohrt, bright*	– *sige, victory*
– *ead, riches*	– *stan, hard, bold*
– *heah, high*	– *weald, power, ruler*
– *leof, love*	– *weard, guard*
– *maer, famous*	– *wig, war*
– *mund, protection*	– *wine, friend*
– *os, divine*	– *wulf, wolf*

*aelf and aedel have been conflated in many modern surnames

Magic is intrinsic to the Anglo-Saxon outlook, where rulers and ruling take on superhuman qualities. These are surnames that originally contain *aelf, wulf* or *os*. Ellwood, Aldrich and some Eliots, are elf rulers and Alfred is elf counsel. (Aelfheah, now Elphick or the Norman Alphege, seems to have been an affectionate name for someone small.) Woolrich and Woolston invoke the power of the wolf. The need for victories was ever present in Anglo-Saxon England. War and victory could be magical, too – Algar is elf spear, and Elsey, elf victory. A Bishop Aelfsige of Chester-le-Street was one of King Alfred's wise men, summoned to his council when he needed advice, and we know of him because he is recorded as staying in a tent in Woodyates, Oakley Down in Wessex when a provost records adding collects to a ritual book

Aelfsige had with him.[18] War, power and victory are also recorded in Harold and Hereweald, many today incorporated in Harold, from *weald*, army power, Rimmel, a rare name meaning border war, Levett, beloved battle, Livesey, dear victory and Sewell, victory ruler, both with *sige* suffixes.

Alaway is elf war, and a record of an Aelfwig at the Conquest gives an insight into the usefulness of specialists. William II (1087–1100) recommended that, despite the massive alienation of English landowners, an English priest called Aelfwig should continue to hold his living in Sutton Courtenay because he was learned in the law.[19] That William specifically recommended an Englishman for the living suggests there was opposition to the idea.

The purpose of magical powers was protection; these are the *-weard* and *-mund* names. Wyman (also Norse) is war protection, Aylward and Aylmer noble protection, Eastman, grace/favour protection, Garman spear protection. Both war and protection from it, or perhaps through it, preserve or win prosperity (*-ead*). Edward and Edmund are prosperity guard and Eddy prosperity war.

An important group of surnames revives Anglo-Saxon ideals. They identify qualities that are admired in rulers and warriors and the importance of friendship. Nobility is a concept that runs through many of these names. It includes the *-aedel* and *-beohrt* names, as well as those adding the concept of fame, or *-maer*. Since *aedel* and *aelf* can no longer be separated in the roots of many surnames now, all the *aelf* names mentioned could also record noble rulers, wars, victories and protection. In addition, Albert is noble bright, Ayliffe a noble gift, Aldred is noble counsel, and Allnatt noble or daring. An Alnoth (Allnatt today) is a military engineer responsible for the royal buildings at Westminster and the Tower of London in 1157, buildings at Windsor in 1166–73, as well as for the restoration of Westminster Abbey after a fire. Nobility is often associated with fame, *maer*, recorded in Gummer, a southern name, which could be from Gnomar, battle famous, or Godmaer, good famous. Cobbold is famous bold and Cuthbert famous bright.

Allaway, can be noble war from Aedelwig, and a story about an Aethelwig gives an insight into the character of that most

246

scorned Anglo-Saxon king, Aethelred the Unready. Aethelwig was the king's reeve in Buckingham and, with his counterpart from Oxford, a Winsige, he illegally gave a Christian burial to two brothers killed while defending, against the law, one of their men who had stolen a bridle. When the ealdorman brought the case to Aethelred, the latter 'did not wish to sadden Aethelwig', and refused to act. Worse, he granted Aethelwig the brothers' forfeited estates.[20] Little wonder that his reign was plagued by lack of support from his ealdormen if he consistently ignored their advice in this way.

The names of heroes as well as kings record the mental and physical attributes needed for good leadership and victory. Harding, brave warrior, Alstan noble stone, Stannard stone hard, Woolston, wolf hard, Kennard is bold/royal guardian, the rare Cobbold, Willard and Kemble are all bold (the latter also means chief war in Welsh). The English name of one Wulfstan who told King Alfred about his travels in northern waters and to Baltic ports in the late eighth/early ninth century, shows the English involved in the Baltic trade even as the Vikings invaded England.[21] Judgement, -raed, is important: Alfred elf counsel, Aldred noble counsel.

Friendship

Among all the names that glorify war and the boldness and guardianship that go with it, is a clutch of Old English names that record more man-sized concepts. One is the importance of friendship, demonstrated by names with the suffix '-win' or '-wine' as in Darwin (dear friend), Goodwin (good friend), Frewen or Frow (generous friend), and Alvin or Alwin (noble or elf friend), which was common in the Middle Ages but rare today – indeed, some Alwins are lost in the more popular Allens. A famous antecedent of our Goodwins was the ambitious Anglo-Saxon Godwine, Earl of Wessex, who rose to prominence under Edward the Confessor, who had taken the throne from Harthacnut in 1042. Godwine's daughter Edith married the king, and one of his sons was Harold II, the king killed in the Battle of Hastings in 1066.

Unwin means the opposite, an enemy, but catches on. A Stephen Onwin assessed for tax in Shrewsbury in 1306, has a packhorse and some grain, and has begun to acummulate some covetable possessions – a little brassware and some clothes worth valuing.[22]

Leof means beloved, and there are many names combined with the word – Levett from Leofgeat, beloved Geat, Lewin with all its variants from Leofwine, beloved friend, Livesey from Leofsige, beloved victory, and so on. Luff, the modern name almost identical with the Anglo-Saxon, just means beloved and was a Bedfordshire/Dorset/Essex name in the fourteenth century.[23] A Lewin ancestor has left a record of how the Anglo-Saxon legal system worked. In about 990 in Berkshire a Leofwine contested a claim by a Wynflaed that his father had given her two estates. Anglo-Saxon lawsuits were settled by the parties bringing character witnesses to establish their trustworthiness rather than the justice of the charge. Leofwine was trounced when Wynflaed produced declarations on her behalf by the Archbishop of Canterbury, the bishop of Rochester, the ealdorman of Hampshire and the king's mother. He handed the estates over, but received in return gold and silver that Wynflaed had received from his father.[24]

Legends Enliven

With these surnames, medieval people engage with Saxon culture and through them the culture comes down to us. Legends both explain the names and give them context.

The kings with superhuman attributes in surnames like Sewell or Oswald go back to Charlemagne in *Chanson de Roland* and a Roger, Hrothgar, in *Beowulf* who led 'The Danes to such glory that comrades and kinsmen/Swore by his sword ... '. Kings are loved, Loveridge is beloved ruler. *Beowulf* records 'Shild's son, ruling as long as his father/And as loved, a famous lord of men'. Kings protect, as examples like Edmond and Wyman suggest. Hrothgar, is 'the Danes' high prince and protector'.[25]

Even an apparently human characteristic like judgement, or counsel, the *raed* in Alfred or Elldred, is the stuff of heroes. 'There is wise valour, and there is recklessness:/Prudence is worth more than foolhardiness' says Oliver in the *Chanson de Roland*.[26]

The nexus of nobility and fame in names like Aldric and Cuthbert comes directly from legend. Nobility is associated with heroism, courage in war, wisdom and gentleness in rule and the willingness to die for a higher cause. 'I'd rather die than thus be put to shame' cries Roland preparing to fight a vastly superior force of Saracens who 'cover all the mountains and the vales'. Heroism in the face of death leads to fame for Beowulf:

> ... he who can earn it should fight
> For the glory of his name; fame after death
> Is the noblest of goals.[27]

Tribes Dig in

The pre-Conquest settlement patterns of the Anglo-Saxons emerge in these surnames chosen in the fourteenth century, suggesting that where people choose their own tribal names they have generally not moved far from their traditional areas over the three centuries since the Norman invasion.

This is clearest in the concentration of Norse names in the east and north of England. For Old English names, which have wider distribution, continuity is easier to prove when names are relatively rare, because rarity gives one more confidence that a single original family is involved. Arden is one of the two names (the other is Berkeley) that can prove descent from a pre-Conquest English family. The name comes from an Arden/Aelfwine who was Sheriff of Warwickshire before the Conquest and Thurkill of Arden, one of only two Englishmen who held tenancies of the first order under William in 1086 (the other being Colswain of Lincoln).[28] There is a place called Arden in the North Riding of Yorkshire. Freelove, from an Anglo-Saxon personal name and now a rare Bedfordshire name, was recorded there in the tenth century and was still only in Bedfordshire, west of Bedford, in 1279.[29]

Some English names become and remain surnames in core Danish areas. The Cobbolds, from Cudbeald, famous bold, are represented by only five families assessed for tax on the north Suffolk border in the fourteenth century. Stannard, from stone hard, goes back to twelve Suffolk taxpayers in 1327; Kerridge, from Cyneric, family ruler, to a John Kerrich recorded in Leiston in Suffolk in 1327; and the Drabbles to the south-west Pennines in the fourteenth century. Most stay true to their roots. Hearth Tax and death records show Cobbolds migrate, but only to south Suffolk in the seventeenth century and almost all the twenty-two Cobbolds dying in the nineteenth century are still there. Stannard is still concentrated in Suffolk in the seventeenth century and Kerridge is still an eastern name in the nineteenth century. Drabble, in north Derbyshire and south-west Yorkshire in the seventeenth century, is back in the Peaks in the nineteenth century, and is still concentrated around Sheffield, Doncaster, Yorkshire and the north Midlands, although some Drabbles have moved south.[30]

Hunt the Meaning

Many of these ancient names survive because they combine with others. In some cases, the word has the same meaning in the different languages; names keep alive the words that united them. So Oswald echoes the English Osweald or the Norse Asvaldr, Algar the English Aelfgar or the Norse Alfgeirr, Harding usually comes from the English Hearding but could be from the German Hardwin brought to England by the Normans and so on.

When personal names combine with other types of names with different roots, it is also often the words that unite them. Thus, Goodman could be an English, Norse or German personal name, or a householder from any of the three languages because the English, Norse and Germanic words for this very basic activity are almost identical. The Coles could hark back to personal names from the Old English Cola or the Old Norse Koli, or they could be a nickname for someone swarthy or black from the English *col* or Norse *kol* that are the roots of the personal names too. Knott could be a Norse personal name from Knutr, or English for a thickset person. Both the derivations for the name come from similar words meaning knot -*knutr* in Norse and *cnotta* in

English. Raven can be the English or Norse name or a nickname for the bird, both based on the English or Norse word *hrafn*.

Often, names with quite dissimilar meanings combine just because they sound the same, which makes it difficult to identify where they come from. This can happen to a single-derivation name in which similar sounding Anglo-Saxon words are conflated. So Seward combines *saeward* with *sigeweard* and Alfred could come from *aelfraed* or *aedelraed*. The merging of the two original meanings suggests how pronunciation evolved and consonants like 'g' or 'd' were lost.

With other names, the different meanings come from very different roots that sound the same. Elliot could come from the English Aedelgeat or Aelfweald or be a diminutive of the French Elias – all personal names – and has spawned, as well as Elliot, Aylett, Ellwand and Ellwood, among other modern names. Lambert could be a French or German personal name meaning land-bright, or denote a shepherd from English words meaning lamb-herd. Many names could either be personal or refer to a place, and clearly there could be a lost connection between the two. Woollard from the Old English name Wulfweard, meaning wolf ward, for example, might also be from Wolford if it occurs in Warwickshire. As well as the German smith Weland, Wayland in Norfolk could be a source of our Waylands and come from the English. Dunstan and Livesey, could, as well as personal names, be place names.

Records Illuminated

A simple illustration of the extensive integration of Anglo-Saxon culture with that in the north of Europe shows how the Conquest was a family affair as well as an invasion. Local volumes of the Domesday Book give a good idea of the names of the conquerors and those of the conquered in 1066. A sample from the Devon volume of the Domesday Book shows that most of the incoming Normans were Hughs, Walters and Williams, while most of the Anglo-Saxons were Dodas, Alwins and Brictrics.

But a number of names could have occurred on either side of the conflict and a few did. They carry heavy irony as the same person seems to continue to own estates but does not. Thus, an Alfred of 'Spain' and Alfred 'the Breton' took some Devon land and an English Alfred lost some. A Norman or Breton Aiulf came in and English Ulfs lost out – both the names from the Norse Ulfr or Danish/Swedish Ufr, meaning wolf. A Norman or Breton Thurstan came in and an English Thorkell went out. These names show that Alfred existed on both sides of the Channel, as did the Norse Thor and Ulf names. Other names of those who lost their land also had continental roots – Algar, English or Norse, Harold, chiefly Norse or Danish and possibly also German and English. Others on the conquerors' side had names that already existed in England – Baldwin, Osbern, Hervey.

Aelfric's Colloquy

A few names bring to light a dramatic connection between Anglo-Saxon and medieval culture. Our modern Alldridge, Aylward, Woolvett, Woolston and Ellwood are purely Old English. Alldridge is from Aelfric or Aedelfric; Aylward from Aedelward; Woolvett from Wolfgeat; Woolston from Wulfstan; and Ellwood from Aelfweald or Aedelweald. People with these names bring down to us the priorities and principles of a remarkable Anglo-Saxon scholar.

This was Aelfric (Alldridge), a monk born about 955, perhaps the greatest scholar of the revival of Benedictine monasticism and certainly the most prolific. Aelfric's teacher and patron at Winchester had been Aethelwold (Ellwood), Bishop of Winchester from 963, who, with Dunstan and Oswald, was a crucial player in bringing the Benedictine revival to England under Eadwig and Edgar (see Chapter 7). Their connections with a Benedictine revival on the European continent and royal support from Eadwig and particularly Edgar helped restore monastic life in England after it had virtually disappeared in the second half of the ninth century.

Despite the turbulent times of Aethelred the Unready and unprecedentedly violent and extortionate Danish raids, this abbot of Eynsham in Oxfordshire devoted himself to a life of study and education. But instead of focusing on monks and the monastic life, he brought religious texts and principles to the secular world, and especially to village priests and students. For this, he wrote in the vernacular – Anglo-Saxon – not Latin. For Aethelweard (Aylward) an ealdorman in west Wessex, Aelfric translated the Old Testament; for a Woolvett, Wulfgeat of Ilmington, an ordinary thane, a theological treatise; for priests, a series of sermons and lives of saints; for Wulfstan (Woolston), Bishop of Sherborne and Archbishop of York, he wrote pastoral letters.[31]

But perhaps the most appealing of Aelfric's educational works is his *Colloquy*. In Latin and Anglo-Saxon, and so a tool to teach Latin, this is a text of questions and answers in which a teacher asks pupils representing various workers what they do. These consist of ploughmen, shepherds, oxherds, hunters, fishermen, bird-catchers, merchants, leatherworkers, salters, akers, cooks, a blacksmith and carpenter and even a lawyer.

From the answers, we get an idea of ordinary Anglo-Saxon life. It is hard for ploughmen, shepherds and oxherds, who depend on 'the lord' and are not free and the ploughman says 'It is never so harsh a winter that I dare lurk at home for fear of my master.' But the hunter works for the king, gives him his prey, and is fed, clothed, and the king 'sometimes gives me a horse or armlet, that I may the more joyfully ply my craft'.[32] He kills a boar. The fishermen, bird catchers and merchants work for themselves, selling their prey or their skills in the towns. The merchant sells abroad, bringing back 'precious objects ... purple cloth and silk, precious stones and gold ... clothes and dyes, wine and oil, ebony and brass, tin and brimstone, glass ...'.[33]

The *Colloquy* tells us about pupils' ambitions: they 'do not want to be a wild beast...we want to be wise' and to learn to speak correctly 'not with meaningless, base words', so in Latin. There is a discussion about wisdom – it is simplicity without hypocrisy. A boy describes what he does at the school, singing the services, and what he eats – meat, vegetables, eggs, fish and cheese. But he does not want to eat 'ravenously, since I am not a glutton'.

More than 400 years later Alldridge, the name taken from Aelfric, begins to appear as a surname and other surnames are to echo Aelfric's choice of the vernacular and the occupations he used to illustrate his world. At the same time, these names inveigh, like his *Colloquy*, and like William Langland in *Piers Plowman*, against hypocrisy and gluttony. So both Aelfric the scholar and his teaching come full circle.

Norse Names

Surnames from Norse are not as numerous as Norman names. (Norse is used to identify Scandinavian names since it was spoken by all Scandinavians in Anglo-Saxon England after the ninth century. Many will have been Old Danish or Swedish as well as Norse.) This is true in medieval times as well. Norse names in popular medieval sources are scarce.

These names range from the rare Arkell, eagle cauldron, and the ancient Gamble – a Lincolnshire surname from the Old Norse personal name Gamel mentioned by Chaucer – to more common names like Rolf, Simmonds and Osborn. The more popular names tend to have other derivations. Roger with its many variants is the only Norse name in the top dozen personal names today (at number eleven). Also German, it was very popular as a first name in England before the Conquest as well as being brought over by the Normans. It recalls the Old Norse Hrothgar, the king living under the threat of Grendel in *Beowulf*. Harold is usually Old Norse but could be Old German, and is sometimes confused with the Old English Hereweald. Norse names with their continental counterparts are closely linked to Norse mythology, the most comprehensive record of the northern European belief system that operated in England throughout the Anglo-Saxon period.

Tribal Settlement

The first pre-surname records of most of these Norse personal names, single then, were concentrated in the Danelaw and surnames follow suit. The Danelaw referred to those large swathes of England north-east of a line running from Dover through Roxborough to Chester, the area first settled by the Vikings and the Danes and recognized by Alfred the Great in the ninth century.

The survival of these relatively scarce names testifies to the local endurance of the invading culture. A sample of those with only Norse roots from Reaney and Wilson shows that 81 per cent of the first records of names, mostly tenth and twelfth century, are in the Danelaw, with a high concentration, 52 per cent, in East Anglia and the rest in the north and north-west of England. Their persistence is remarkable since the last Danish King of York had left in 954 and the Danelaw had been part of a united England since then.

Scarce records show how some of these names survived in the Danish areas after the consolidation of England. Many Norse names have pre-Conquest records, including only Norse names like Arkell, Askell (Ankell in Normandy) and Ingall, as well as Norse/German names like Ralph and Reynolds, and, of course, the Norse/English Harold that combines Haraldr with Hereweald. Osburn, a West Riding name, probably came directly from Scandinavia, and a Kettle (the original form of Arkell), was in Northamptonshire in 972.

For other Norse names, records start in the eleventh or twelfth century. A Copsi who was Earl of Northumberland is remembered in about 1100 for giving a cup to Durham Cathedral in about 1066, that 'is preserved in the church and retains the memory of that deed for ever'.[34] Great halls identified the magnates of a particular place and the names of the owners that have survived from the eleventh century record England's racial structure. So on the eve of the Conquest, halls in Lincoln and Colchester were held by Toki and Thurbert, both with Norse names, while the Englishman Godwine had his in Southwark. In about 1086, a Colswain of Lincoln, with a Norse name, one of the few Englishmen to prosper after the Conquest, built two churches for thirty-six new houses and is remembered for not endowing them. Grime, from the Norse Grim, helmet, was the name of a Danish fisherman who sold his catch in Lincoln and is said to have founded Grimsby, according to a twelfth-century story.[35] In Teutonic legend Grim was a predatory giant with the strength of twelve men whose head was cut off by the hero Dietrich who had stolen his sword.

The Norse surnames that clearly keep these distribution patterns generally have few variants and no other etymology to boost popularity and survival. They include the Kettles taxed in Cumberland, Essex and Hereford in the fourteenth century and rarely elsewhere; and the Algoods, from Algot, only recorded in Colchester, the Cinque Ports and two other places in Essex in 1377–81. Families like the Randolphs from South Croxton in Leicestershire can be traced back more narrowly, with a Robert Randolph recorded on a Poll Tax return of 1377. The surname survives as Randall in Leicestershire.[36] Other quintessentially Norse surnames are recorded in the Danelaw: Collings from the Norse Kolungr, Copsey, Hacon, Orme, Storey, Osborn and Osmund, Rolf, a peasant recorded in Danish Lincolnshire and Tovey, from Tovi the Proud, a follower of Cnut. Many have Danish or Swedish roots as well as Norse – Allgood, Grave, Grime, Knott, Orme, Swain and Thurgood. Names like Allgood and Arkell, common before and after the Conquest, were also popular in Normandy.

Most are still concentrated in the Viking stamping grounds. Osburn is still a West Riding name, Oman in Orkney and the Shetlands, Grime, Grimes and Knott in Lancashire, Orme and Arkell in the Midlands and the north-west, Storey in the north and Gamble mainly in the north and the Midlands. Rare today but common then, Dowsing, which could also be Huguenot, is thought to be an '-ing' derivative of the Old Danish Dusi, is popular in Norfolk and Suffolk in the Middle Ages and is still particularly strong in Suffolk.

Many of these names of course moved out of the Danelaw. Later records show that Gunn, Hemming and Osborne have scattered; Toope, Tubb, Toovey, Drabble, Seagrim, Turk and Tookey have all wandered south.[37]

But the picture is confused because so many of these ancient names have acquired other meanings and can emerge anywhere. The Norse/English names – Goodman, Harold, Raven, Algar – will always have had wide distribution. Other Norse personal names could also be English or Norse nicknames: Grime, fierce; Gunn, forceful; Knott, portly and Gambell, old. So the John Gamel in the Shrewsbury tax assessments for 1313 could be an out-of-area Nordic or an old-looking Englishman. Gamel seems to be prosperous. He has a twenty-shilling riding horse, jewellery, brassware and the meat of the rich. The cash, four carthorses and cart, tanned hides and cloth in his inventory suggest he is a merchant.[38]

Just as English surnames emerge in the Danelaw, Norse appear outside it, some even in the south-west. Names like Osbern, Osbert, Osmund, Siward, and Turbern are recorded in Devon; and Asketill, Colbern, Colebrand, Ordlof, Thurkyld and Thurstan in Somerset in the fourteenth century. A Richard Ketell is a customary tenant in Somerset in the thirteenth century. And there are Anketils, Colswains and Thurstans in Dorset.[39] Of these, seven of the eleven with identifiable roots are Norse, two Norse/English and only one, Osbert, is probably English. Although never a Danish area, there were at least nine Danish raids on Devon between 851 and 1003, the final one burning and plundering Exeter, including, probably, its abbey. King Alfred is said to have captured from the Danes in Devon a banner displaying the iconic Danish *hraefn*, or raven, the bird of death who fed on the corpses of Odin's battlefields.[40]

Violence and Magic

The persistence of Norse names in the Danelaw demonstrates the existence of a traditional society there, so when these single names become surnames it is highly likely they carry with them their baggage of legend and myth. It is thought that Norse culture survived at least into the tenth century in England. Certainly, invaders continued to speak their own language after they had settled and as late as the fourteenth century Chaucer is including Scandinavian slang within *The Canterbury Tales* and fully expecting his audience to understand it. The documentation of the Norse legends in the twelfth and especially thirteenth centuries could have contributed to the revival of the names they contained, whether by reminding people about them or by making names current in oral history more acceptable.

Norse surnames carry echoes of this culture. They also suggest that the English namers identify with the world they described. The legends record a universe in uneasy balance between warring gods and giants, good and evil, with man in between. This world is ultimately to go up in flames in a comprehensive final battle, the Ragnarok. Both good and evil re-emerge from the ashes. The chief god, Odin, is the god of war and poetry, the preferred god of the educated, who promotes strife and murders his favourites in order to fill the halls of Valhalla with heroes for Ragnarok. Thor, Odin's eldest son, who became the most important god of the Viking invaders and settlers, maintains the order of the universe, defending the world of man, holding the forces of chaos in check. These are stories that record peoples' perceptions of a world so hostile and terrifying that only gods could be responsible for the events they encounter and only magic and heroes could protect people from them. Whether you were a Norse warrior or his enemy, a raider or a victim, you responded to legends of victorious heroes, protective yet unreliable gods and magical weapons. The culture reflected the times.

Its themes are similar to those recorded in English names, but because the Norse mythology is better recorded and more comprehensive than the English we can relate many names precisely to the legends that have correlations with the continental myths discussed in Chapter 7. This allows us to be more specific about the cultural heritage the medieval namers were, consciously or not, reviving.

An analysis of Norse names by theme shows a culture of war – armies, weapons, battles and magic, with a preponderance to do with battles and protection from them. Several of these names have other roots, demonstrating their continental inheritance. Ottar or Otter, terrible army (or the human lover of Freyja, the fertility goddess); Gunn, battle; Gunnell, battle-battle; Goodhew, battle spirit; Harold, army power. An Ottar from Norway is remembered for bringing King Alfred an offering of some walrus tusks.[41]

Craving for Protection

War and violence are associated with the magic of protection. Surnames echo this idea. Thor is the guardian of men and gods. Thorburn, Thor bear, invokes both the god and a fierce animal and Osmond is god-protection while Hammond and Oman mean high protector. Thurgood and Thorogood, Thor-Geats, call on the legendary tribe of Geats celebrated in *Beowulf* and discussed in Chapter 7. Wyman is war-protection, Goodman, can be battle-protection and Simmonds, victory-protection. Seagrim is sea-protection.

Many surnames have to do with weapons. Roger from Hrothgar is fame spear, introduced from Normandy; Algar is elf or noble spear; Thurgar, Thor's spear; Brand, sword or firebrand; Geary just a spear (and also one of the pet wolves of Odin, an omen of good luck); and Grimes is helmet or mask. They invoke the strength and weapons of the victorious. Many of these have other roots. Weapons in legend are important enough to have their own names and attributes, often magical. Odin's spear was Gungnir. Thor, with his belt and his iron gloves, had a double-headed hammer, which came back to him when thrown, called Mjölnir. Siguro had a sword Gramr, which cut in two a fleck of wool floating down the Rhine. Roland's sword in the *Chanson de Roland* was Durandel, once owned by Hector and won from the giant Jutmundus.

These names echo the Ragnarok and Thor's battles with the giants and the struggles of heroes like Sigmund and Harald Wartooth against adversity. The chief source of Harold is the Norse Haraldr, the name of kings. The Harald Finehair who centralized government in Norway in about 885 was a tyrant. Harald Greycloak, a Christian, seized the kingdom about a century later, smashing the pagan temples and putting an end to sacrifice. It is said that as a result, crops failed and snow fell in midsummer. Harald Wartooth was a legendary hero, a favourite of Odin, said to have lived 150 years and conquered, among other countries, Denmark and Sweden, called after two gigantic tusks growing in place of his molars. Odin made him quarrel with his nephew Hring and when they met on the battlefield of Bravellir, Odin became Hring's charioteer and battered Harald to death with his own club. The story of another Harald is rather more human. Harald Gormsson, a late tenth-century king of the Danes, disliked the Icelanders and took on a wizard who went there as a malevolent whale. This whale met first with a dragon and other monsters who spat poison at him, next a gigantic and terrifying bird, then a bull with a tremendous bellow, and finally a rock giant higher than the hills and carrying an iron pole. The whale/wizard made off.[42]

Harding, hard, usually Old English, could also come from the

Norse tribe of Hadding (called Hearding by the Saxons), named after the grandson of Thor and son of Halfdan (our Haldanes). A Viking namesake of Hadding's father Halfdan was one of the leaders of the Danish army that attacked East Anglia in 865 and entered York a year later, defeating and martyring King Edmund on its return to East Anglia in 869.

Invoking the Power of Animals

Heroes are remembered in names like Howard, from Haward or Hugihead, brave spirit, and all the names that invoke fierce animals to absorb their powers and/or call on their protection – Orme, snake or dragon, Osborn, god bear, Randolph, shield wolf, Raven, Rolf, fame wolf and Thorburn, Thor-warrior or bear. Some names carry the idea that judgement as well as brute force is important. So Reynolds could come from the Old Norse Ragnaldr meaning counsel might, mostly introduced by the Normans.

In legends as in names, gods and fierce animals substitute for each other. Ravens and wolves accompanied Odin and fed on the carrion of his battlefields. It was a wolf, Fenrir, chained to confine his destructive potential, which brought on the Ragnorok. In one legend dark dwarves manufactured these chains from the sound of a cat's footsteps, a woman's beard, the spittle of birds and the longing of the bear.[43] No man could break them. But at Ragnarok, Fenrir did and caused the final battle that destroyed the world, killing Odin. In Norse legend, the sun was carried on a chariot through the sky during the day, chased by wolves intent on devouring it and plunging the world into darkness and chaos. The snake Jormungand, the symbol of evil, coiled around the earth, was Thor's most formidable enemy. At Ragnarok, they were to kill each other. The Randolphs and Ormes recalling these legends invoke the protection of these all-powerful animals.

A Geoffrey Rondulf assessed for tax in Shrewsbury in 1306 is a namesake of such a shield wolf. And, indeed, life seems to have been magical for him. Out of the Norse area, his inventory shows he might be a grain trader, with substantial quantities of wheat, barley, peas and oats, together with three packhorses and a cart.

He also has a riding horse, cash, valuable clothes, a cup with silver fittings, jewellery and some brassware. Someone or something must have been watching out for him.[44]

The Heroes

All the 'sig-' names, like Simmonds and Simmons, are names of heroes and discussed in Chapter 7. Finn is another hero along 'sig-' lines, but with a Norse/Irish name. He is thought originally to have been a god, transformed into a hero once Christianity had driven out paganism.[45] *Beowulf* includes the tale of Finn's armies half wiping out a Danish tribe, killing its king, his brother-in-law and his son and of his murder by Hengest, the leader of the surviving Danes, who 'drove his new sword / into Finn's belly, butchering that king/ Under his own roof.' Beowulf personifies heroism, killing the monstrous Grendel who 'had bewitched all men's weapons, laid spells ...' with his bare hands.[46]

Norse heroes are driven by the search for glory, fame overcoming death an essential element of northern myths. In a world that honours independence and self-belief, courage in death is rewarded by esteem, even of enemies. Where all is brutal and transitory, heroism and its reputation live on.[47]

Poetry

Poetry, akin to magic, is a vital part of this world. Odin was the Norse god of poetry as well as war, emphasizing its importance. No names seem to preserve him. Finn, in his Norse/Irish persona, steals water from the well of wisdom, a sign of initiation into the cult of poetry that arises from wisdom. Bragg, noted earlier, could come from the Old Norse name of Bragi Bodason the Old, a poet probably from south-western Norway in about 830–40. He wrote *The Lay of Ragnar*, describing pictures painted on a shield, including Thor's struggle with the World Serpent. There is also a god of poetry called Bragi, who has runes or spells carved on his tongue, bickers a lot with the sinister half-god Loki, and is said to be the husband of Idunn, who guards the apples of eternal youth to keep the gods young. He is thought to be the poet, promoted to a god after his death. The Norse were illiterate, but used runes – the letters of the Germanic alphabet – for inscriptions and believed that they had magical powers if put in the right order.

Nothing says more about the Viking admiration of courage and glorification of violence than the language used by their poets. It's one thing to describe violence, but even in translation the Scandinavian poets gloat in it. Our Thoburns – Thor bears – have namesakes in Thorbjorn Dlsonskald, the poet of Dis, and Thorbjorn Hornklofi, the favourite poet of Harald Finehair. The former praises Thor's exploits '[Your hammer] rang on Keila's skull/ You crushed the body of Kjallandi...' in an episode when Thor killed two giants and six giantesses. Hornklofi's most famous work is the *Lay of Harald and Words of the Raven*, a dialogue between a valkyrie and a raven, that describes how, ever since he was hatched, the bird has followed the young Thor, rejoicing in the carrion left on his battlefields.[48]

Northumbrian Names Illuminate the Political Record

Understanding names casts a new light on Northumbrian tribal politics around the time of the Conquest. In 1035 Cnut appointed as earl of Northumberland a warrior called Siward to control its western borders and the Scots who had been challenging English authority under Malcolm. Siward married Aelflaed from the indigenous Bernician dynasty, and had a son, Waltheof.

Siward's name (Seward today) could have been English or Norse. He was in fact a Dane, appointed by a Danish king to subdue the most fractious and vulnerable part of his kingdom. And a Dane he remained; although he had married into the indigenous elite, his son's name was Norse or Anglo-Scandinavian, not English. The names show that for both Siward and Cnut, tribal and political priorities were identical. Cnut wanted a Dane to sort out the Scots and Siward was and stayed a Dane. This is borne out by later events. After the Conquest and his father's death, Waltheof was to support two attempts by the Danes to invade

England and supplant William I. After the first, he was able to persuade William of his repentance, but not after the second, and he was executed in 1076 when he was still only thirty-one years old. Waltheof's opposition to William was not an act of English resistance, but an attempt by a Dane to take control of England from an invading Norman.

Before he died, Waltheof was to end with extraordinary barbarity a famous eleventh-century blood feud involving his family that had lasted three generations. Thurbrand of Yorkshire engineered the murder of Earl Uhtred of Northumbria as the latter made his obeisance to Cnut in 1016. Uhtred's son Aldred killed Thurbrand. Mutual reparations were paid by Aldred and Thurbrand's son Carl, and the two planned a pilgrimage together to Rome. The feud seemed to be over. But, caught together in a storm, Carl killed Aldred. The feud then lapsed; Aldred's heir was Aelflaed, Waltheof's mother, who married Siward, the Dane. But in 1073, Waltheof sent assassins to kill all Carl's sons and grandsons, as they were feasting. Only two escaped.[49] Look at the names: Uhtred's side – Uhtred, Aldred, Aelflaed – are English. Thurbrand's side – Thurbrand, Carl, and the eldest grandson, another Thurbrand – are Norse. An underlying cause of the feud is surely racial, the result of the influx of the Norse into English territory and the competition for land and power. Siward's marriage to Aelflaed might have been an attempt to end the tribal emnity through a mixed marriage. But Waltheof was unable to let go; the mixed marriage had produced another Dane.

Celtic Names

Between the Roman occupation and the Conquest, the Celtic territories on Britain extended northward from south-west England through Wales and Carlisle in a great wavering arc across to Edinburgh. There were close connections between the Welsh and southern Scotland, and between Wales, the south-west and Armorica, the heart of present-day Brittany, where north-western European Celts were concentrated. In Britain, the Celts survived between the Irish to the west, the Picts to the north and to the east the encroaching Anglo-Saxons, pushing up from Northumberland and west into Somerset and beyond. Their influence is captured in the Celtic names of important landmarks: the Clyde, from Clota; the Severn from Sabrina; and Carlisle from Caer Lugubalion. Celtic names can be Welsh, Irish, Gaelic or Breton.

The language mainly persisted in these peripheral areas, and, particularly, along the routes of ancient Irish settlement. This travelled along the north Cornish coast and the shores of the Severn to southern and western Wales as far as Caernarvonshire. By the fifth century, as the Saxon invaders began to penetrate the far south-west, migrants from there, following the pull of language and race, were going to Armorica, then in western Gaul. Many of the saints discussed in Chapter 7 tracked the paths they had taken in the fifth and sixth centuries, from south Wales to Cornwall and on to Brittany, some staying where they landed, as Petroc did in Padstow. More than 150 church dedications in Cornwall and Brittany to Irish monks suggest some also followed the trajectory of the Welsh saints. So obvious fantasies like that of Saint Ia, who gave his name to St Ives, and is said to have come across from Ireland to Cornwall on a leaf, might have a kernel of truth.

Boosted by Immigrants

There are few early records of people with Celtic names. The first documentation of Petroc is of a Cornishman called Petherick in the mid-sixteenth century, yet ancient church dedications and place names from Saint Petroc, a sixth-century saint, are widespread and frequent in the south-west where Pethericks must be too.

Somewhat after the missionaries were boarding their little ships to Cornwall and Brittany, the Vikings were bringing to Cumbria and northern England the Irish/Norse names – Coleman and Gille, Brian, Neal and Duncan – discussed in Chapter 7. They are striking examples of how the Celts survived attached to a more vigorous culture. Their Old Irish derivations are evidence that the Norse were at least to some extent acculturated by the Irish Celts as Neal and Duncan are tied to the Gaels, Murdoch to the Welsh and Brian to the Bretons as well as the Irish.

Brian and Neal are both well entrenched in Celtic myth. In Irish legend, Brian was one of the three sons of Dannnan, the mother of the Irish gods, the ancient inhabitants of Ireland, who killed Cian, the father of the sun-god Lug.[50] There are many Neal saints in Irish legend, but in one a Niall seems to have been close to the hero of the Grimm tale about the princess and the frog. In this, he is looked down on by his four stepbrothers because his mother was treated as a slave. Out hunting with them, they come to a well guarded by a horrendously ugly hag who demands a kiss. When Niall gives her one, she becomes the most beautiful woman in the world, and he is destined to be king.

Some two centuries later, at the Conquest, Irish/Norse (and Norse) names were brought back with the Normans from their own Norse past to southern and eastern England. Simultaneously, the Bretons soldiering with William re-introduced their Celtic names, expanding the areas where they were heard and identifying where the Breton contingents of the invasion went.

Broadly speaking, the Bretons brought names like Allan, Joel and Sampson to the Midlands and these plus Harvey, Griffin and Howell came east. Allen, Martin and Joel, particularly, were to become popular surnames. The Bretons also brought Welsh names back to the west; Griffin to Cornwall in 1066 and around 1100 to Devon. First records of Allens just after the Conquest are in Suffolk, Leicestershire and Lincolnshire; the Breton magnate, Earl Allen of Richmond, established himself with his followers in Lincolnshire around Boston and the name was popular after the Conquest. In Irish myth, Aillen mac Midna was a malevolent arsonist, enemy of the hero Finn, who, blowing fire from his mouth, burnt Tara, the royal court, at the annual Samain feast on 1 November, and who, every year, was slain. The Earl came from Brittany, but his name had its roots in Ireland.[51]

Survival

Logic suggests that many of these names must have already been in Celtic England before these invasions and their Breton roots record earlier continental influence. Allen, an Old French/Old

Breton name was Gaelic in Scotland, like Duncan, and carried by early Welsh and Breton saints. Martin, whose namesake was St Martin of Tours, was recorded in Gaul in the fourth and fifth centuries and in Llangian churchyard, Caernarvonshire, lies the fifth- or sixth-century burial stone of Melus the doctor, son of Martin – *Meli medici fili Martini j[a]cet.*[52] The Bretons who went to Devon at the Conquest brought first Judhael of Totnes, one of William's knights, and then, in 1166, arrived Joel de Sancto Winnoco and Joel de Moles, all holding versions of the same Celtic Breton name Judicael. Joel slowly became a name of free and then unfree peasants there. Yet Devon was a late Saxon conquest and some of these local versions of the name, particularly the Jekylls, are likely to have continued unrecorded until the Bretons arrived.

In the Welsh borders, names like Joel and Sampson, Howell and Griffin – a pet form of Gryffydd, one of the few Welsh pet names – already existed and the Welsh there were making them hereditary. Following the Celtic trail, Griffin was already in Devon in the early tenth century and Howell and Griffin in Devon and Cornwall by the twelfth century.

Howell is a distinguished ancient Welsh name. Hywel Dda (the Good) is remembered for pledging allegiance to England under Athelstan, mostly due to royal marriages, and from 942 seems to have consolidated Wales under his rule. Laws from throughout Wales were promulgated under his name from his seat 'Ty Gwyn', the White House, on the River Taf.[53] Another Howell, Hywel ap Owain, has left information on a less well-known Celtic trail, from northern Wales to Cumbria along the Irish Sea. This Hywel was a famous medieval bard from north Wales who died in 1170. He recorded a prince of Gwynedd said to have ridden from Maelinydd, between the Wye and the Severn in northern Wales, to Rheged in Cumbria, probably Carlisle, in twenty-four hours:

> I mounted my bay steed and from Maelinydd
> To the land of Rheged I rode both night and day.[54]

One group of these Celtic names that does not seem to have had Breton connections is common in the Welsh borders in the twelfth and thirteenth centuries – including names like Bowen from ap Owen, Kemble, Meredith and Maddock, Morgan and Cadwallader, in use since at least the seventh century, and Cadogan, thought to be the origins of our Cades.[55] There are eleventh-century records for Owen in Herefordshire and Rhys in Cheshire and twelfth-century records for Cadogan, Maddock and Cadwallader in Shrewsbury. Several of these – Morgan, Bowen, Meredith – are still popular there and have penetrated Wales as well, although when the Welsh choose surnames in the sixteenth century many other Welsh names lose out to Norman names. Morgan is a very ancient Celtic name. Old Welsh, Cornish, Pictish and Breton, it is still common in south Wales.

Maddock, meaning goodly, has a namesake in Madawg, Prince of Powys in about the mid-twelfth century. One myth has him to be a son of Owain Gwynedd who crossed to America in 1170, pre-dating Columbus by 322 years. The bard of *The Dream of Rhonabwy* belonged to his retinue. Cadwallon and his son Cadwaladr were from a powerful Welsh dynasty from the heroic Welsh age, covering the fifth to ninth centuries. 'The Eulogy of Cadwallon' is an important poem dating from the sixth to the seventh centuries. Thought to have had direct contact with continental culture, Cadwallon was the most powerful enemy of the English in the north. He killed King Edwin of Northumbria and died himself in 633 after being defeated by the Northumbrian King Oswald.[56]

Morgan has several incarnations. The name was associated with Morrigan, the maiden, the young and first part of the Celtic Triple Goddess of fertility who presided over birth, life and death. The other two parts were Macha, the woman, and Badh, the old hag. A corbel in the church of St Mary and St David in Kilpeck, Herefordshire shows the Triple Goddess as a devouring mother. The church is Norman, but thought to have replaced a Saxon church built on Celtic foundations originally dedicated to St David. In Arthurian legend, Arthur's sister and Uther Pendragon's daughter was Morgan le Fay, a witch. In Mallory's *Morte d'Arthur* she tries to kill Arthur. In another version, the rebellion against Arthur is led by her son, Mordred. After the rebellion, Morgan le Fay is one of the three black-robed women who take the mortally wounded Arthur away to Avalon. The Cornish version of the name was Morcant. A Morcant was one of the four seventh-century British princes fighting the invading Saxons under Urien from Carlisle, the most important prince of Cumbria. Morcant's subsequent jealousy and murder of Urien marked the end of the Britons' ability to form effective alliances against the invaders.[57]

Various forms of Ewan and Owen had Celtic origins in Gaelic, Irish and Welsh and an Ewan Britto is recorded in Herefordshire in the Domesday Book. These became the Welsh form of John, adopted in the Welsh Authorized Version of the Bible, and eventually Jones. These names have broad Celtic roots in early medieval times, with Ewens in Scotland and the Welsh borders and Evens in eastern counties from Brittany. The *Book of Taliesin*, written in about 1275 by the bard Taliesin recording sixth-century poems, includes nine in praise of an Ewan, Urien of Rheged and his son, the hero Owain ap Urien. 'The Battle of Llwyfein Wood' reports a celebrated victory of Owain over the English:

> Urien, lord of Erechwydd shouted:
> 'Let us carry our spearshafts over the mountain
> And lift our faces above the ridge.'[58]

In about 1195, a Welsh Owen, Owain Cyfeiliog, the last of the Welsh princes, went to die at the Abbey of Strata Marcella at the ford of the Severn. *The Dream of Rhonabwy* could have been about his arrival. There is a direct connection between this place of the death of the last prince and Arthur's camp, said to have been where the abbey stood at Rhyd-y-Groes, the Ford of the Cross, north of Welshpool at Buttington.[59]

Distribution

Medieval Celtic surnames, like the Norse names, often arise where a single name had first appeared. Brian, Neal and Duncan are still in Yorkshire in the twelfth and thirteenth centuries, and Duncan, also a common Scottish name, is in Berwick in the fourteenth century. Many names introduced to East Anglia by Bretons at the Conquest – Griffin, Harvey, Joel – are in the same areas two and three centuries later and the same names are in the same pockets of Celtic settlement in the Welsh borders.

Many medieval personal surnames still record the trajectory of language from Wales to the south-west. A tenth-century Owen appears in Devon and Rhys, Owen, Morgan and Maddock are inherited names in Devon in the thirteenth and fourteenth centuries.[60] David and, particularly, Davy (often a saint's name), Sampson, and Cade are similarly common. Many of these names have suffixes that suggest their origin, like the David de Cornwaille and the David Walshe recorded in medieval Devon that show the Celtic trail to be still vigorous. The trail operated northwards too. The south-west has many medieval Alans, Brians and, particularly Martins from Brittany. Joels, Juls and then Jewells from the original Judicael from Brittany become fairly common medieval surnames in Devon, and, indeed, are popular there still.

Like so many other surnames, many Celtic names persist where their history had scattered them. Allen and Brian are carried by the Bretons as well as the Gaels or the Norse; Morgan and Griffin by the Bretons as well as the Cornish and the Welsh; Lewis by the French and the Welsh from Llewellyn and so on. Others become hereditary outside Celtic areas because they have other meanings. Howell or Sampson/Samson, are place names too, and people coming from the places take on the names. Many combine different meanings that sound the same, like Powell, ap Howell from the Welsh, that is a variant of Paul or a dweller by a pool from Old English. Some are also nicknames, such as Griffin, the Welsh or Breton personal name, which means someone fierce or a dragon in Middle English.

Heroes and Legends

Our knowledge of Celtic Welsh beliefs and traditions comes from oral poetry written down in about the ninth century and thought to originate mainly in southern Scotland. Four manuscripts from the mid-twelfth to the mid-fourteenth centuries record almost all early Welsh poetry. Rather elegies and panegyrics than epics, the most famous is the *Book of Aneirin* and its poem '*Gododdin*' about a disastrous expedition of a small band of Britons against the Saxons in about 600. Prose stories about heroes and feuds are thought to date from about 1100.[61]

There are many similarities between the Celtic and Norse traditions and beliefs underlying the names. Heroes with magical or superhuman qualities were warriors, fighting for survival, hunting animals, sometimes taking on their attributes. Poets and minstrels, as in Teutonic myth, were honoured. Kings claimed divine origins. The focus is on the prowess of individuals. Heroes of the north mingle with those of the west.

Finn

Finn – the name is still the same – had many incarnations as a Celtic hero. In Scottish legend, Finn mac Cumhaill (or Finn MacCoul) was a Highland hunting giant, sixty feet tall, with a hammer like Thor and matchless swords made by a smith whom he killed. Ancient stories about a third-century Irish warrior, poet and diviner called Finn passed into twelfth-century troubadour romances from stories common among ordinary people from the eleventh century. A comprehensive text on the Fenian Cycle was written at the end of the twelfth century. Finn is recorded as leading men in war and hunting wild boar, and a story about a great boar hunt is the prelude to an account of his death.[62] Like Odin, a warrior and also god of poetry, Finn was a poet and had eaten the salmon of Fec, so that whenever he put his thumb in his mouth, knowledge was revealed to him.

Arthur

Arthur is a well-known Celtic name. It is derived from Arturius, which is Roman, although etymologists classify it as 'Celtic, with disputed etymology'. First records of the name are found in Cumberland and Yorkshire, Essex and Worcester.

Medieval people dispute Arthur's parentage and where he lived. Geoffrey of Monmouth connects him with the royal family in Devon and identifies his father as the early king, Uther Pendragon;

others link him with the Scottish King Constantine. According to Welsh tradition, Arthur's court was in south-east Wales. The medieval Welsh prose saga, the *Dream of Rhonabwy*, has his camp at Rhyd-y-Groes on the Severn. Others placed it in Cornwall, with Camelot at Camelford and Merlin's Cave at Tintagel with Arthur's castle at Dozmary Pool, where Excalibur was thrown.[63]

People will nevertheless have been familiar with Arthurian legends. They would not have known Thomas Mallory's *Morte d'Arthur* printed by Caxton in 1485. They would, however, have known many of Mallory's sources (the French romances common from the late twelfth century) that reworked ancient myths of a Celtic hero called Arthur. After Eleanor of Aquitaine had married Henry II, the literary and courtly culture she brought of chivalric knights, courtesy and honour became profoundly influential in the violent and unpredictable times that followed. In the early twelfth century, people in Wales, Cornwall and Brittany believed that Arthur would come back and deliver them from their enemies.[64]

The medieval romance is well known. Reared by the wizard Merlin, Arthur pulls the magic sword Excalibur from its stone and takes the crown, defeating a hostile league of eleven kings. His life and actions set the standards of medieval chivalry. From his court in Camelot his knights of the Round Table set out on daring exploits. His faithfulness in his unhappy marriage to Guinevere, the tragic destruction of his court and the disappearance of the chivalric life, the return of Excalibur to the lake and his own removal at his death to Avalon are the core of many contemporary *chansons de geste*.

These medieval Arthurian stories of king and courtly love crowded out older, late fifth-century, Welsh legends of a courageous warrior called Arthur who fought the Anglo-Saxons and early twelfth-century writers are recorded as objecting to the later 'distortion of the truth'.[65] Rather than a chivalric ruler, early poetry talks of an Arthur who, among other heroes, is a warrior like Finn who defends his country and fights witches, giants and magic animals, including boar.

It seems there probably was a fifth-century Celtic chieftain called Arthur who did fight the Saxons. But there is no contemporary evidence for his existence and Bede, the best source of pre-eighth-century history of England, does not mention him in his *Ecclesiastical History of the English People*. Early records are few and unreliable. The longest is by Nennius in his *Historia Brittonum*, written around the early tenth century, who refers to twelve British victories over Saxon leaders associated with an Arthur. The biographer of St Columba writing before 704 has an Arthur among the sons of Columba's King of Argyll, Aedan mac Gabrain, who had Welsh links. This Arthur was killed in southeast Scotland fighting an army that included Saxons. *'Goddodin'*, probably written in about 600, mentions an Arthur who stands for the highest standard of courage who could be the source for the transformation of the sixth-century warrior into the medieval chivalric knight.[66]

There are few Arthurs in fourteenth-century records in Devon, Somerset and Dorset, where you might expect to find them, showing a lack of engagement by ordinary people with the legend.[67] In Dartmouth, a Symon Arthur witnessed a land grant in about 1280 (paid for in wine and cumin), and there are references to a Johanna Artour and a John Dartour in 1339 and 1377 respectively.[68] From 1313 to 1344 a Geoffrey Arthur was living not far away at Uplyme.[69] Four people with the same name over a century is not a resounding proof of the success of a legend.

Tristram

The surname Tristram, like Arthur, records another hero cited in Welsh poems from about the sixth century. The Celtic name means tumult or din. Like Arthur, he was taken up by the medieval romances in a similar three-way love triangle with Iseult, the wife of King Mark of Cornwall. Scholars have not found the Tristan-Iseult story in Celtic sources, but it is very similar to Irish stories about Diarmid and Grainne. In one of the later romances, *The Pursuit of Diarmid and Grainne*, Finn pursued the eloping couple and allowed Diarmid to die after he was wounded in a boar hunt. Tristram is given veracity by a sixth-century inscription on what is called the Castle Dore stone, near Fowey in Cornwall. It reads: *'Drustans ... hic jacit Cunomori filius'*, or 'Here lies

Drusta ... the son of Cunomorus'. Cunomorus was King Mark, so this could commemorate a Tristram connected with Mark and Iseult.[70] Tristram as a surname is most common in Lancashire and Staffordshire, but in medieval times it was usually a first name. The only references to the name as a surname in Dartmouth are to a Tristram supplying the churchwardens with stone, ropes and horses for building projects in the sixteenth century.

Records of Disappearing Celts

But specifically Celtic surnames are far less common than generic names like Wallis, Walsh, Welshman, Cornwallis or all the similar names for the Irish and it is these names that record most of the Celts in medieval England. These generic names far outnumber individual Celtic names in medieval records; in early fourteenth-century Devon almost all Celtic taxpayers had them. With *wealas* meaning a slave as well as a Welshman, Celtic names seem to have pejorative connotations. The Domesday Book for Cornwall shows most Cornish land before the Conquest was held by people with English names – possibly evidence that the Cornish changed their names to become landholders.

There are strikingly few references to the Celts in medieval literature and those few are deprecating. William Langland in *Piers Plowman,* written in the late fourteenth century, refers to a drunken Griffin the Welshman in the tavern that Glutton frequents, the name almost certainly popular because of Gruyffydd ap Llewlyn who became the virtual ruler of Wales in the early eleventh century.[71] He also refers to a Sir Harvey (who wears Welsh flannel). Chaucer, in *The Canterbury Tales,* has an Alan in the Reeve's Tale, another Old French/Breton name that came with the Conquest. He has several references to Arthurian legends, from the Wife of Bath, who begins her tale: 'In th'olde days of the king Arthour,/Of which that speken greet honour/Al was this land fulfild of fayerye [fairies] ... ' to the cock in the Nun's Priest's Tale who maintains: 'This storie is al – so trewe, I undertake,/As is the book of Launcelot de Lake ...'[72]

The attitude in these references towards the English Celts

is very clear. Few as the names are, they are almost all Breton. Moreover, although the Wife of Bath clearly hopes to impress with her reference to Arthur, the book referred to by the cock is believed to be a version by Walter Map known for its lack of accuracy.[73] If these books reflect popular preferences, they show a clear reluctance to take these names.

The names in the Cornwall Domesday Book show the status of the Celts there at the time of the Conquest. One would expect to find land owned by the Celts since Saxon control had largely ended at the Tamar and the borders of Devon. But the first, very striking, feature is that the vast majority of the pre-1066 landowners in Cornwall carried English names – Edwy, Brictmer, Aelfric, Aelmer, Alwin and so on. Apparently, the Celts scarcely possessed any land in the far south-west that was their home. To be Celt was to be subservient. Alternatively, the Celts had taken English names to become landowners. Either you did not belong to the landowning class, or you hid your race. There were a few Celt names, Griffin and Cadwallon – both recalling the traditional links with Wales. There were a few landowners with Norse names: these included Ketel, Grim and Algar, also English, and Ralph, which is usually German. This is less surprising, since Cornwall had never been a Norse area, although there was, as mentioned, a persistent, if small, group of Norse names in Somerset, Dorset and Devon recalling Danish raids.

Most of the Norman tenants and subtenants who took the land in the Cornish volume of the Domesday Book had Norman, mostly German, names. These included Geoffrey, the Count of Mortain and the Conqueror's half-brother, and Gotshelm, tenants of the first degree, and then Reginald, Richard, Hamelin, William, Erchenbald, Humphrey, Ralph and Roger as subtenants.

But in the Cornish, as in other Domesday Books, some names record the close links between invaders and invaded. There are Celtic names on both sides: Griffin and Cadwallon lost land while Judhael, Nigel (or Neal) and Brian took it. The Norse Thurstan, also English, was a land-grabber, while the Norse Ketel and Grim lost it. Alfred and Algar appears both as grabbers and losers.

The names that occur on both sides are complicated by another unusual feature of this volume of the Domesday Book that

274

suggests some, particularly Algar, might actually have been the same person. Quite a number of names are specifically recorded as renewing their ownership of the same land in 1086. The list includes Osferth, Alfward, Alnoth, Ednoth, Alric, Alfsi, Aelmer, Brictric, Wulfsi, Cola, Leofnoth, Doda, Sheerwold, Hwata and Iovin. This could mean that nobody wanted that land – it is usually only one entry and not always valuable – or that these people, almost all of whom had English names, cooperated with the invaders and were rewarded by having their land restored.

So knowing something of these indigenous personal names adds to our understanding of the England that the Normans invaded, of the apparently English ownership of the land that was taken that could hide a Celtic presence, of the links that drew the invaders and even, perhaps, that they were welcomed.

GLOSSARY OF KEY SURNAMES

This glossary covers many, but not all, surnames mentioned in the text. Note that the spelling of most was fluid until the nineteenth century. Some variants are given.

Abbot, 23, 24, 38, 167, 186, 196
Agar, *see* Edgar
Alabaster, 40, 76, 103
Alaway, 246
Aldred, 209, 243, 246, 247, 263
Aldrich, 244, 245 (*see also* Alldridge)
Alfred, 209, 230, 242, 243, 245, 247, 248, 251, 252, 254, 257, 258, 274
Algar, 207, 208, 209, 245, 250, 252, 256, 259, 274, 275
Allain, *see* Allen
Allan, *see* Allen
Alldridge, 232, 252, 253 (*see also* Aldrich)
Allen, 39, 220, 226–7, 247, 265–6, 269
Alphege, 223, 229, 245 (*see also* Elphick)
Alstone, 243
Alured, 230 (*see also* Alfred)
Ambler, 56, 64, 88, 89, 149
Angel, 141, 158, 165
Angove, 49, 50, 72, 73, 101
Appleton, 117
Archer, 25, 103, 106, 108
Arden, 19, 127, 128, 249
Arm, *see* Harmes
Armes, 157
Armstrong, 103, 147, 164
Arrowsmith, 25, 103, 104
Arthur, 270–2
Ash, 113, 116 (*see also* Nash)
Ashburner, 21, 76, 79, 108
Aston, 243
Attree, 18, 19, 116
Atwell, 113, 121
Austen, 220, 221, 229
Ayer, *see* Ayres

Ayres, 159, 160
Ayliffe, 202, 246
Aylward, 209, 246, 252, 253

Bacchus, 76 (*see also* Backhouse)
Backhouse, 86, 107
Bailey, 75, 77
Bailiff, 20, 38, 77, 78, 107, 109
Baird, *see* Beard
Baker, 26, 38, 57, 75, 93, 107
Baldree, *see* Baldry
Baldry, 202, 209
Baldwin, 18, 239, 240, 252
Ball, 146
Barber, 56, 73
Barclay, *see* Berkeley
Berkeley, 19, 58, 61, 85, 90, 128, 249
Bachelor, *see* Batchelor
Barefoot, 160
Barker, 40, 54, 76, 79, 108
Barnes, 118
Barnett, 22, 117, 120
Baron, 103, 170, 186, 187, 194, 195, 196
Barrat, 164 (*see also* Barratt)
Barratt, 75, 91, 154, 164 (*see also* Barrat)
Barrel, 21, 34, 53, 71, 145, 166
Barrett, *see* Barratt
Bartholomew, 218
Barton, 118, 128
Bassett, 142, 145
Batchelor, 56, 103, 158
Bates, 39, 118, 127
Baxter, 86
Beauchamp, see Beecham
Bear, *see* Beer

Carr, 118, 122, 127
Carswell, 115
Carter, 21, 46, 50, 86, 102, 107
Cartwright, 52
Catchpole, 11, 15, 163
Caunter, 94, 96
Challinor, 48, 66, 69
Chamberlain, 20, 37, 46, 47, 59, 71, 73
Champion, 42, 162
Champness, 28, 132
Chandler, 48, 57
Chant, 94
Chantrell, 94, 96, 190
Chaplin, 56
Chapman, 26, 38, 91, 107, 108, 109
Chase, 81, 108
Cheeseman, 86
Chester, 123, 124, 245, 254
Child, 159
Chubb, 171, 182, 183
Clapp, 141, 145
Clarke, 29
Clough, 115
Clouter, 66, 72
Cock, 172, 182, 183
Codner, 64, 66, 72
Coffin, 48, 53, 71, 102
Coldwell, 115, 120
Cole, 164, 230, 242, 250
Coleman, 31, 76, 79, 206, 207, 220, 226, 264
Collier, 53, 79
Colman, 206, 226 (*see also* Coleman)
Colswain, 246, 255, 257
Combe, 113, 114, 120, 121, 125, 137
Combes, *see* Combe
Comber, *see* Combe
Cope, 66
Cook, 21, 26, 56, 73, 75
Cooper, 17, 52, 53, 71, 116
Coot, 168, 169, 182
Copeman, 91, 108
Copsey, 256
Corben, *see* Corbin
Corbett, 157, 174, 176, 177
Corbin, 176, 177
Corbyn, *see* Corbin
Corder, 54, 66
Cork, 40, 76, 88
Cornell, 180
Cortis, *see* Curtis
Cottell, 103
Cousans, 42, 138, 159, 160
Cousen, 164 (*see also* Cousans)
Cousin, *see* Cousans
Coward, 21, 40, 76, 79, 107

Crane, 34, 172, 183, 185, 186
Crawcour, 158 (*see also* Crocker)
Cripps, 146
Crisp, 146, 166
Crocker, 17, 54, 158
Crook, 19, 31, 39, 140, 142, 148, 154, 164, 166
Crookshank, 147, 164
Cross, 119
Crow, 34, 176, 184
Crowther, 94
Cruise, 141, 156, 166, 179
Curtis, 30, 140, 152
Cuthbert, 23, 33, 218, 222, 227, 229, 242, 246, 249
Cutler, 54, 72, 103

Darby, *see* Derby
Darling, 158
Darlow, *see* Dearlove
Dart, 103
Darwin, 247
David, 218, 224, 225, 226, 227, 235, 267, 269
Davies, 235 (*see also* Davy)
Daw, 180, 237, 238
Dawkins, 232, 238
Day, 56, 59, 73
Davy, 225, 228, 236, 240, 269
Deacon, 85, 186, 190, 196
Deakin, *see* Deacon
Dean, 119, 120, 186, 196
Dearlove, 158
Denis, *see* Dennis
Dennis, 133, 199, 220, 221, 227, 228
Derby, 27, 124, 131
Derbyshire, 128
Dobb, 37, 238 (*see also* Robert)
Dobbins, 42, 238
Dodd, 31, 153, 238
Doe, 174
Dorset, 128
Dove, 30, 172, 174, 177
Dover, 126, 219, 254
Down, 115
Drabble, 242, 250, 256
Drake, 157, 171, 176, 177, 178
Draper, 26, 27, 38, 76, 88, 91, 107
Drew, 147, 158, 164, 166
Drewery, *see* Drury
Drinkale, *see* Drinkall
Drinkall, 34, 138, 163
Drury, 158
Duke, 103, 170, 194
Dullard, 153, 181
Dumble, 153

ENDNOTES

Chapter 1

1   Hakluyt, R., *Hakluyt's Voyages* (J.M. Dent & Sons, 1926), p.178.
2   Hoskins, W.G., 'Three Studies in Family History' in W.G. Hoskins and H.P.R. Finberg, *Devonshire Studies* (Jonathan Cape, 1952), p.102, quoting *Devon Fines*, Nos 281, 323.
3   Reaney, P.H. & Wilson, R.M., *A Dictionary of English Surnames* (Oxford University Press, 1995), p.xxiii.
4   Hey, D., *Family Names and Family History* (Hambledon & London, 2000), p.52.
5   Ibid, p.34.
6   Local genealogical research has nevertheless come up with links between a few rare names and early families. See in particular Hey (2000).
7   Hey (2000), p.82, quoting R. McKinley (1981) and G. Redmonds (1973).
8   Cromarty, D. & Cromarty, R. (eds), *The Wealth of Shrewsbury in the Early Fourteenth Century: Six Local Subsidy Rolls, 1297–1322* (Alan Sutton, 1993), p.103.
9   Hakluyt (1926), p.183.
10 Blair, P.H., *Anglo-Saxon England* (The Folio Society, 1997), Plate 14.
11 Although romances about Arthur fit into the French chivalric mode and are common in the literature and the lives of the Celtic saints are recorded.
12 Hopper, V. F., *Chaucer's Canterbury Tales: An Interlinear Translation* (Barron's Educational Series, 1970), p.211.
13 Hey (2000), p.37.
14 Blair (1997), Plate 13.

Chapter 2

1   Dyer, C., *Making a Living in the Middle Ages* (Yale University Press, 2002), p.187.
2   Postles, D., *The Surnames of Devon* (Leopard's Head Press, 1995), Table 8.1.
3   Dyer (2002), p.202.
4   Dyer, C., *Standards of Living in the Later Middle Ages* (Cambridge University Press, 1989), p.213.
5   Cromarty, D. & Cromarty, R. *The Wealth of Shrewsbury in the Early Fourteenth Century: Six Local Subsidy Rolls, 1297–1322* (Alan Sutton Publishing, 1993), p.101.
6   Hey, D., *Family Names and Family History* (Hambledon & London, 2000), pp.72, 159.
7   Sayers, D.L. (trs.), *Chanson de Roland* (Penguin, 1957), p.147.
8   Heaney, S. (trs.), *Beowulf* (Farrar, Straus & Giroux, 2000), pp. 107, 111.
9   Sullivan, K.E., *Viking Myth & Legend* (Brockhampton Press, 1998), p.122.
10 Dyer (1989), p.169.

11 Dyer (2002), pp.288–92.
12 Cromarty & Cromarty (1993), p.102.
13 Madicott, J.R. in *Landlords, Peasants and Politics in Medieval England*, T.H. Aston (ed.), (Cambridge University Press, 2006), pp. 324–5, quotes a 1300–9 study of wages in Winchester manors, where a carpenter earns 2.82d a day, less than half the wages of a tiler, who earns 6.19d a day; by 1330–9 the carpenter has narrowed the gap (mostly because the tiler's wages have fallen) and is earning 3.18d, while an unskilled labourer earns 1.49d–1.87d a day.
14 Dyer (2002), p.321.
15 See Cromarty & Cromarty (1993).
16 Dyer (2002), p.201.
17 Razi, Z. (ed.) in Aston (2006), pp.388–9.
18 Postles (1995), p.38.
19 Mortimer, I., *The Time Traveller's Guide to Medieval England* (The Bodley Head, 2008), p.158.
20 Beaumann, R., *Charters of the Redvers Family ... 1090–1217* (Devon & Cornwall Record Society, 1994), Vol.37, p.90, Charter 44.
21 Dyer (2002), pp.209–10.
22 Clanchy, M.T., *Early Medieval England* (The Folio Society, 1997), p.22.
23 Watkin, H.R., *Dartmouth Pre-Reformation*, (Devonshire Association, 1935), Vol.1, p.250.
24 Dyer (2002), Table 3; Dyer (1989), p.52.
25 Ibid, p.56.
26 Ibid, p.71.
27 Ibid, Table 5.
28 A quarter is used for dry goods, such as grain. Eight bushels made one quarter.
29 Dyer (1989), p.65.
30 Cromarty & Cromarty (1993), p.90.
31 Kowaleski, M., *Local Customs Accounts of the Port of Exeter, 1266–1321* (Devon & Cornwall Record Society, 1993), Vol.36, p.159.
32 Dyer (1989), p.14, quoting *Statutes of the Realm* (Record Commission, 1810–28), Vol. 1, p.380.
33 Mortimer (2008), p.103.
34 Watkin (1935), p.208.
35 Dyer (1989), pp.70, 170.
36 Dyer (2002), p.296.
37 Hopper, V.F., *Chaucer's Canterbury Tales: an Interlinear Translation* (Barron's Educational Series, 1970), p.29.
38 Dyer (2002), p.280.
39 Keen, M.H., *England in the Later Middle Ages* (The Folio Society, 1997), p.163.
40 Dyer (2002), p.321.
41 Hopper (1970), p.28.
42 Dyer (2002), p.315.
43 Morris, C. (ed.), *The Journeys of Celia Fiennes* (The Cresset Press, 1949), pp.245–6.
44 Dyer (1989), p.193.
45 Coss, P. (ed.), *Thomas Wright's Political Songs of England* (Cambridge University Press, 1996), p.52.
46 Dyer (1989), Tables 5, 15, 17.
47 Finberg, H.P.R., *West Country Historical Studies* (Augustus M. Kelley, 1969), p.182.
48 Kendrick, A.F., *English Needlework* (Adam & Charles Black, 1967), p.16.
49 Erlande-Brandenburg, A., *The Cathedral Builders of the Middle Ages* (Thames & Hudson, 2009), p.114.
50 Dyer (2002), p.302.
51 Dyer (2002), p.315; Dyer (1989), p.68.
52 Dyer (1989), p.105; Dyer (2002), p.322; Dyer (1989), p.79.

53   Blair, P.H., *Anglo-Saxon England* (The Folio Society, 1997), p.284.
54   Hopper (1970), pp.6, 7.
55   Kendrick (1967), p.41.
56   Dyer (1989), pp.175, 177.
57   Barber, R. (ed.), *The Paston Letters* (The Folio Society, 1981), pp.23, 19.
58   Rebold Benton, J., *Medieval Mischief: Wit and Humour in the Art of the Middle Ages* (Sutton Publishing, 2004), p.57. Misericords are ledges under the tip-up seats in choir stalls so you can still technically be standing while taking the weight off your feet. The seats are usually up and the carving visible. Their name comes from the blessing they are to priests who have to stand for church offices.
59   Hatcher, J., *The Black Death* (Weidenfeld & Nicolson, 2008), pp.81–2.
60   Cromarty & Cromarty (1993), pp.105, 92, 103, 96.
61   Dyer (2002), p.319.

Chapter 3

1   Dyer, C., *Making a Living in the Middle Ages* (Yale University Press, 2002), p.212.
2   Kowaleski, M., *Local Customs Accounts of the Port of Exeter, 1266–1321* (Devon & Cornwall Record Society, 1993), Vol. 36, p.93.
3   Hopper, V.F., *Chaucer's Canterbury Tales: an Interlinear Translation* (Barron's Educational Series, 1970), p.38.
4   Finberg, H.P.R., *West Country Historical Studies* (Augustus M. Kelley, 1969), pp.13–14.
5   Dyer (2002), p.180.
6   Hallam, M.E., *Rural England, 1066–1348* (Harvester Press, 1981), p.167; Madicott, J.R. (ed.), in *Landlords, Peasants and Politics in Medieval England*, T.H. Aston (Cambridge University Press, 1987), p. 325.
7   Stamper, P. , in *The Countryside of Medieval England*, Grenville Astill and Annie Grant (eds) (Blackwell, 1988), p.129.
8   Hopper (1970), p.7.
9   Dyer (2002), p.113.
10   Grant, A., in Astill and Grant (1988), pp.168–9.
11   Finberg (1969), p.97.
12   A charming fourteenth-century drawing in the Bodleian Library shows a shaky-looking windmill pivoting on a sort of trestle with its door open for the sack of corn carried by the peasant approaching on the left, with a buyer for the flour already trotting up on the right. MS Bodl 264 fol 811; Dyer (2002), plate 7.
13   Finberg (1969), pp.160–2.
14   Beaumann, R., *Charters of the Redvers Family* (Devon & Cornwall Record Society, 1994), Vol. 37, pp.32, 36.
15   Hopper (1970), p.39.
16   Cromarty, D. and Cromarty, R. (eds), *The Wealth of Shrewsbury in the Early Fourteenth Century* (Alan Sutton Publishing, 1993), p.108.
17   Dyer (2002), pp.288–91.
18   Hoskins, W.G. & Finberg, H.P. R., 'Three Studies in Family History', *Devonshire Studies* (Jonathon Cape, 1952), p. 102, quoting *Devon Fines*, Nos 281, 323.
19   Cromarty & Cromarty (1993), pp.112, 111, 120, 121.
20   Dyer (2002), p.310.
21   See John Hatcher in Aston, p.269.
22   Finberg (1969), p.39.
23   Hopper, (1970) pp.19, 20.
24   Watkin, H.R., *Dartmouth: Pre-Reformation* (Devonshire Association, 1935), p.5.
25   Although elementary schools had been provided for by the Council of Clovesho in AD 747.
26   Coulton, G.G., *Medieval Panorama* (Cambridge University Press, 1938), pp.388–9.

27 Coulton (1938), pp.392–3.
28 Postles, D., *The Surnames of Devon* (Leopard's Head Press, 1995), p.239, Table 7.6.
29 Dyer, C., *Standards of Living in the Later Middle Ages* (Cambridge University Press, 1989), p.47; Dyer (2002), p.341; Dyer (1989), Table 5.
30 By 1300, 87 per cent of transport on demesnes in England involved the use of horses, compared with 24 per cent a century earlier. See John Langdon in Aston (1987), pp.34–59.
31 Dyer (2002), p.202.
32 Dyer (1989), Table 3.
33 Dyer (2002), pp.131, 203.
34 Grant, A., in Astill and Grant (1988), p. 172; Dyer (1989), p.62.
35 The Duke of Buckingham's household drinks 30,000 to 40,000 gallons of ale a year. See Dyer (1989), pp.197, 58.
36 Razi, Z., in Aston (1987), p.367.
37 Dyer (1989), Table 6.
38 Watkin (1935), p.237.
39 Cromarty & Cromarty (1993), pp.84, 102.
40 Brooke, C. & Keir, G., *London 800–1216: The Shaping of a City*, (University of California Press, 1975), p.271.
41 Schmidt, A.V.C. (trs), *William Langland, Piers Plowman: A New Translation of the B-Text*, (Oxford University Press, 1992).
42 Dyer (2002), p.206; Dyer (1989), p.63.
43 Dyer (1989), Table 3 and p. 63.
44 Ibid, Table 14.
45 Dyer (2002), p.208.
46 Hopper (1970), pp.357, 358.
47 Dyer (2002), p.164.
48 Hopper (1970), p.18.
49 Dyer (1989), p.193; Dyer (1989), pp.193–4.
50 Schmidt (1992), pp.21, 75.
51 Roud, S., *The English Year* (Penguin, 2006), p.371.
52 Power, E., *Medieval People* (The Folio Society, 2001), p.187.
53 Cromarty & Cromarty (1993), p.103.
54 Ibid, (1993), pp.84, 52.
55 Dyer (1989), p.93.
56 Cromarty & Cromarty (1993), pp.92, 106, 112, 120.
57 Jackson, C.J., quoted in 'The Crozier of William of Wykeham', Jeremy Montagu (*Early Music*, November 2002), p.542.
58 Quite apart from being a stunning work, this crozier is academically important because some of these instruments – the woodwind/recorder, conical and domed cymbals, the single kettledrum and the transverse flute – were thought not to exist, or at any rate not in this form and that this time.
59 Hopper (1970), p.7.
60 Beaumann (1994), p.100.
61 In Tutbury in Lincolnshire the Court had an annual celebration, abolished in 1778, that involved bull-running. First minstrels and later others would chase a bull covered with soap across the open fields. Anyone managing to catch the bull long enough to cut off some hair could keep the animal. See Roud (2006), pp.364–5.
62 Heaney, S. (trs.), *Beowulf* (Farrar, Straus & Giroux, 2000), p.143.
63 Eleanor had a favourite troubadour, Bertrand de Born.
64 Hopper (1970), pp.352–3.
65 Whitelock, D., *The Beginnings of English Society* (Penguin, 1956), p.107.
66 Benton, J., *Medieval Mischief: Wit and Humour in the Art of the Middle Ages* (Alan Sutton Publishing, 2004), p.82.
67 Hopper (1970), pp.205, 16.
68 Clanchy, M.T., *Early Medieval England* (The Folio Society, 1997), p.44; Coulton

(1938), p.581, quoting Honarius of Augsburg.
69 Montagu (2002), p.547.
70 Cromarty & Cromarty (1993), p.111.
71 Dyer (2002), p.214.
72 Erlande-Brandenburg, A., *The Cathedral Builders of the Middle Ages* (Thames & Hudson, 2009), p.132.
73 Dyer (1989), p.80.
74 All references in this paragraph are from Erlande-Brandenburg (1995), pp.132, 162; 89, 163.
75 Erlande-Brandenburg (2009), pp.148, 150–1.
76 Ibid, p.135.
77 There is still a treadwheel in working order at the base of the spire of Canterbury Cathedral where William of England's men must have left it at the end of the twelfth century.
78 Erlande-Brandenburg (2009), p.164.
79 Cherry, B. & Pevsner, N., *The Buildings of England: Devon* (Penguin, 1999), pp.368–9.
80 The contract for £300 going to William Horwood for Fotheringay details £6 13s 4d to be paid after excavation and so on up to the last £3. See Erlande-Brandenburg, pp.162–3.
81 Cherry & Pevsner (1999), p.367.
82 Erlande-Brandenburg (2009), p.151.
83 His appointment is particularly appropriate: Thomas à Becket, murdered at Canterbury in 1170, spent time at Sens during his refuge in France after 1160. Sens Cathedral still has an early thirteenth-century stained glass window depicting Becket's last days, while he is buried in the crypt at Canterbury where a chapel is dedicated to him.
84 Cherry & Pevsner (1999), pp.372–3, 369.
85 Dyer (2002), p.172.
86 Erlande-Brandenburg (2009), pp.90 and 171 for ref.
87 Ibid, pp.92–3.
88 Benton (2004), p.17.
89 Hoskins, W.G., *Local History in England* (Longmans, 1984), p.109.
90 Hoskins (1984), p.134.
91 Hayter, Sir William, *William of Wykeham* (Chatto & Windus, 1970), p.97 *et seq.* for more on Glazier.
92 Erlande-Brandenburg (2009), p.164.
93 Ibid, pp.116–7.
94 After the mid-fourteenth century thatch roofs are replaced with shingles or ceramic tiles in towns to limit fire risk. See Dyer (1989), p.191.
95 Erlande-Brandenburg (2009), p.137.
96 Dyer (1989), pp.220–5.
97 Dyer (2002), p.316.
98 Keen, M.H., *England in the Later Middle Ages* (The Folio Society, 1997), pp.6–7.
99 Keen (1997), p. 115; Geoffrey le Baker chronicle quoted in *Mad Dogs and Englishmen*, R. Fiennes (Hodder & Stoughton, 2009), p.75.
100 Madicott in Aston (1987), pp.322–5.
101 A charter from 1394–5 records that Richard II reminds the burgesses of Dartmouth they have 'to maintain at their own expense two warships always ready to sail anywhere at the King's command'. *Torre Abbey*, Deryck Seymour, (James Townsend, 1977), p.204.
102 The tax is levied on movable goods worth more than 10 shillings in the country and 6 shillings in the towns; for animal equivalents, see Madicott in Aston (1987), p.294.
103 Finberg (1969), p.152.
104 Keen (1997), p.7.
105 Roud (2006), p.352.

Chapter 4

1   North, D.C., Wallis, J.J. & Weingast, B.R., *Violence and Social Orders* (Cambridge University Press, 2009), p.108.
2   Hatcher, J., *The Black Death* (Weidenfeld & Nicolson, 2008), pp.47, 57, 75 and map on p.48.
3   Reaney, P.H. & Wilson, R.M., *A Dictionary of English Surnames* (Oxford University Press, 1995), p.xvii.
4   Postles, D., *The Surnames of Devon* (The Leopard's Head Press, 1995), Table 8.1 and p.254.
5   Dyer, C., *Making a Living in the Middle Ages* (Yale University Press, 2002), p.161.
6   Addison, Sir William, *Understanding English Place Names* (B.T. Batsford, 1978), p.19.
7   Dyer, C., *Standards of Living in the Later Middle Ages* (Cambridge University Press, 1989), p.76.
8   Hallam, H.E., *Rural England, 1066–1348* (Harvester Press, 1981), p.167.
9   Hey, D., *Family Names and Family History* (Hambledon & London, 2000), p.177.
10 Hallam (1981), p.167.
11 Dyer (1989), p.194.
12 Kowaleski, M., *Local Customs Accounts of the Port of Exeter, 1266–1321* (Devon & Cornwall Record Society, 1993), Vol. 36, Appendix 2, p.215.
13 McKinley, R.A., in Postles (1995), pp.102–3.
14 Dyer (2002), p.187.
15 Ibid, p.212.
16 Postles (1995), p.254.
17 Cromarty, D. & Cromarty, R. (eds), *The Wealth of Shrewsbury in the Early Fourteenth Century* (Alan Sutton, 1993), p.118.
18 Dyer (1989) p.230–1.
19 Dyer (2002), pp.193–4.
20 Cromarty & Cromarty (1993), p.115.
21 Dyer (2002), p.296.
22 York has houses for artisans built in the early fourteenth century that are still used.
23 Keen, M.E., *England in the Later Middle Ages* (The Folio Society, 1997), p.165.
24 Robinson, J., *Blue Stockings* (Viking, 2010), p.xii.
25 Kowaleski (1993), p.24.
26 Mclure, P., 'Patterns of Migration in the Late Middle Ages' (*Economic History Review*, 1979).
27 Hey (2000); Reaney & Wilson (1995); Titford, J., *British Surnames* (Penguin, 2009).
28 Hey (2000), p.52.
29 Addison (1978), p.58.
30 Ibid, pp.19–21.
31 Dyer (2002), p.207.
32 Hakluyt, R., *Hakluyt's Voyages* (J.M. Dent and Sons, 1926), Vol. 1, p.187.
33 Hakluyt (1926), p.183.
34 Ibid, p.183.
35 Power, E., *Medieval People* (The Folio Society, 2001), p.217.
36 Tengvik, G., *Old English Bynames* (Almqvist & Wiksells boktryckeri-a.-b., 1938), quoted in Hey (2000), p.38.
37 Hey (2000), p.40.
38 Ibid, p.45, quoting Reaney (1995).
39 Ibid, p.40.
40 Keen (1997), p.161.
41 Hey (2000), p.47, from poll taxes of 1377, 1379, 1381.
42 Kowaleski (1993), p.150.
43 Dyer (2002), p.137.
44 Ibid, p.208.

45 Hampden, J. (ed.), *Richard Hakluyt. Voyages & Documents* (Oxford University Press, 1958), p.xi.
46 Hakluyt (1926), p.178.
47 Postles (1995), pp.64–6, Table 3.2.
48 Hey (2000), p.48; Watkin, H.R., *Dartmouth: Pre-Reformation* (The Devonshire Association, 1935), p.4.
49 Watkin (1935), p.205.
50 Watkin (1935), p.378. The reference is to a commission to the sheriff of Devon to bring to the king Breton prisoners captured at Blackpool Sands in April 1404.
51 From Reaney & Wilson (1995); Cherry & Pevsner (1999); Watkin (1935); and Hoskins, W.G.H. & Finberg, H.P.R., 'The Making of the Agrarian Landscape' in *Devonshire Studies* (Jonathan Cape, 1952).
52 Hey (2000), p.82, quoting R. Mckinley (1981) and G. Redmonds (1973).

Chapter 5

1   Postles, D., *The Surnames of Devon* (Leopard's Head Press, 1995), Table 8.1, p.253.
2   Watkin, H.R., *Dartmouth: Pre-Reformation* (The Devonshire Association, 1935), pp.355, 34–7.
3   Dyer, C., *Standards of Living in the Later Middle Ages* (Cambridge University Press, 1989), p.253.
4   Hopper, V.F., *Chaucer's Canterbury Tales: An Interlinear Translation* (Barron's Educational Series, 1970), Prologue, pp.35–6, 40.
5   Hopper (1970), pp.66–7.
6   Schmidt, A.V.C. (trs), *William Langland, Piers Plowman: A New Translation of the B-Text*, (Oxford University Press, 1992), p.30 and note.
7   Hopper (1970), Prologue, p.38.
8   Benton, J.R., *Medieval Mischief: Wit and Humour in the Art of the Middle Ages* (Alan Sutton Publishing, 2004), p.34.
9   Benton (2004), pp.100–3.
10 Sharkey, J., *Celtic Mysteries: the Ancient Religion* (Thames & Hudson, 1975), p.14.
11 Hopper (1970), Prologue p.5, p.307.
12 Watkin (1935), p.24.
13 Ibid, p.355.
14 Hopper (1970), pp.351, 354.
15 Schmidt (1992), p.156, from Peter Cantor and Ezekiel 16:49.
16 Benton (2004), p.56.
17 Dyer, C., *Making a Living in the Middle Ages* (Yale University Press, 2002), p.207.
18 Hopper (1970), Prologue, p.32.
19 Whitelock, D., *The Beginnings of English Society* (Penguin, repr. 1956), p.120.
20 Schmidt (1992), p.96.
21 Benton (2004), p.68.
22 Watkin (1935), pp.221–58.
23 Hopper (1970) , Prologue, p.4.
24 Schmidt (1992), notes, p.280.
25 Hopper (1970), pp.352–3.
26 Schmidt (1992), p.147.
27 Coulton, G.G., *Medieval Studies* (Simpkin, Marshall, Hamilton & Kent, 1915), p.30.
28 Hopper (1970), p.36.
29 Ibid, Prologue, pp.38–40.
30 Watkin (1935), pp.385–6.
31 Schmidt (1992), p.49.
32 Benton (2004), p.52.
33 Benton (2004), pp.53–4.
34 Aesop's Fables: Mercury and the Tradesmen.

35 This is before England became a country of merchants, although in Victorian times, Charles Dickens is calling London City merchants 'sleek, slobbering, bow-paunched, overfed, apoplectic, snorting cattle'.

36 Schmidt (1992), p.11.

37 Matthews, C.M., *English Surnames* (Weidenfeld & Nicolson, 1966), pp.38–9.

38 Sayers, D.L. (trs), *The Song of Roland* (Penguin, 1957), p.94.

39 Taylor, M.H. & Ching, D., *Medieval Woodcarvings of Ripon Cathedral* (The Friends of Ripon Cathedral, 2009), p.54.

40 Hopper (1970), p.243.

41 Coulton, G.G., *Medieval Panorama* (Cambridge University Press, 1938), p.523.

42 Hopper (1970), p.6.

43 Bloch, M., *Feudal Society* (Routledge & Kegan Paul, 1961), pp.123–4. Quoted from *Cartulaire de Sainte Madeleine de Davron*, bibl.Nat.MS Latin 5288 fol. 77.

44 Hopper (1970), Prologue, p.2.

45 Skeat, W.W. (ed), *Notes on The Works of Geoffrey Chaucer* (Oxford, Clarendon, 1934) after Tyrwhitt, p.3.

46 Collis, L., *Memoirs of a Medieval Woman: the Life and Times of Marjory Kempe* (Harper & Row, 1964).

47 Schmidt (1992), p.2.

48 Ibid, p.60.

49 See Chapter 7 for Neal as a personal surname.

50 Reaney, P.H. & Wilson, R.M., *Dictionary of English Surnames* (Oxford University Press, 1995), p.90.

51 Hatcher, J., *The Black Death* (Weidenfeld & Nicolson, 2008), p.276.

52 Roud, S., *The English Year* (Penguin, 2006).

53 Cromarty, D. & Cromarty, R. (eds), *The Wealth of Shrewsbury in the Fourteenth Century* (Alan Sutton Publishing, 1993), p.86.

Chapter 6

1   Aesop can be unreliable because his moral is more important than the consistency of his characters. Some are stupid in one story but shrewd in another. For instance, the crow losing his cheese to the fox, but then throwing stones into the pitcher to raise the water level so he can drink.

2   Turville-Petre, E.O.G., *Myth and Religion of the North* (Weidenfeld & Nicolson, 1964), p.280.

3   Schmidt, A.V.C. (trs), *William Langland, Piers Plowman: A New Translation of the B-Text* (Oxford University Press, 1992), p.175.

4   Ibid, p.182.

5   Rees, A. & Rees, B., *Celtic Heritage* (Thames & Hudson, 1961), p.192.

6   Sharkey, J., *Celtic Mysteries* (Thames & Hudson, 1975), p.15.

7   Coulton, G.G., *Medieval Panorama* (Cambridge University Press, 1938), pp.106, 112, quoting *Lives of the Brethren*, transl. by F. Conway (1896).

8   Turville-Petre (1964), pp.57–8.

9   Heaney, S. (trs.) *Beowulf* (Farrar, Straus & Giroux, 2000), p.49.

10 Turville-Petre (1964), pp.75–6, 279.

11 Schmidt (1992), pp.88, 48, 189.

12 Ibid, pp.146–7.

13 Reaney, P.H. & Wilson, R.M., *A Dictionary of English Surnames* (Oxford University Press, 1995).

14 Dyer, C., *Standards of Living in the Later Middle Ages* (Cambridge University Press, 1989), p.224.

15 Benton, J., *Medieval Mischief* (Alan Sutton Publishing, 2004), p.18.

16 Hopper, V.F., *Chaucer's Canterbury Tales: An Interlinear Translation* (Barron's Educational Series, 1970), p.40.

17 Schmidt (1992), pp.148, 134.
18 Benton (2004), pp.59–60.
19 MS Gg.6.19, fol.148, repr. in *The Cambridge Illuminations*, Paul Binski and Stella Panayatova (eds), (Harvey Miller Publishers, 2005), p.293.
20 Schmidt (1992), p.151.
21 Raffel, B. (trs), *Beowulf* (Mentor, 1963), p.51.
22 Hopper (1970), pp.330, 332.
23 Hey, D., *Family Names and Family History* (Hambledon & London, 2000), p.68.
24 Whitelock, D., *The Beginnings of English Society* (Penguin, 1956), p.26.
25 McKinley, R., in *Devon Surnames* by David Postles (Leopard's Head Press, 1995), p.90.
26 Schmidt (1992), p.134.
27 Hopper (1970), p.1.
28 Benton (2004), p.23.
29 Ibid, p.14.
30 Schmidt (1992), pp.180, 14.
31 Reaney & Wilson (1995); Titford, J., *Penguin Dictionary of British Surnames* (Penguin, 2009).
32 Finberg, H.P.R., *West Country Historical Studies* (Augustus M. Kelley, 1969), p.171.
33 Roud, S., *The English Year* (Penguin, 2006), pp.196–7.
34 He can lead processions and hold services, but not undermine the dignity of the church; his sermons are generally written by adults. See Roud (2006), p.494.
35 Benton (2004), p.77; Taylor, M.H. & Ching, D., *Medieval Wood Carvings of Ripon Cathedral* (Friends of Ripon Cathedral, 2009), p.51.
36 Coulton (1938), p.123.
37 Under Bishop Stapeldon of Exeter (1308–24) only a little over a third of rectors in the diocese are ordained, but the reforming Bishop Grandisson (1327–69), ordains 31 priests versus 40 non-priests in his first five years, and later 115 priests versus 63 non-priests.
38 Dyer (1989), p.247.
39 Schmidt (1992), pp.55–6, 3.
40 Hopper (1970), p.31.
41 Dyer, C., *Making a Living in the Middle Ages* (Yale University Press, 2002), pp.348–9.
42 Beaumann, R. *Charters of the Redvers Family ... 1090–1217* (Devon & Cornwall Record Society, 1994) Vol. 37, p.37.
43 Quoted by Coulton (1938), p.136.
44 Coulton (1938), p.128, quoting Hist. Dunelm.Scriptores.
45 Schmidt (1992), p.39.
46 Benton (2004), pp.75, xii.
47 Finberg (1969), p.180.
48 Hopper (1970), pp.13–14.
49 Schmidt (1992), p.104.
50 Hopper (1970), p.16.
51 Schmidt (1992), p.4.
52 Benton (2004), p.16.
53 Coulton, G.G., *Medieval Studies* (Simpkin, Marshall, Hamilton & Kent & Co., 1915), p.5.
54 Finberg (1969), p.170.
55 Coulton, G.G. (1915), pp.6, 5.
56 Cromarty, D. & Cromarty, R. (eds), *The Wealth of Shrewsbury in the Early Fourteenth Century: Six Lay Subsidy Rolls, 1297–1322* (Alan Sutton Publishing, 1993), p.97.
57 Dyer (1989), p.110.
58 Watkin, H.R., *Dartmouth: Pre-Reformation* (The Devonshire Association, 1935), Vol. 1, p.380.

59 Dyer (1989), p.23.
60 Hopper (1970), p.4.
61 Postles, D. p.122; Erskine, A.M. (ed.), *The Devonshire Lay Subsidy of 1332* (Devon & Cornwall Record Society, 1969), Vol. 14.

Chapter 7

1   Postles, D., *The Surnames of Devon* (Leopard's Head Press, 1995), p.10, Table 5.1.
2   Ibid, p.163.
3   Although Chaucer has the nun's priest quote the Icelandic proverb 'Women's counsels are often fatal enough' and St Cuthbert appears in the Reeve's Tale [see line 207 among others]. Under Edward III, forked beards (a pre-Conquest Danish fashion) were adopted by the bourgeoisie. See Skeat, Rev. W.W., *Notes to The Works of Geoffrey Chaucer* (Oxford University Press, 1934), p.29.
4   Watkin, H.R., *Dartmouth: Pre-Reformation* (The Devonshire Association, 1935), Proceedings of Mayors' Courts, pp.227, 230, 236, 240.
5   Bragg, M., *The Adventure of English* (Hodder & Stoughton, 2003), p.33.
6   Blair, P.H., *Anglo-Saxon England* (The Folio Society, 1997), p.290.
7   Skeat (1934), p.113.
8   Blair (1997), p.164.
9   Ibid, p.166.
10 Ibid, p.269.
11 Thursberg Moor in Germany, Porlakshafin in south Iceland and Thursley, Thunderfield, Thundersley and Thurstable in southern England.
12 Reaney, P.H. & Wilson, R.M., *A Dictionary of English Surnames* (Oxford University Press, 1995), pp.xxxii–xxxiii.
13 Hey, D., *Family Names and Family History* (Hambledon & London, 2000), pp.60–1.
14 Whitelock, D., *The Beginnings of English Society* (Penguin, 1956), p.128.
15 Hey (2000), p.60.
16 Whitelock (1956), p.235.
17 Hey (2000), pp.68–9.
18 Blair (1997), p.188.
19 Whitelock (1956), pp.44–5.
20 Ibid, p.69.
21 Sayers, D.L. (trs), *The Song of Roland* (Penguin, 1957), pp.99–100.
22 Turville-Petre, E.O.G., *Myth and Religion of the North* (Weidenfeld & Nicolson, 1964), p.252.
23 Mackenzie, D.A., *Teutonic Myth and Legend* (Gresham Publishing Co., 1912), p.78.
24 Raffel, B. (trs), *Beowulf* (New American Library, 1963), p.51.
25 In a late tenth-century Devon charter, a 'Grendel's Pit' is marked near West Rowthorne. It surely relates to the den of Beowulf's monster and records tenth-century memories of Beowulf. A nearby Pitt Farm now records the feature but has lost the memory of its inhabitant. Dragons like Grendel were associated with demons at pagan rituals, and this place might have marked an earlier heathen worship site. See Finberg, H.P.R., *West Country Historical Studies* (Augustus M. Kelley, 1969), p.46.
26 Whitelock (1956), p.106.
27 Watkin (1935), p.233.
28 Sayers (1957), p.92.
29 Sacrifices, mostly of animals, allowed people to absorb the power of the god.
30 Turville-Petre (1964), p.93.
31 Ibid, p.264.
32 Raffel (1963), p.37.
33 Skeat (1934), pp.356–7.
34 Kowaleski, M., *Local Customs Accounts of the Port of Exeter, 1266–1321* (Devon & Cornwall Record Society, 1993) and Watkin (1935), p.375.

35 Attwater, D. with John, C. R., *Penguin Dictionary of Saints* (Penguin, 1994), pp.3–5.
36 Collis, L., *Memoirs of a Medieval Woman: The Life and Times of Margery Kempe* (Harper & Row, 1964).
37 Skeat (1934), p.166.
38 Watkin (1935), pp.371–2.
39 Erlande-Brandenburg, A., *The Cathedral Builders of the Middle Ages* (Thames & Hudson, 2009), p.132.
40 Hopper, V.F., *Chaucer's Canterbury Tales: An Interlinear Translation* (Barron's Educational Series, 1970), The Prioress's Tale.
41 Hopper (1970), pp.11, 277.
42 Clanchy, M.T., *Early Medieval England* (The Folio Society, 1997), p.19.
43 Blair (1997), pp.165–70.
44 Whitelock (1956), pp.69–70.

Chapter 8

1 Clanchy, M.T., *Early Medieval England* (The Folio Society, 1997), p.35.
2 Postles, D., *The Surnames of Devon* (Leopard's Head Press, 1995), p.161. Indigenous names probably continued orally after the Conquest. Kinman from Cynemann (royal man), and Kemble, from Cynebeald (family/kin–bold) are, for instance, only recorded once, in about AD 770, in Worcester and before the ninth century, respectively, before becoming surnames centuries later.
3 Hopper, V.F., *Chaucer's Canterbury Tales: An Interlinear Translation* (Barron's Educational Series, 1970), p.465.
4 Blair, P.H., *Anglo-Saxon England* (The Folio Society, 1997), pp.98–9.
5 Reaney, P.H. & Wilson, R.M., *A Dictionary of English Surnames* (Oxford University Press, 1995), p.xxiii.
6 Genealogies for these times are rare, but as an example, an Elric with an English name is recorded in twelfth-century Lincolnshire with a daughter with a Scandinavian name who had called her son William, and he called his Roger and Robert (see Reaney & Wilson (1995), p.xxi).
7 Hey, D., *Family Names and Family History* (Hambledon & London, 2000), p.64.
8 Schmidt, A.V.C., (trs.), *William Langland, Piers Plowman: A New Translation of the B-Text* (Oxford University Press, 1992), pp.66, 95.
9 Hey (2000), pp.25–6, 61–2.
10 Cromarty, D. & Cromarty, R. (eds), *The Wealth of Shrewsbury in the Early Fourteenth Century* (Alan Sutton Publishing, 1993), p.107.
11 Beaumann, R., *Charters of the Redvers Family* (Devon & Cornwall Record Society, 1994), Vol. 37, pp.8–9.
12 Blair (1997), p.146.
13 Edward the Aetheling, son of Edmund Ironside and grandson of Aethelred the Unready, went to Hungary when Cnut took the throne in 1016. He returned in 1057, a strong candidate to replace Cnut when he died, but died shortly afterwards.
14 Whitelock, D., *The Beginnings of English Society* (Penguin, 1956), p.123.
15 Blair (1997), p.87.
16 Whitelock (1956), pp.106, 113.
17 Blair (1997), p.188.
18 Whitelock (1956), pp.55–6.
19 Ibid, p.135.
20 Ibid, p.82.
21 Ibid, pp.59, 123.
22 Cromarty & Cromarty (1993), p.94.
23 Hey (2000), p.61.
24 Blair ((1997), p.218.
25 Raffel, B. (trs.), *Beowulf* (New American Library, 1963), pp.25, 35.

26 Sayers, D.L., *The Song of Roland* (Penguin, 1957), p.118.
27 Ibid, p.94; Raffel (1963), p.67.
28 Hey (2000), p.52.
29 Ibid, pp.169–70.
30 Ibid, pp.23–4 for Drabble; pp.162–3 for Cobbold; p.166 for Stannard and Kerridge.
31 Blair (1997), pp.340–1.
32 Whitelock (1956), pp.110, 105.
33 Watkins, A.E. (trs.), *Aelfric's Colloquy* (Gutenberg).
34 Clanchy (1997), p.227.
35 Reynolds, S., *An Introduction to the History of English Medieval Towns* (Oxford University Press, 1982), pp.85, 38.
36 Hey (2000); p.63 for Kettle; p.155 for Algood; p.64 for Randolf, quoting Hoskins.
37 Reaney & Wilson (1995); Hey (2000).
38 Cromarty & Cromarty (1993), p.112.
39 Postles, (1995), p.162.
40 Turville-Petre, E.O.G., *Myth and Religion of the North* (Weidenfeld & Nicolson, 1964) p.47.
41 Whitelock (1956), p.63.
42 Turville-Petre (1964), pp.119, 193, 210–3, 233.
43 Sullivan, K.E., *Viking Myth and Legend* (Brockhampton Press, 1998), p.122.
44 Cromarty & Cromarty (1993), pp.92–3.
45 Turville-Petre (1964), pp.203–4.
46 Raffel (1963), pp.59, 48.
47 Turville-Petre (1964), p.274.
48 Ibid, pp.85–6, 14.
49 Whitelock (1956), pp.44–5.
50 Rees, A. & Rees, B., *Celtic Heritage* (Thames & Hudson, 1961), p.53.
51 Ibid, pp.66, 156.
52 Chadwick, N., *Celtic Britain* (Thames & Hudson, 1963), p.119.
53 Ibid, pp.71, 82, 86.
54 Ibid, p.65.
55 Postles (1995), p.165.
56 Chadwick (1963), pp.71, 72.
57 Ibid, p.63.
58 Ibid, pp.101–5.
59 Ibid, p.112.
60 Postles (1995), p.167.
61 Chadwick (1963), pp.102–11.
62 Rees and Rees (1961), pp.26, 67, 71.
63 Addison, Sir William, *Understanding English Place Names* (B.T. Batsford, 1978), p.61.
64 Rees and Rees (1961), p.71.
65 Ibid, p.71.
66 Chadwick (1963), pp.46–8.
67 Postles (1995), p.161.
68 Watkin, H.R., *Dartmouth: Pre-Reformation* (Devonshire Association, 1935), pp.11, 35, 62.
69 Postles (1995), p.224.
70 Chadwick (1963), p.106.
71 Schmidt (1992), p.53.
72 Hopper (1970), pp.438, 325.
73 Ibid, p.526.

BIBLIOGRAPHY

Addison, Sir William, *Understanding English Place Names* (B.T. Batsford, 1978).

Astill, G. & Grant, A. (eds) *The Countryside of Medieval England* (Blackwell, 1988).

Aston, T.H. (ed), *Landlords, Peasants and Politics in Medieval England* (Cambridge University Press, 1987)

Attwater, D. & John, C. R., *Penguin Dictionary of Saints* (Penguin, 1994).

Barber, R. (ed), *The Paston Letters* (The Folio Society, 1981).

Beaumann, R., *Charters of the Redvers Family ... 1090–1217* (Devon & Cornwall Record Society, 1994), Vol.37.

Benton, J., *Medieval Mischief: Wit and Humour in the Art of the Middle Ages* (Alan Sutton, 2004).

Blair, P.H., *Anglo-Saxon England* (The Folio Society, 1997).

Bloch, M., *Feudal Society* (Routledge & Kegan Paul, 1961).

Bragg, M., The Adventure of English (Hodder & Stoughton, 2003).

Brooke, C. & Keir, G., *London, 800–1216: the Shaping of a City* (University of California Press, 1975).

Chadwick, N., *Celtic Britain* (Thames & Hudson, 1963).

Cherry, B. & Pevsner, N., *The Buildings of England: Devon* (Penguin, 1999).

Clanchy, M.T., *Early Medieval England* (The Folio Society, 1997).

Collis, L., *Memoirs of a Medieval Woman: the Life and Times of Marjory Kempe* (Harper and Row, 1964).

Coss, P. (ed), *Thomas Wright's Political Songs of England* (Cambridge University Press, 1996).

Coulton, G.G., *Medieval Studies* (Simpkin, Marshall, Hamilton & Kent, 1915).

Coulton, G.G., *Medieval Panorama* (Cambridge University Press, 1938).

Cromarty, D. & Cromarty, R. (eds), *The Wealth of Shrewsbury in the Early Fourteenth Century: Six Local Subsidy Rolls, 1297–1322* (Alan Sutton, 1993).

Dyer, C., *Standards of Living in the Later Middle Ages* (Cambridge University Press, 1989).

Dyer, C., *Making a Living in the Middle Ages* (Yale University Press, 2002).

Erlande-Brandenburg, A., *The Cathedral Builders of the Middle Ages* (Thames & Hudson, 2009).

Erskine, A.M. (ed), *The Devonshire Lay Subsidy of 1332* (Devon & Cornwall Record Society, Vol. 14., 1969).

Fiennes, R., *Mad Dogs and Englishmen* (Hodder & Stoughton, 2009),

Finberg, H.P.R, *West Country Historical Studies* (Augustus M. Kelley, 1969).

Hakluyt, R., *Hakluyt's Voyages* (J.M. Dent & Sons, 1926).

Hallam, M.E., *Rural England, 1066–1348* (Harvester Press, 1981).

Hatcher, J., *The Black Death* (Weidenfeld & Nicolson, 2008).

Hayter, Sir William, *William of Wykeham* (Chatto & Windus, 1970).

Heaney, S. (trs), *Beowulf* (Farrar, Straus & Giroux, 2000).

Hey, D., *Family Names and Family History* (Hambledon & London, 2000).

Hopper, V. F., *Chaucer's Canterbury Tales: An Interlinear Translation* (Barron's Educational Series, 1970).

Hoskins, W.G., 'Three Studies in Family History' in W.G. Hoskins and H.P.R. Finberg, *Devonshire Studies* (Jonathan Cape, 1952).

Hoskins, W.G., *Local History in England* (Longmans, 1984).

Keen, M.H., *England in the Later Middle Ages* (The Folio Society, 1997).

Kendrick, A.F., *English Needlework* (Adam & Charles Black, 1967).

Kowaleski, M., *Local Customs Accounts of the Port of Exeter, 1266–1321* (Devon & Cornwall Record Society, 1993).

Mackenzie, D.A.,*Teutonic Myth and Legend* (Gresham, 1912).

Madicott, J.R. in *Landlords, Peasants and Politics in Medieval England*, T.H. Aston (ed.) (Cambridge University Press, 1987).

Matthews, C.M., *English Surnames* (Weidenfeld & Nicolson, 1966).

Mclure, P., 'Patterns of Migration in the Late Middle Ages' (*Economic History Review*, 1979).

Morris, C. (ed), *The Journeys of Celia Fiennes* (The Cresset Press, 1949).

Morris, J. (ed), Domesday Book: Cornwall (Phillimore, 1979).

Mortimer, I., *The Time Traveller's Guide to Medieval England* (The Bodley Head, 2008).

North, D.C., Wallis, J.J. & Weingast, B.R., *Violence and Social Orders* (Cambridge University Press, 2009).

Postles, D., *The Surnames of Devon* (Leopard's Head Press, 1995).

Power, E., *Medieval People* (The Folio Society, 2001).

Raffel, B. (trs), *Beowulf* (Mentor, 1963).

Razi, Z. (ed) in T.H. Aston (Cambridge University Press, 1987).

Reaney, P.H. and Wilson, R.M., *A Dictionary of English Surnames* (Oxford University Press, 1995).

Rebold Benton, J., *Medieval Mischief: Wit and Humour in the Art of the Middle Ages* (Alan Sutton, 2004).

Rees, A. & Rees, B., *Celtic Heritage* (Thames & Hudson, 1961).

Reynolds, S., An Introduction to the History of English Medieval Towns (Clarendon, 1977).

Robinson, J., *Blue Stockings* (Viking, 2010).

Roud, S., *The English Year* (Penguin, 2006).

Sayers, D.L. (trs), *Chanson de Roland* (Penguin, 1957), p.147.

Schmidt, A.V.C. (trs), *William Langland, Piers Plowman: A New Translation of the B-Text* (Oxford University Press, 1992).

Seymour, D., *Torre Abbey* (James Townsend, 1977)

Sharkey, J., *Celtic Mysteries: the Ancient Religion* (Thames & Hudson, 1975).

Skeat, W.W. (ed), *Notes on The Works of Geoffrey Chaucer* (Oxford, Clarendon, 1934).

Stamper, P., in *The Countryside of Medieval England*, G. Astill and A. Grant (eds) (Blackwell, 1988).

Sullivan, K.E., *Viking Myth & Legend* (Brockhampton Press, 1998).

Taylor, M.H. & Ching, D., *Medieval Woodcarvings of Ripon Cathedral* (The Friends of Ripon Cathedral, 2009).

Titford, J., *British Surnames* (Penguin, 2009).

Turville-Petre, E.O.G., *Myth and Religion of the North* (Weidenfeld & Nicolson, 1964).

Watkin, H.R., *Dartmouth: Pre-Reformation* (Devonshire Association, 1935), Vol.1.

Whitelock, D., *The Beginnings of English Society* (Penguin, 1956).

Wright, T., *Political Songs of England*, (Cambridge University Press, 1996).

INDEX